Also by John K. Roth

AFTER-WORDS: Post-Holocaust Struggles with Forgiveness, Reconciliation, Justice (*edited with David Patterson*)

AMERICAN DIVERSITY, AMERICAN IDENTITY (*ed.*)

THE AMERICAN DREAM (*with Robert H. Fossum*)

AMERICAN DREAMS: Meditations on Life in the United States

AMERICAN DREAMS AND HOLOCAUST QUESTIONS

AMERICAN GROUND: Vistas, Visions & Revisions (*edited with Robert H. Fossum*)

THE AMERICAN RELIGIOUS EXPERIENCE: The Roots, Trends and the Future of American Theology (*with Frederick Sontag*)

APPROACHES TO AUSCHWITZ: The Holocaust and its Legacy (*with Richard L. Rubenstein*)

A CONSUMING FIRE: Encounters with Elie Wiesel and the Holocaust

THE DEATH OF GOD MOVEMENT AND THE HOLOCAUST: Radical Theology Encounters the Shoah (*edited with Stephen R. Haynes*)

THE DEFENSE OF GOD (*edited with Frederick Sontag*)

DIFFERENT VOICES: Women and the Holocaust (*edited with Carol Rittner*)

ENCYCLOPEDIA OF SOCIAL ISSUES (*ed.*)

ETHICS AFTER THE HOLOCAUST: Perspectives, Critiques, and Responses (*ed.*)

ETHICS: An Annotated Bibliography

ETHICS: Ready Reference (*ed.*)

FIRE IN THE ASHES: God, Evil, and the Holocaust (*edited with David Patterson*)

FREEDOM AND THE MORAL LIFE: The Ethics of William James

FROM THE UNTHINKABLE TO THE UNAVOIDABLE: American Christian and Jewish Scholars Encounter the Holocaust (*edited with Carol Rittner*)

GENOCIDE AND HUMAN RIGHTS: A Philosophical Guide (*ed.*)

GENOCIDE IN RWANDA: Complicity of the Churches? (*edited with Carol Rittner and Wendy Whitworth*)

GOD AND AMERICA'S FUTURE (*with Frederick Sontag*)

"GOOD NEWS" AFTER AUSCHWITZ?: Christian Faith within a Post-Holocaust World (*edited with Carol Rittner*)

GRAY ZONES: Ambiguity and Compromise in the Holocaust and Its Aftermath (*edited with Jonathan Petropoulos*)

HOLOCAUST: Religious and Philosophical Implications (*edited with Michael Berenbaum*)

THE HOLOCAUST CHRONICLE (*with Marilyn Harran* et al.)

HOLOCAUST POLITICS

INSPIRING TEACHING (*ed.*)

MEMORY OFFENDED: The Auschwitz Convent Controversy (*edited with Carol Rittner*)

IDEOLOGY AND AMERICAN EXPERIENCE: Essays on Theory and Practice in the United States (*edited with Robert C. Whittemore*)

THE MORAL EQUIVALENT OF WAR AND OTHER ESSAYS (*ed.*)

THE MORAL PHILOSOPHY OF WILLIAM JAMES (*ed.*)

POPE PIUS XII AND THE HOLOCAUST (*edited with Carol Rittner*)

THE PHILOSOPHY OF JOSIAH ROYCE (*ed.*)

PRIVATE NEEDS, PUBLIC SELVES: Talk about Religion in America

THE POLITICS OF LATIN AMERICAN LIBERATION THEOLOGY: The Challenge to U.S. Public Policy (*edited with Richard L. Rubenstein*)

PROBLEMS OF THE PHILOSOPHY OF RELIGION

THE QUESTIONS OF PHILOSOPHY (*with Frederick Sontag*)

REMEMBERING FOR THE FUTURE: The Holocaust in an Age of Genocide (*edited with Elisabeth Maxwell*)

RIGHTS, JUSTICE, AND COMMUNITY (*edited with Creighton Peden*)

WILL GENOCIDE EVER END? (*edited with Carol Rittner and James M. Smith*)

WORLD PHILOSOPHERS AND THEIR WORKS (*ed.*)

"There is an integrity, consistency, rigor and even poetry to all of John Roth's work. His wrestling with *Ethics During and After the Holocaust: In the Shadow of Birkenau* is deep and penetrating. It is the mature work of a distinguished scholar who asks all the difficult questions and refuses to accept the simple answers; thus the questions deepen and they are shared with the reader. Roth refuses to accept cheap grace. All issues are handled not just with care but with a sensitivity, and a depth of intellect that is matched by compassion. Roth's grasp is wide; his understanding profound, his insights glisten, and even the most complex of ideas are expressed with clarity, sensibility and wisdom."—Michael Berenbaum, director, Sigi Ziering Institute, Professor of Theology, The University of Judaism, former president and CEO of the Survivors of the Shoah Visual History Foundation, former director, Holocaust Research Institute, United States Holocaust Memorial Museum.

Ethics During and After the Holocaust

In the Shadow of Birkenau

John K. Roth

palgrave
macmillan

First published in hardback 2005

First published in paperback 2007 by
PALGRAVE MACMILLAN
Houndmills, Basingstoke, Hampshire RG21 6XS and
175 Fifth Avenue, New York, N.Y. 10010
Companies and representatives throughout the world.

PALGRAVE MACMILLAN is the global academic imprint of the Palgrave Macmillan division of St. Martin's Press, LLC and of Palgrave Macmillan Ltd. Macmillan® is a registered trademark in the United States, United Kingdom and other countries. Palgrave is a registered trademark in the European Union and other countries.

ISBN-13: 978–1–4039–3377–5 hardback
ISBN-10: 1–4039–3377–4   hardback
ISBN-13: 978–1–4039–3378–2 paperback
ISBN-10: 1–4039–3378–2   paperback

This book is printed on paper suitable for recycling and made from fully managed and sustained forest sources.

A catalogue record for this book is available from the British Library.

Library of Congress Cataloging-in-Publication Data

Roth, John K.
    Ethics during and after the Holocaust: in the shadow of Birkenau/
John K. Roth.
        p. cm.
    Includes bibliographical references and index.
    ISBN 1–4039–3377–4 (cloth) 1–4039–3378–2 (pbk)
        1. Holocaust, Jewish (1939–1945) – Moral and ethical aspects.
    2. Holocaust, Jewish (1939–1945) – Influence. I. Title.

D804.7.M67R68 2005
940.53'18'01—dc22   2005051391

10 9 8 7 6 5 4 3 2 1
16 15 14 13 12 11 10 09 08 07

Printed and bound in Great Britain by
Antony Rowe Ltd, Chippenham and Eastbourne

To
Keeley Jane Brooks
... The girl was fair and beautiful ....
Esther 2:7

The Holocaust demands interrogation and calls everything into question. Traditional ideas and acquired values, philosophical systems and social theories—all must be revised in the shadow of Birkenau.

Elie Wiesel

Contents

Prologue: Only the Darkness?

> And what of human ideals, or of the beauty of innocence or the
> weight of justice? ... Why all these deaths?
>
> Elie Wiesel, *All Rivers Run to the Sea*

In his classic Holocaust memoir called *Night*, Elie Wiesel describes the deportation of Jews from Sighet, his hometown in Nazi-occupied Hungary, during the spring of 1944. That railroad journey reduced his world to "a cattle car hermetically sealed."[1] Wiesel recalls "the heat, the thirst, the pestilential stench, the suffocating lack of air" but emphasizes that they were "as nothing compared with [the] screams which tore us to shreds."[2]

The screams were those of a middle-aged woman whom Wiesel identifies only as Madame Schächter, although he adds that he knew her well. She was imprisoned in the cattle car with her ten-year-old son, but her husband and two older boys had been deported earlier. "The separation," says Wiesel, "had completely broken her. ... Madame Schächter had gone out of her mind."[3] Her disorientation was revealed not only by moans and increasingly hysterical screams but also by the visions that provoked them.

Madame Schächter could not see outside, but on the third night of the seemingly endless journey she saw flames in the darkness. " ' ... Listen, listen to me,' she kept exclaiming, 'I can see a fire! There are huge flames! It is a furnace.' "[4] At first the screams led some of the men to look through the small windows that allowed a little air into their cattle-car prison, but they saw no flames. "There was nothing there," reports Wiesel, "only the darkness."[5]

Some took pity and tried to calm Madame Schächter. Others were less kind. Wanting her quiet, they bound, gagged, and even struck Madame Schächter—"blows," Wiesel acknowledges, "that might have killed her." Meanwhile, he observes, "her little boy clung to her; he did not cry out; he did not say a word. He was not even weeping now."[6] Dawn's arrival stilled the bewildered woman. She remained quiet throughout the next day, but the fourth night again brought her screaming visions of fire. On the following day, the train stopped at a station. None of Madame Schächter's flames were to be seen, but signs indicated that the train had reached Auschwitz. "No one," says Wiesel, "had ever heard that name."[7]

For an afternoon and on into the evening, the train did not move, but with nightfall Madame Schächter's mad cries were again renewed. At last the train began to move again, and as it took the rail spur that had been recently constructed to facilitate the arrival of transports at Birkenau, the killing center at Auschwitz, Madame Schächter once more became quiet, but other voices echoed hers with terrible screams of their own. They accurately reported what could be clearly seen. "Look! Look through the window! Flames! Look!"[8] Lighting up the darkness as they reached skyward from Birkenau's crematorium furnaces, those flames turned Jewish lives into smoke and ash.

With the transport's arrival at Birkenau, the cattle cars opened, and the prisoners were rousted toward the selection process that determined their fate: a gas-chamber murder or the slave labor that eventually resulted in death for most of those who were chosen. The selection process began. It spared Wiesel and his father Shlomo but condemned his mother Sarah and his little sister Tsiporah. *Night* also indicates that Wiesel caught one last glimpse of Madame Schächter and the little boy who held her hand.

Madame Schächter and her son were of no use to the Germans. Birkenau's furnaces soon consumed them. As for Wiesel and his father, their Auschwitz path took them toward a fiery pit in which little children were being burned. Wiesel recalls his father's words: "Do you remember Madame Schächter, in the train?"[9] The immediate response in *Night* does not contain an explicit answer to his father's question, but the words that follow are among Wiesel's most powerful:

> Never shall I forget that night, the first night in camp, which has turned my life into one long night, seven times cursed and seven times sealed. Never shall I forget that smoke. Never shall I forget the little faces of the children, whose bodies I saw turned into wreaths of smoke beneath a silent blue sky.
>
> Never shall I forget those flames which consumed my faith forever.
>
> Never shall I forget that nocturnal silence which deprived me, for all eternity, of the desire to live. Never shall I forget those moments which murdered my God and my soul and turned my dreams to dust. Never shall I forget these things, even if I am condemned to live as long as God Himself. Never.[10]

Initially studying Wiesel's *Night* some thirty-five years ago, I became a philosopher tripped up by Holocaust history. In my early thirties at the time, my American life was progressing well, and, despite the fact that my philosophical interests focused on questions about injustice, suffering, and evil, the Holocaust was not at the center of my attention. The experiences that Wiesel reported in *Night*, even his use of words and silences, were distant from my experience. Nevertheless, what had happened to Madame Schächter and her son, to Elie Wiesel and his family, had taken place during my lifetime. My life, their lives, indeed all of *our* lives, are realities of one world, and the resulting collisions of consciousness and concern would drive me to find out as much as I could about how and why the Holocaust happened. My study convinced me that Wiesel was correct when he went on to say that "the Holocaust demands interrogation and calls everything into question. Traditional ideas and acquired values, philosophical systems and social theories—all must be revised in the shadow of Birkenau."[11]

Those words, along with others that Wiesel has written, indicate that his memory of Madame Schächter has never left him. Decades after writing *Night*, Wiesel recalled her in his 1995 memoir, *All Rivers Run to the Sea*. "Certain images of the days and nights spent on that train invade my dreams even now," he wrote, "anticipation of danger, fear of the dark, the screams of poor Mrs. Schecter, who, in her delirium, saw flames in the distance; the efforts to make her stop; the terror in her little boy's eyes."[12] Such recollections make Wiesel wonder: "And what of human ideals, or of the beauty of innocence or the weight of justice? ... Why all these deaths?"[13]

Questions shape the Holocaust's legacy. "What happened to ethics during the Holocaust? What should ethics be and what can it do after the Holocaust?" are questions that loom large among them. Absent the overriding of moral sensibilities, if not the collapse or collaboration of ethical traditions, the Holocaust could not have happened. Its devastation may have deepened conviction that there is a crucial difference between right and wrong; its destruction may have renewed awareness about the importance of ethical standards and conduct. But Birkenau also continues to cast a disturbing shadow over basic beliefs concerning right and wrong, human rights, and the hope that human beings will learn from the past. Given what happened there, how could it not?

The Holocaust did not pronounce the death of ethics, but it did prove that ethics is immensely vulnerable, that it can be misused and perverted, and that no simple reaffirmation of pre-Holocaust ethics, as if nothing had happened, will do any more. Too much has happened for that, including the fact that the shadow of Birkenau so often shows Western religious, philosophical, and ethical traditions to be problematic. Far from preventing the Holocaust, they were at times seriously implicated in that catastrophe. This book explores those realities and the issues they contain. It does so not to discourage but to encourage, not to deepen darkness and despair but to face those realities honestly and in ways that can make post-Holocaust ethics more credible and realistic. No book, however, can deal responsibly with all of the dimensions that those challenges contain. Thus, the chapters that follow direct attention to pieces of a very large puzzle. They do so in ways akin to Raul Hilberg's. That preeminent scholar of the Holocaust seeks to avoid small answers to big question by focusing on "details in order that I might then be able to put together in a gestalt a picture, which, if not an explanation, is at least a description, a more full description, of what transpired."[14] Likewise, my methods in Holocaust studies draw both on my philosophical training and perspective and on a commitment to write about the Holocaust's particularity and detail. At every turn, I try to keep my reflections focused as accurately as I can on the history of the Holocaust. Philosophically, I try to avoid abstraction and to explore instead the practical meanings and applications of ethical analysis. My approach is to consider, first, what happened to ethics during the Holocaust by concentrating on specific persons and places, on particular moments and memories that identify how that catastrophe did immense harm to ethics. My attempts to reconsider and retrieve ethics, to recover and renew its vitality in the ruins of a post-Holocaust world, also draw on specific concerns and particular needs. They include children and education, antisemitism and racism, relativism and credible responses to it, torture and political power, genocide and aspects of religious life, such as forgiveness and prayer, to mention a few at the outset.[15]

As the shadow of Birkenau continues to shed its gloom on the earth, does only the darkness remain? The thesis that rivets the book's attention, sums up its major findings, and responds to that question in particular is as follows:

> The Holocaust did not have to happen; it resulted from human choices and decisions. Those facts mean that nothing human, natural, or divine guarantees respect for the ethical values and commitments that are most needed in contemporary human existence, but nothing is more important than our commitment to defend them, for they remain as fundamental as they are fragile, as precious as they are endangered.

Many good people helped me to write this book. I shall name only a few, but I am grateful to them all. At Palgrave Macmillan, it was Jennifer

Nelson who initially encouraged me to develop this volume. Her successor, Luciana O'Flaherty, focused the project further, and then Daniel Bunyard managed the final editorial and production process, which was also facilitated expertly by Vidhya Jayaprakash. Excellent copyediting was done by Perviz Dara Bhote. I am thankful for their professional expertise and friendly support.

I completed my writing at the United States Holocaust Memorial Museum in Washington, DC, where I was privileged to spend the 2004–05 academic year as the Ina Levine Invitational Scholar at the Center for Advanced Holocaust Studies. I am deeply indebted to William S. Levine, whose thoughtful generosity endowed the fellowship that honors his late wife and that it was my privilege to hold. I am also immensely grateful to Paul Shapiro, the Center's dedicated director, and to his superb staff. They make the Center a wonderful place to work. My thanks also go to Sara J. Bloomfield, the director of the United States Holocaust Memorial Museum, and to the Center's scholars, visiting and permanent, who did so much to create a stimulating, challenging, and congenial exchange of ideas and research. I am particularly grateful to Lisa Yavnai and Lisa Zaid, who coordinated the Visiting Fellows Program in 2004–05. Jerry Fowler, who works persistently and creatively on genocide prevention as he guides the Museum's influential Committee on Conscience, also gave encouragement and guidance when they were much needed.

With special help from Ellen Blalock, who coordinated the Center's outreach program, I was able to test my research and writing in lectures and seminars at numerous colleges and universities. I thank my hosts at these places: Lawrence Baron at San Diego State University; Omer Bartov at Brown University; Beth Benedix at DePauw University; Jacquelyn Bussie at Capital University; Kenneth Cmiel at the University of Iowa; Ward "Skip" Cornett, III, at Trinity Lutheran Seminary; Charles Fishman at the State University of New York, Farmingdale; Jennifer Geddes at the University of Virginia; James Glass at the University of Maryland; Barton Lee at Arizona State University; Rochelle Millen at Wittenberg University; Albert Pierce at the US Naval Academy; Michael Popich at Westminster College, Salt Lake City; Richard Rubenstein at the University of Bridgeport; and Mary Todd at Ohio Dominican University.

This book is dedicated to Keeley Jane Brooks, my grandchild, who has inspired my reflection in more ways than she is ever likely to know. My friend Michael Berenbaum, who became a grandfather just as I began to enjoy that special status in 2003, said to me one day, "Many things in life are oversold, but being a grandparent is not one of them." I agree, but one of the reasons is scarcely a cause for celebration. Anticipating the joys of grandparenthood, I was not fully prepared for the awesome responsibility that grandparenting confers.

As Keeley's grandfather, I want more than ever for her post-Holocaust world to be one in which human rights abuses, genocide among them, are minimized if not eliminated. I want more than ever—for her, for all children and grandchildren—a world that embodies higher ethical standards and conduct than ours exhibits in the early twenty-first century. Having become a grandfather, my time to work for those goals grows shorter, and therefore the work seems increasingly urgent, more intensely required because it will remain so far from being done when my death comes. A book about ethics during and after the Holocaust is, at best, a modest contribution in response to that urgency, but its completion coincided with Keeley Brooks's second birthday, April 30, 2005. So I offer it as a present to her world, as well as to her, hoping that it may help to encourage justice, healing, and compassion.

The book in the Hebrew Bible that bears her name says that Esther, who grew up to save her people from annihilation, was a girl "fair and beautiful." No grandfather worthy of that name would say less of his grandchildren. Keeley is fair and beautiful. So are all granddaughters and grandsons, at least when they are small children. Sensitive ethical judgment is essential if they are all to grow and thrive as they deserve to do. Such judgment must be intergenerational, which means not only that the generations of Keeley's grandparents and parents must cultivate and care for it, but also that Keeley, her peers, and their children will have to learn to do the same. Like Esther of old, they will have to grow up in ways that equip and enable them to save their people so that human life, fair and beautiful, can continue and so that much more than darkness will remain.

1
The Philosopher's Project

> Since some philosophers lived in a different age—and perhaps
> in a completely different culture from ours—it is a good idea to
> try and see what each philosopher's *project* is. By this I mean
> that we must try to grasp precisely what it is that each particular
> philosopher is especially concerned with finding out.
>
> Jostein Gaarder, *Sophie's World*[1]

As a philosopher tripped up by history, my aim is to find out what
happened to ethics during and after the Holocaust, Nazi Germany's
genocide against the Jewish people. That project also entails reflection
on what ethics can and should be in our post-Holocaust world. In the
history of philosophy, such concerns are recent and particular. Usually
they are not at the center of contemporary philosophical reflection.
Their particularity, however, does connect with the history of philosophy.
By tracing those connections, one can see why the project undertaken
in *Ethics During and After the Holocaust* should concern not only philosophers but also every critically thinking person who lives after Auschwitz.

To test the validity of those claims, note that Jostein Gaarder's *Sophie's
World* (1991) narrates the philosophical adventures of a teenager named
Sophie Amundsen, who finds strange mail waiting for her when she
comes home from school. Its messages ask questions. *Who are you?* and
Where did the world come from? are the first two.

Those questions make Sophie wonder. Along with her, Gaarder's readers
learn that the mysterious mail originates with the enigmatic Alberto
Knox, who becomes Sophie's philosophy teacher. Before many pages are
turned, the reader is drawn into Gaarder's project. One of its parts
involves reflection about wonder. Pursuit of that theme, followed by
consideration of several others related to Gaarder's project in *Sophie's*

World, helps to identify the project advanced by *Ethics During and After the Holocaust*.

Wondering about wonder

Philosophy means "the love of wisdom," but that definition needs unpacking. Doing so requires reflection on wonder, which Plato regarded as philosophy's beginning. That reflection, in turn, invites inquiry about questions—their variety, power, and fundamental role in philosophy. Questions raised early on by Socrates, Plato, and Aristotle provide much of philosophy's inspiration, but theirs was a pre-Holocaust world. As I believe this book will help to show, philosophy after Auschwitz cannot be true to its ancient calling unless it involves the deepest wonder about the Holocaust and its implications, especially those that pertain to ethics.

What do people wonder about? How does wondering feel? Where can wonder lead? Where should it go? What do such questions and responses to them reveal about philosophy? Encountering the Holocaust affects what such questions mean and how they can and should be approached. Aristotle's teacher was Plato (427–347 B.C.E.), who had learned philosophy's ways from Socrates (c. 470–399 B.C.E.). Little would be known of Socrates if we had to depend on his writings, for he apparently left none behind. Socrates preferred question-filled conversation, but Plato made sure that Socratic discussion was not lost when the talking stopped. Plato reconstructed versions of those Socratic inquiries in a series of classic dialogues. Although we cannot be sure where Plato blurred the line between historical fact and imaginative creation, he did preserve the memory and method of Socrates while developing ideas of his own.

Theaetetus is one of Plato's most important dialogues. Its name comes from a character in the narrative. A brilliant young man, Theaetetus knows mathematics. Plato has Socrates show, however, that even Theaetetus may not know as much as he thinks he does, because a clear account of what it means to know something is much harder to pin down than it seems. As Theaetetus and Socrates talk, experience becomes perplexing, and they find more questions than answers. Theaetetus says these puzzles amaze him. He wants to find out more about what the questions mean and what the answers to them are, but he confesses that thinking about them makes him dizzy. When philosophy encounters the Holocaust something akin to dizziness does and should take place. A human catastrophe of that magnitude, as Elie Wiesel underscores, calls everything into question. The Holocaust is not the only human event that has this power, but as the chapters that follow will indicate, that event has compelling power to do so, and that power deserves attention.

Socrates understood how Theaetetus felt. Long ago one of Socrates' friends had gone to the sacred site at Delphi and asked the Oracle, a religious visionary, to indicate whether anyone was wiser than Socrates. "No one," the priestess replied. Socrates wondered about the Oracle's answer, for self-study made him feel that he lacked wisdom. His sense of wonder about the Oracle's meaning led Socrates to spend his life looking for people who were truly wise. This search was what made him ask so many questions. Socrates found that people often claimed to know more than they had a right to do. At least he was wiser than they in recognizing his own ignorance and working to move beyond it.

Signs of a disposition similar to Socrates' exist in *Theaetetus*. They show the makings of a philosopher, even of what it would take to be a post-Holocaust philosopher. In fact, their mutual friend, Theodorus, was right to call Theaetetus a philosopher, Socrates tells the young mathe- matician, because "wonder is the feeling of a philosopher, and philosophy begins in wonder." Plato's dialogue about Theaetetus and Socrates suggests several points that Aristotle (384–322 B.C.E.), who knew the account, summed up effectively later on. Philosophy attempts to escape ignorance, Aristotle agreed with Socrates, and awareness of ignorance emerges from wonder. Wondering dwells in the human capacity to ask questions: who, what, where, when, how, and, above all, *why*? The Holocaust does and should provoke wonder, especially in the form of anguish, with respect to all of those questions.

Aristotle did not believe, however, that we plunge into philosophy originally or automatically at the level found in *Theaetetus*. Wondering develops. Driving deeper than it does at the beginning, wonder concentrates in time on things that are more rather than less important. Wondering what's for dinner, for example—important though that may be—is not on the same level as the questions about knowledge that concerned Socrates and Theaetetus. Something analogous to this process exists in the relationship between Holocaust history and the philosophical inquiry to which it can and ought to lead. We can ask: How did the Holocaust happen? Historical research provides many reliable answers to that question. But in the process, that same research can make us wonder because it raises questions that go beyond the findings that historical study can produce. Among them is the question "What can be made of ethics after Auschwitz?"

Aristotle thought human beings naturally desire to know. So he believed that one kind of wonder will probably lead to another. While our sense of wonder may be aroused first by questions such as "What's for dinner?," Aristotle argued that experience typically provokes "wonder about less mundane matters such as the changes of the moon, sun, and stars, and the beginnings of the universe." At least initially, he added, the result of this wondering is "an awesome feeling of ignorance." Asking how the Holocaust happened and finding out how it did can have similar effects. We are led to think about human rights, about justice, about relationships between might and right. Moreover, to the extent that the Holocaust is confronted deeply, that encounter will scarcely leave us confident that we have convincing answers ready for the questioning wonder that remains. Something akin to an awesome feeling of ignorance is more likely to be our condition.

The feeling of wonder involves puzzlement, uncertainty, and unclarity. Encounters with the Holocaust may also lace feelings of wonder with despair. Such qualities link up with the dizziness of Theaetetus. Wonder also includes awareness, sensitivity, and amazement—features connected to the "awesome feeling" Aristotle emphasized. In addition, it reflects wanting, yearning, and hope. Only now, with the Holocaust in view, those qualities may have to be pursued in spite of the realization that the Holocaust's immense destruction may leave those feelings in ruins. Dark though they are, however, those elements still relate to the desire and determination to know that Socrates embodied. Socrates, Plato, and Aristotle shared the conviction that philosophy begins in wonder and reflects our need and capacity to ask insightful questions about fundamental matters. Failure to make our feelings of wonder the occasions for inquiry, they thought, dooms us to ignorance and folly. After Auschwitz, one can add, such failure could also doom us to despair and cynicism. But if we can use wonder not only to keep ourselves curious but also to resist despair, philosophical wonder can be a key ingredient in mending the world and in enhancing life in a post-Holocaust world. Of course, wondering that leads from darkness into light is a difficult path to take. The rewards can make the journey worthwhile, but that outcome is not simply assured. This we know because Socrates got into serious trouble for being a philosopher. Such facts become additional occasions for wonder.

The word *philosophy* derives from two Greek words: *philein* (to love) and *sophia* (wisdom). The practice of philosophy, if not the word itself, probably appeared in India even before its birth in the Greek world, but some traditions hold that the word *philosophy* was coined by Pythagoras, a Greek thinker who lived nearly two centuries before Socrates and called himself a lover of wisdom. Thus, philosophy is the love of wisdom, and, following that definition, a philosopher is or should be a lover of wisdom. Socrates fitted that description. The love of wisdom, however, cost him his life.

Why did the love of wisdom get Socrates into such difficulty? If that is where philosophy leads, why should Sophie Amundsen or anyone else be introduced to it? Socrates' often-quoted reply to versions of the second question—"the unexamined life is not worth living"—also helps to provide an answer to the first. In a nutshell, Socrates challenged too many assumptions and beliefs that Athenian authorities preferred to leave uncriticized. In the *Apology*, which deals with Socrates' trial before an Athenian jury, Plato reports that Socrates made his famous claim as he defended himself against charges of atheism and corrupting the city's youth.

Socrates posed too many hard questions about fundamental issues. He might wonder, for example, what is justice? What does justice mean? What, if anything, do all just acts have in common? Aristotle credited Socrates for being the first thinker to stress the importance of obtaining sound definitions for the most basic ideas. Indeed, getting truthful definitions for basic ideas such as justice was at the core of wisdom as far as Socrates was concerned. Such questioning, however, could make people intensely uncomfortable. If they could answer such questions at all, the answers people gave as they tried to define key terms that they used all the time—good, true, right, wrong—were unlikely to withstand the further questions that Socrates stood ready to ask. Unrelenting in his love of wisdom, Socrates questioned and questioned. He unmasked pretense, uncovered confusion, undermined dogmatism, undid false certitude, and, in general, left very little unexamined. This activity instructed and delighted the friends of Socrates—Plato among them—but it also put Athenian leaders on the defensive, which made them uneasy and angry. Philosophy and philosophers may not face trial and execution as Socrates did, but their encounters with the Holocaust are unlikely to comfort anyone because their reflection will call into question many of humankind's fondest hopes and cherished assumptions. The best post-Holocaust philosophy and philosophers will intensify calls for human responsibility and accountability. Those calls are unlikely to be popular, but they cannot be ignored with impunity.

Socrates wanted people to discover truth for themselves. He believed they could do so if they tried. That is why he raised so many questions. The love of wisdom and the ways of thinking that encourage it, believed

Socrates, require dialogue. Obtaining wisdom is a personal experience because wisdom is found, if it is obtained at all, only by the individual who seeks it. The journey and the destination are inseparable. But the seeking is also a communal activity in many ways. We need to be corrected by discussion with others, if we are not to go astray. Without the give and take of discussion, we may settle too easily for an insufficiently examined "truth."

Among those who offered such truth were teachers known as *Sophists*. Typically, they taught that power, prestige, and property measure success. They also emphasized that the right techniques—learning, for example, how to speak and argue cleverly—could produce those results. Like Socrates, the Sophists challenged traditional Athenian values. Unlike Socrates, they were more interested in getting ahead than in knowing the truth. Socrates contested their views. His dialogue with the Sophists showed their "wisdom" to be sophistry, for their "knowledge" was more apparent than real.

Dialogue requires what Socrates called dialectic, which is the core of what we still call the "Socratic method." Dialectic is the disciplined and sustained use of questioning, responding, and questioning some more. That rhythm is philosophy's heartbeat. Such inquiry weighs the strengths and weaknesses of different views. It aims at a more balanced and complete perspective than one's starting points provide. Socrates was a master of dialectic, and Plato portrays him as the questioner *par excellence*. The context for Socrates' exercise of dialectic was typically a search for the wisdom he loved but felt he possessed inadequately. Publicly Socrates would engage people who presumed to be wise, and he would ask that they share their enlightenment. Unwittingly they would oblige and start to "tell" him about goodness, justice, truth, beauty, or whatever the fundamental topic might be. Then Socrates would probe away. His questioning turned appearance into reality: "Knowledge" dissolved into opinion and usually into unsubstantiated opinion at that. "Wisdom" collapsed into ignorance, if not into sheer foolishness. Philosophy touched by Auschwitz will be profoundly dialectical in post-Holocaust Socratic ways because it will have to test its findings and even its questioning by asking: Is this inquiry credible in the shadow of Birkenau?

What wisdom means

The wisdom Socrates loved was not a matter of collecting facts or obtaining information, though facts and information were important to him.

A person can have a lot of data and still be arrogant and foolish—the opposite of wise. What Socrates wanted was understanding, insight, ways of thinking that make sound judgments about truth and goodness. Socrates yearned for these but never claimed that he possessed them completely.

In his *Symposium*, a dialogue about love, Plato has Socrates explain further by noting that a philosopher, a lover of wisdom, "is in a mean between the wise and the ignorant." The philosopher does not possess wisdom lock, stock, and barrel. No one does. But the philosopher senses what is lacking and seeks what is not possessed or completely obtainable. He or she does so because the lack of wisdom leads to folly and foolishness of the tragic kind that Athens produced when it took Socrates' life or to arrogance and hatred that paved the way for Nazi Germany's genocidal antisemitism.

In making us aware of ignorance and the arrogance and prejudice that usually accompany it, wondering shows that we do not know as much as we may assume but also that we are not necessarily condemned to ignorance. The possibility of learning can create a yearning for the knowledge that goes beyond information to wisdom. That yearning can become passionate. When it does, love is the right word to use for the desire that keeps us asking and searching for wisdom. After Auschwitz, wondering about what happened to ethics during and after the Holocaust is a key part of any genuine search for wisdom.

Socrates' love of wisdom embodied at least four principles that further define philosophy at its best. Each of them has a place in one of the most memorable scenes in all of philosophy's history. It comes from Plato's *Republic*, a classic dialogue on the nature of justice and the ideal state. The scene is his famous "Allegory of the Cave."

An allegory is a story whose characters, circumstances, events, and the relations among them, function symbolically to illustrate a basic idea. The idea illustrated by the "Allegory of the Cave" is that of philosophy itself. For the story that Plato has Socrates tell to Glaucon in Book VII of the *Republic* is about a crucial activity, the climb from the shadows and darkness of ignorance to the enlightenment of wisdom.

Socrates describes prisoners who spend their lives in a cave. Dwelling there since childhood, they are chained so that all they can do is to watch the shadows cast on a wall by fire. They cannot even turn their heads to discover why the shadows exist. Behind the prisoners there are objects moving before a fire that burns near the entrance. Unaware, the prisoners mistake the shadows for reality. If "the unexamined life is not worth living," the prisoners' predicament is not a good one. Socrates suggests that those prisoners are like ourselves—less than the fully human persons we might become. To move toward that full humanity we need to be unchained from the bondage of taking experience for granted. This principle—our need to question and evaluate experience critically—is one that defines philosophy Socratically.

In the allegory, at least one of the prisoners is set free, forced out of the cave, and even dragged into the sun's full light. This journey is anything but easy. The glare from the fire is blinding; the objects that made the shadows on the cave's wall cannot be clearly identified. Confused, the released prisoner may think that the previous circumstances were clearer, more comfortable, than the new ones. The disorientation may even get worse when the sun itself is glimpsed, for no one can look directly at the very source of light. Gradually, however, adjustment to the light can happen. Then confusion may give way to clarity. Disorientation can recede in favor of reorientation that sees the difference between appearance and reality. The Holocaust is scarcely analogous to the sun in Plato's allegory. Plato's sun stands for pure truth and goodness, while the Holocaust is a darkness that engulfed them both. Nevertheless, we remain in a cave of deception if the Holocaust is not confronted openly and honestly. Doing so ought not to produce accommodation with evil, but it may produce much-needed clarity that can result in reorientations that expose the difference between appearance and reality.

Here, then, is a second Socratic principle that defines philosophy: Appearance and reality are not the same any more than falsity and truth are identical or right and wrong are indistinguishable. Confusion reigns, disorientation rules, where those basic distinctions are blurred, forgotten, or left unexamined. It is hard work to distinguish appearance from reality. A philosopher-teacher like Socrates or, in Sophie Amundsen's case, Alberto Knox can lend a hand. But even in those situations philosophy requires inquiry for oneself. Socrates liked to call himself a gadfly who provoked others to think by prodding them, even against their wills, into the light of the sun. A gentler self-image, although it too entails pain, was that of the midwife who helps a mother deliver the child that is within her. Both images, but especially the latter, suggest a third Socratic principle that defines philosophy: We can learn, and truth awaits discovery within our own experience if only we keep prodding one another and ourselves to give it birth.

As Socrates concludes the allegory, the former prisoner's enlightenment brings new understanding. When the former prisoner thinks about the cave, there is sympathy for those who remain within it.

But the liberated one would endure almost anything rather than going back to living and thinking as before. Indeed, if he or she had to return to the cave, the darkness would cause problems. The former prisoner might appear ridiculous to those who had never left the cave. If he or she tried to teach them, they might be so offended that they would even try to put the teacher to death.

Plato alluded to Socrates' fate as the allegory ended, but he also had Socrates discuss the story with Glaucon. In that discussion, Socrates stressed that those who obtained philosophy's understanding had a responsibility. It was to reenter the cave and to try to set the other prisoners free so that they would also see the light. To Socrates—and this is a fourth Socratic principle—philosophy meant freedom to inquire and responsibility to learn and teach.

The Holocaust was and is no allegory. It is about unrelenting mass murder. Nevertheless, the four themes underscored in Plato's story about the cave have their place in *Ethics During and After the Holocaust*. Critical thinking could have prevented the Holocaust, and human well-being depends on it now and in the future. Unmasking of deception that blurs differences between appearance and reality, especially as those differences pertain to judgments about right and wrong, justice and injustice, are of fundamental importance. Even in the aftermath of mass destruction, it is possible for ethical learning to take place. Freedom of inquiry must be protected and used to teach ways of thinking and living that can help us to become the responsible men and women we ought to be.

The questions of philosophy

There are many kinds of questions, but not every one is a question of philosophy. What makes the difference? What are the questions of philosophy? To clarify those issues, consider some examples. "What time is it?" is a question frequently asked. The answer we want for it is usually specific—for instance, "It's four o'clock." A different question might ask "What is time?" "Four o'clock" will not be very helpful in that case. It may be an instance of time, but it is not time itself. Philosophers need to know what time it is, but they are also likely to be concerned about the nature of time itself.

Another question might go like this: "Is it true that you are going out tonight?" This time the answer could be a simple "yes" or "no." But such answers will not make sense if the question becomes "What is truth?" Few things are more important than distinguishing true judgments from false ones. Knowing how to do that well depends on having sound insight about the conditions that constitute truth. Philosophers need to know whether "yes" or "no" is the answer to a question with the form "Is it true that ... ?" But they also want to know about the nature of truth itself.

"Is she a good doctor?" "Is this sculpture better than that one?" "Was his decision fair?" Those are common questions too. Sometimes they can be answered "yes" or "no," but often they require careful evaluation. That may be because we feel the need to wonder about some other questions along the way. These might include: "What does goodness mean?" "How can works of art be compared?" "What's the difference between fair and unfair treatment?" Questions of the latter kind, which defy quick and easy answers, guide the philosopher's search for wisdom.

Lines between philosophical and non-philosophical questions are not hard and fast. They often blur into shades of gray. Asking "Is she a good doctor?" is a case in point. If that question wonders whether the doctor has mastered the latest surgical technique, it might not be very philosophical because its answer depends simply on easily obtainable facts. But that same question may wonder about a larger cluster of qualities evoked by the word *good*. Among them, for example, might be signs of character, care, and conscientiousness that go beyond technique.

In any case, a question will be philosophical to the extent that it checks quick, easy, simple yes-or-no answers and invites instead inquiry that examines—critically and rationally—our most basic concepts and ideas, assumptions and beliefs. What is happiness? Does God exist? Why is there so much suffering? What purpose and meaning do life have? In what sense do human rights exist? Those are just a few other examples of the questions of philosophy. One does not have to think about them very long to discover that they are not abstractions remote from our lives but rather expressions of the concerns that are closest to our hearts. One aspect of the project that governs *Ethics During and After the Holocaust* is to show how encounters with the Holocaust drive home that point in especially compelling ways.

As *Sophie's World* suggests, every self-reflective person is likely to ask at least some of the questions of philosophy. Philosophers, however, sustain the inquiry that the questions provoke. Over time they have organized these investigations so that several major fields—distinguishable but overlapping—characterize philosophy. Traditionally, one major area of philosophy is *metaphysics*. That name appeared in the first century B.C.E. when a scholar named Andronicus edited Aristotle's writings. Not knowing how to classify some of those works, he placed them after

Aristotle's writings on what was then called physics. Hence those writings got labeled *meta ta physica*—"after the physical works." The coincidence was a happy one because the Aristotelian writings now called *Metaphysics* did indeed deal with questions that come after physics in the sense that they go beyond that subject.

Metaphysics is by no means found only in the ancient Greek world. Focused on being and becoming, it pervades philosophy. What is reality? What are its most general or ultimate qualities? What kinds of beings are there? Why do some things exist and not others? Why is there a world at all? Why do some things change while others remain the same? How are causes and effects related? Is there a human nature, and, if so, what is it? Are human beings free or determined? What are the connections, if any, between spirit and matter, mind and brain? Physics, or science in general, may have important things to say about these questions. But metaphysical questions, such as the ones just mentioned, go beyond those of science. The latter's perspectives and findings do not encompass everything that exists. Metaphysics tries to deal with nothing less than that, but the problems of metaphysics are compounded by the fact that reality includes Auschwitz and genocide. How philosophy responds to those realities will affect the world significantly.

Beliefs, judgments, theories, arguments—these, too, exist. There are also falsity and truth, error and knowledge. Metaphysics involves these realities, but typically philosophy organizes inquiry about them under a category called *epistemology*. Taken from a Greek word for knowledge (*episteme*), epistemology—or the theory of knowledge—is what philosophers often call the study of questions about knowledge and knowing.

What does knowing mean? Can I be certain of anything? What are the best ways to inquire? Does reason have limits or is it possible, in principle, for us to know everything? To what extent is sense experience trustworthy? Does truth change or is it eternal? How do concepts work and how does language function? These are some of the questions that epistemology involves. When the questions ask "How do arguments work?" or "How do we know that reasoning is consistent or contradictory?" then issues about knowing lead to logic, another key area of philosophy. Like those that characterize metaphysics, the issues of epistemology and logic are as important as they are fundamental. Encounters with the Holocaust impact them as well, for we see that reasoning and argumentation can be the allies as well as the enemies of antisemitism and genocide. We see, too, that inquiry can lead to murderous "Final Solutions" as well as to imperatives to resist them. Such tensions require reconsiderations about what knowing means.

Good and evil, right and wrong, beauty and ugliness—these are also real. The ways in which they are and our knowing about them make these elements parts of metaphysics and epistemology too. But philosophers also find that there is an emphasis on values that deserves a focus of its own: What should we value? What should we care about and why? Most often this third major area of philosophy is identified as *ethics*. In that case the emphasis falls on questions such as: What makes one act wrong and another right? What is the difference between good and evil? How should we treat one another? How should we treat the environment in which we live? Are there eternal moral truths, or is moral judgment relative, simply a reflection of the time and place in which it occurs? How does ethical discourse work? What are its strengths and weaknesses? The Holocaust puts these issues in bold relief. How we deal with them will make a huge difference in the quality of life after Auschwitz.

Closely related to ethics is social and political philosophy. Here the emphasis falls on inquiry about the communal and political nature of human life. For example, what are the best forms of government? What rights and responsibilities does political life entail? How does social organization affect individual existence? Can individuals exist apart from society? Closely related to both ethics and philosophy that is social and political in its emphases is aesthetics, which concentrates on the values found in the arts and our experiences of beauty. What is art? Are there rational standards by which it can be judged, or is its evaluation a matter of taste and liking alone? Does art serve politics? Should it? Questions like those open up inquiries that philosophers often categorize as aesthetics. All of these topics emerge as matters of life and death when they encounter the Holocaust or when that catastrophe is brought to bear on them. The Holocaust was systematic, state-sponsored murder. It depended on politics and government, and Nazi Germany put art in the service of genocide even as that regime destroyed works of art that Nazi ideology defined as degenerate.

In addition to metaphysics, epistemology and logic, and value-oriented inquiries focusing on ethics, politics, society, and aesthetics, there are still other dimensions of philosophy that intersect with those major fields while retaining an identity of their own. Typically these fields of inquiry are called "the philosophy of ____." The blank could be filled with religion, history, science, education, law, or some other discipline. In these cases, the philosopher's project will be to examine the methods, practices, findings, and implications of these particular areas of human experience. Philosophers in Nazi Germany worked in this terrain, and they put philosophy itself in the service of a genocidal regime. Such facts show that philosophy has to be self-critical; it even has to atone for its own sin. Concerns of that kind also have their place in *Ethics During and After the Holocaust*.

What matters most?

The questions of philosophy are many and diverse. This is so because experience is vast and rich—intense, new, and personal on the one hand and far-reaching, perennial, and communal on the other. In all of their variety, and at their best, the questions of philosophy try to do one thing in common: They keep focusing attention on what matters most.

Think of all the ways one might answer the question, "What matters most?" One might say "my career" or "our country." Friends, family, fortune, the future—these could be candidates too. For some, God might matter most. Others would emphasize truth and goodness. Socrates, Plato, and Aristotle favored answers such as the latter two. Yet their development of those answers also differed. So another way to answer "What matters most?" is to say, "It all depends."

Wondering does not occur in a vacuum. The priorities of our questioning and inquiry depend on factors such as time, place, circumstance, and personal as well as communal experience. The fact that philosophy has a history and is embedded in history reflects that pattern. Philosophy's history shows that its way rarely deviates far from the basic priorities of Socrates, Plato, and Aristotle. Nevertheless that same history shows that philosophy's way takes turns and reaches destinations distant from its origins. The Holocaust can and should affect philosophy in that way.

Gaarder's project in *Sophie's World* emphasizes four additional dimensions that relate to these perspectives of philosophy and to their post-Holocaust outlooks in particular. Here is how they unfold. First, Gaarder created *Sophie's World* from his teaching, which included introducing philosophy to students who, like Sophie, were unacquainted with its key questions, major figures, and seminal texts, its delights and frustrations, even though these students might have already puzzled over at least some of philosophy's issues without realizing they were doing so. Informed by Holocaust studies, philosophy has important contributions to make in that regard.

Second, Gaarder thought his students would find philosophy most appealing if their introduction to it took the form of a story, a special story in which the characters themselves embodied key philosophical themes. *Ethics During and After the Holocaust* is not exactly a story, let alone a novel, but there are stories in it, and all of them explore versions of the distinction between appearance and reality that are so central to *Sophie's World*.

Next, Gaarder wanted his students and readers to see the several ways in which philosophy is world philosophy. In *Sophie's World*, four of those ways stand out. First, philosophy is world philosophy because *philosophy exists worldwide*. Along with humanity's development, philosophy appears here, there, and everywhere. It does so because questioning and question-asking are basic elements of human experience. The capacity to question takes individuals and communities on journeys that can scarcely be imagined in advance. Journeys to Auschwitz that engage philosophy are important cases in point. Wherever questions are asked, philosophy is not far to find, for philosophy is defined by questions. The forms taken by philosophy's questioning ways have been multiple and diverse. They include short essays and long discourses, but philosophy also finds expression in poetry, memoirs, and fiction. Study of the Holocaust illustrates this fact significantly. While writing is indispensable for philosophy's transmission, face-to-face discussion and community dialogue are essential too. So is the thoughtful reflection that takes place in the silence of personal inquiry. Philosophical study of the Holocaust entails silence of that kind.

Second, philosophy is world philosophy because *philosophy has a history*. No one can date philosophy's birthday exactly. One reason is that philosophy's origins are not easy to separate from religion. Distinctively philosophical ways of thought were under way in India, China, and the Greek world about 2500 years ago. Hinduism and Buddhism, two traditions whose spiritual emphases keep religion and philosophy closely intertwined, were emerging in India. They became most overtly philosophical when analytical questioning and argumentative commentary about the meaning of older traditions and texts asserted themselves. In ancient China, Confucius (551–479 B.C.E.) was planting the seeds of the ethical and political traditions that would bear his name and spawn diverse schools of interpretation, again characterized by analytical questioning and argumentative commentary. Only fragments of their writings remain, but in the Greek world even before Pythagoras introduced the word *philosophy*, thinkers such as Thales, Anaximander, Parmenides, and Heraclitus were discussing the world's origins, change, and the basic physical elements of the natural order through questioning and discussion that separated their inquiry from religion.

Strictly speaking, religion is older than philosophy, but in the twenty-first century—and beyond—the two will continue to have much to do with each other, for religion is a key topic for philosophical investigation, and religion continues to draw on philosophical perspectives to explain, if not to justify, itself. Be that as it may, philosophy is world philosophy because philosophy's history, already multiple in its origins, has unfolded in diverse ways. Its variety continues to increase as global communication permits greater contact between traditions that were previously much more isolated from each other.

When Alberto Knox sent Sophie Amundsen a note that asked "Where does the world come from?," she might have thought about the Hebrew Bible's creation accounts in Genesis. Those narratives have been crucial in the development of philosophy's history, at least in the West, but whether those written texts, let alone the oral traditions behind them, are early examples of philosophy is far from clear. What is more clear is that biblical traditions are among those interrogated by the shadow of Birkenau, and a philosophical analysis of what can and cannot, should and should not, remain of them is one of the most important matters taken up in *Ethics During and After the Holocaust*.

A third way in which philosophy is world philosophy involves the fact that *philosophy seeks to interpret and understand the world*. The word *world* can make us wonder, for it invites questioning. Over time, human beings have come to understand that they exist within a reality as vast as it is varied, complex, ordered, and mysterious. As creatures who can think, inquire, and reason, we try to find out where in the world we are and not only where the world came from but what, in fact, it is.

Sometimes the word *world* refers to Planet Earth. Such uses of *world* are complex enough, but even they are too simple, for the meanings of *world* are rightly more expansive than that. To speak of *the world* can be to speak about all that we can think of and imagine—and maybe even more. It is even appropriate for us to observe that *the* world, whatever it may be, contains *worlds*, for one of the most amazing things about the world is not only the vast expanse of the heavens but also the realms of experience—art, for instance, politics, and commerce—which are part of the world. In addition, the natural order itself contains domains of animal, plant, and even so-called inorganic relationships so extensive and complex as to require ongoing revision of what we can rightly claim to comprehend. If philosophy did not try to understand the world—in all the rich and ambiguous senses of the term—it would not be itself. Philosophy was born to understand the world. It lives to pursue that aim. But the task of philosophy is immensely complicated by the fact that the world includes the event now called the Holocaust and places such as Birkenau, which once was the epicenter of a world of mass destruction and now stands, quietly, as a reminder that the world is also full of absence, in this case the absence of a multitude of Jews who were turned into smoke and ash and have no resting place in the earth.

A fourth way in which philosophy is world philosophy is revealed in *philosophy's power to change the world and to create worlds of its own*. A world with philosophy is very different from a world without it. Philosophy makes the world so different, in fact, that if philosophy were erased from history, the world would scarcely be recognizable. Think of it: No Buddha, no Socrates, no Confucius, no Aristotle—whatever the world might be without them, it would not be ours. With them and the influence of other major philosophical voices, world history contains not only individual philosophers and their works but also philosophical traditions that affect culture, politics, ethics, business, education, and a host of other factors. The world—or worlds—of philosophy make an impact on the world. That impact, however, has not always been good. Philosophy and philosophers have not always stood for justice. Sometimes they have been complicit in the Holocaust and other genocides. Encounters with that history are needed to keep philosophy true to its best identity.

As philosophy develops and changes, the world does too. One way in which this happens involves our understanding of the results of inquiry. Human inquiry takes place in the world, not outside of it. Human inquiry brings about changes in the world too. As the world—or worlds—of philosophy interact with the world, our senses of the world's reality have to take account of the interaction. Doing so can result in even greater diversity within philosophy, for the meaning of that interaction can be interpreted in more than one way that makes sense.

As Gaarder constructs *Sophie's World*, Sophie Amundsen's world is not what it first seems to be. Not only is her world fictional. It is also a world within other fictional worlds. Those worlds, in turn, are realms—important ones, because imagination is such a powerful dimension of experience—of our own world. Without imagination, no Auschwitz could have been planned. It will also take sound ethical imagination to devise the planning and the commitment necessary if genocide and other human rights abuses are to be curbed in the future. There are worlds within worlds, worlds within the world. As Gaarder's reflections amplify understanding about the ways in which philosophy is world philosophy, they also connect with a fourth dimension—philosophy's variety—that is central to his project.

Philosophy's self-defeat and its success

Philosophy's variety helps to focus the historical development of philosophy's story. That development is dialectical—that is, one thing leads to another, but not always in expected ways. Philosophy's development is also paradoxical—that is, philosophy is self-defeating, but its self-defeat, as *Ethics During and After the Holocaust* seeks to show, is related to its most important contributions.

To explain these points, note further what especially struck Gaarder, namely, that every philosopher—at least those who have been most influential in world history—has a project. That project, moreover, involves two elements that are in tension as much as they are linked. On the one hand, the philosopher's project is shared with all philosophers. Wherever philosophy exists, it involves reflection on questions that are likely to interest every human being—no matter who they are, when they live, or where they are situated. True, these questions can be phrased in various ways, but they reflect common human interests in, and reasoned reflection on, topics such as the ones that the German philosopher Immanuel Kant (1724–1804) and the French thinker Henri Bergson (1859–1941) used to define philosophy.

For Kant, philosophy's defining and interrelated issues were these: What can I know? What should I do? For what may I hope?[2] The first question concentrates on what was previously identified as epistemology—inquiry about how we obtain knowledge, how we discern the differences between sound and erroneous judgments, appearance and reality, truth and falsity, and how we use and sometimes abuse language and argumentation that make claims about those matters. Kant understood the second question to deal with ethics, another major philosophical field that was previously mentioned. It involves inquiry about what is good, just, and right, and what is not. Its questions pertain not only to personal life but also to social policy and political power. Kant's third question focused on religion and indirectly—Kant doubted that philosophy could do more—on the fundamental nature of reality. It was prompted by the fact that all human beings die, which can make us wonder what, if anything, life means and what its ultimate destiny, if any, may be. Rare is the philosopher's project that does not attend in some way to questions raised by life's finite duration, the widespread impact of religion, and questions about what endures, perhaps eternally, beyond an individual's existence or even humanity's history.

Bergson would have been more comfortable than Kant in speaking of the category signaled by Kant's third question as metaphysics; that part of philosophy, we noted earlier, that considers what is fundamentally and ultimately real, including what our limited human points of view enable us—and prevent us—from saying about such matters. Metaphysics includes inquiry about the origins of the world and the human life that inhabits it. In addition, metaphysics involves questions about what we are doing here, an issue that is not only ethical but one that can invite inquiry about the nature and structure of human action, freedom and determinism, even the relationship between causes and effects, mind and body, spirit and matter. To his first two defining philosophical questions—Where do we come from? What are we doing here?— Bergson added one more, a version of Kant's third theme: Where are we going?[3] That question is about destination but about direction too. Where is history taking us, and where are we taking it? How should history be understood? To what extent can we govern it, and to what extent does it direct us? Neither Kant nor Bergson could have had Auschwitz in mind when they formed their version of philosophy's defining questions, but as *Ethics During and After the Holocaust* will show, those questions are now indelibly Holocaust-related.

Gaarder saw that, in one way or another, every philosopher's project deals with epistemology, ethics, and metaphysics. On the other hand, he also discerned something else. What he saw brought to the fore philosophy's dialectical development and its paradoxical mixture of self-defeat and success. Gaarder's key insight was that philosophy's universality, its common ground, manifests itself concretely in particularity. The particularity, in turn, involves so much differentiation and disagreement that the unity of philosophy is inseparable from its diversity. Philosophy's diversity—it results from the finding that no particular philosophical view deserves to have the last word—defeats philosophy insofar as philosophy's quest aims at what is taken to be the complete and final attainment of some single, unified, and knowable truth. That diversity, moreover, is extended and intensified by encounters with the Holocaust because that event unavoidably has the effect of eluding the closure that theories or explanations might try to impose upon it. Although philosophy defeats itself and is also defeated by history, especially by the Holocaust and other genocides, it nevertheless may achieve an important kind of limited success. That success consists of awareness that, finite and limited though every philosopher's project surely is, philosophical inquiry can focus questions that humankind ignores at its peril. By doing so, philosophy dispels ignorance and creates insight by means of its questioning, which is often more persistent and penetrating than any other. These successes constitute philosophy's most important contributions to human life.

One philosopher's project, then, is both the same as and different from every other's. No philosopher is so different that the work he or she does cannot be properly placed in one or more of the three major philosophical fields: epistemology, ethics, or metaphysics. But within those fields, the opportunities for difference are considerable. Philosophers seize those opportunities.

As Gaarder sensed, philosophers do so for at least two major reasons. First, one philosopher will honestly believe that previous thinkers missed something important. Correction seems needed. Self-proclaimed, modestly or immodestly, as more discerning, the successor conveniently steps up to provide it. Second, the history of philosophy suggests that philosophers want to be different. They may claim and sincerely believe that philosophical inquiry should ultimately produce universal and even eternal agreement among everyone who inquires rationally about a given issue. Nevertheless, the frequent implication is that such universal and eternal agreement entails accepting what a particular philosopher identifies as the direction to take, even if the philosopher adds the caveat that his or her views may need additional refinement, elaboration, or even further correction.

Philosophers are not copycats. Individually, their project is not primarily to say, "Oh, I just agree with Confucius." or "I think Aristotle is great—he got everything exactly right and there's nothing more to say." To the contrary, philosophers tend to think that no one—at least nobody before them—got enough right, to say nothing of everything, and thus there is much that needs to be said that no one else can say as well. Philosophers may employ humility ironically—Socrates comes to mind—but humility is not usually the philosopher's most obvious virtue. It is no exaggeration to say that philosophers are stubborn, arrogant at times, even as they insist that philosophy's inquiry must be open-ended and self-corrective because, like every form of human inquiry, it is prone to error. In these ways, philosophers can be irritating. They may rub things the wrong way as far as conventional wisdom and received opinion are concerned. In addition, they may fall short of practicing the philosophical virtues that they preach. By no means do I exempt myself from this description as I try to show what philosophy should be, what it should emphasize, and what its limitations have been and will probably continue to be after Auschwitz.

Philosophy's virtues are persistent questioning, critical argumentation, boldly reasoned assertion and testing of hypotheses, and a deep commitment to discerning what is true, good, and right insofar as human minds are capable of doing so. At the end of the day, philosophy and philosophers are interesting, significant, and important because they hold that some fundamental views are true and others false, some key ideas about reality are sound and others unsound, and they question, discuss, argue, and inquire about these matters. If hopes for complete acceptance of their particular views get dashed, they typically return to the fray expecting that greater clarity and insight will emerge. If philosophy defeats itself by showing that the truth it seeks, especially after the Holocaust, is harder to pin down than philosophy sometimes suggested it would be, philosophy still can claim important successes whenever the virtues of a philosophical life are practiced well. No part of the philosopher's project, whether we think of the universality or the particularity of the project, is more valuable and important than that.

The richness of the philosopher's project resides not only in the fact that it involves complex relationships between universality and individuality, between philosophers' common concerns and their insistence on difference. It also depends upon the ways in which particular groups of philosophers share enough specific interests and approaches that traditions or "schools" of philosophy begin to form. Often these traditions or schools originate with individual thinkers who exert such an important influence that a sustained following advances the founder's thought. Buddha, Confucius, Plato, and Aristotle are four striking examples. Each of these formidable thinkers exerted not only far-reaching general influence on world philosophy and world history, but also each of them impressed later individuals so much that their particular ways of thinking—sometimes in style as well as substance—were consciously carried forward.

One tradition usually leads to another. Buddha himself modified the Hindu tradition into which he was born. Aristotle's departures from Platonic thought developed a different philosophical approach in the Greek world. As both of those cases illustrate, the breaks between the earlier and the later movements were not absolute. To the contrary, the differentiation depended on reaction and response to what had gone before. Within the differentiation, new and often unexpected developments do take place. The philosophical approaches of Zen Buddhism, which emerged in thirteenth- and fourteenth-century Japan, had clear connections to Buddha's original ways, but Buddha himself would not have been able to anticipate all that Zen philosophy contains. In recent Western philosophy, influential movements such as existentialism, pragmatism, and the philosophy of language all have roots in impatience with traditions that made bold claims for the power of human reason to develop metaphysical systems that explained everything. Sharing a more skeptical outlook, those three approaches emerged through rebellion against philosophy's past. That rebellion took markedly different paths, and thus new traditions were formed. It is unlikely that a tradition called post-Holocaust philosophy will emerge, but there are signs that the impact of the Holocaust on philosophy and on ethics in particular is being felt. To the extent that this effect takes hold, I believe that philosophy will be the better for it and also that philosophy's contributions to ethics and human well-being after Auschwitz will be improved.

Mavericks that they often tend to be, philosophers are not fond of being pigeon-holed as members of a tradition or school, but the fact is that few, if any, philosophers are traditionless. There are philosophical "birds of a feather," and they do—more or less—flock together. The flocks, however, do not always mix and mingle easily. Disputes erupt. Rivalries form. These results are not only between philosophical traditions and schools but also within them. Such relationships keep philosophy on the move.

One philosopher's project can be classified with those of others. Individual though they are, philosophers are social creatures too. Certainly each one's work has distinctive approaches and themes. For example, just as people are unlikely to mistake Monet's painting for van Gogh's, it is not hard to see that Ludwig Wittgenstein's philosophizing is different from Martha Nussbaum's. Nevertheless, philosophers also belong to philosophical families whose members resemble one another. None of these relationships stays absolutely fixed. Individually and sometimes together, philosophers break away from well-worn paths and blaze new trails. This process is ongoing and never ending. It defeats the philosopher's project, because none of those projects proves to be entirely complete. In philosophy's self-defeat, however, wisdom is found. Even a project destined to be eclipsed can advance our knowledge and understanding. Perhaps especially a project bound to fail can help us to sift and sort what is most important and deserving of our loyalty.

Never give up

As Gaarder's story about Sophie Amundsen and Alberto Knox draws to a close, philosophy has taken them to many an unintended destination. Neither they nor Gaarder's readers are sure what will happen next, and not least of all because the philosophical journey they have taken together makes the world different than it was before. At the end of the book, Sophie is still facing in new ways the question "Who am I?," which started her encounters with Alberto and the world of philosophy.

If the answer to that question, and to all the other questions of philosophy, is not crystal clear, Sophie has apparently taken to heart what may be the most important lesson that the projects of *Sophie's World* and all of philosophy impart: "A true philosopher," Gaarder writes, "must never give up."[4] As well as any representative of world philosophy, the Spanish thinker José Ortega y Gasset (1883–1955) understood what that teaching means.

Born into an aristocratic family in Madrid, Ortega studied philosophy at Spanish and German universities before receiving a teaching appointment at the University of Madrid in 1910. He taught there until the Spanish Civil War began in 1936, but meanwhile he was also active as a journalist and a politician. An opponent of monarchies and dictatorships, Ortega supported democracy in Spain. He served in the parliament of the Second Spanish Republic and for a time was Madrid's civil governor. When the political tide turned during the Civil War, he had to flee from his country. Not until 1948 was he able to return permanently to Madrid after years of exile in Argentina and several European states.

Much of Ortega's writing was first published in newspaper and magazine articles, and he often reworked this material for his numerous books. The best known of these is *The Revolt of the Masses* (1930), which sets forth Ortega's social philosophy. By the time of his death, Ortega was acknowledged to be among the outstanding thinkers in Spanish history and the major contributors to the existential tradition in philosophy. Sophie, Alberto, and almost any person could identify with key themes that were central to his philosophical project.

In *What Is Philosophy?* a book published after his death, Ortega asserted, for example, that "life is a constant series of collisions with the future."[5] Consistently, he might have added that these collisions with the future are also collisions with the past, for events such as the Holocaust keep reverberating in human memory and experience in ways—often ominous and menacing—that inform the future. What he called life's "unforeseen character" is present from the beginning and continues until the end. Ortega believed that every person's birth is something like a shipwreck that puts us, without previous consent, "in a world we neither built nor thought about." No one chooses to be born or to exist in the world we enter at birth. But soon enough, contended Ortega, living becomes "a constant process of deciding what we are going to do." That process makes human identity paradoxical, he thought, because one's life "consists not so much in what it is as in what it is going to be: therefore in what it has not yet become." Those who were murdered in the Holocaust are beyond that existential condition, but those of us who live after them are not. How we are informed about and touched by the Holocaust, existentially and philosophically, can make a big and important difference regarding who we will be and what will come to be.

For Ortega, philosophy is rooted in our collisions with the future. Feeling, thinking, questioning as we do, the undecided, yet-to-be-determined, and therefore unknown elements of existence make philosophy "a thing which is inevitable." But if philosophy is a form of life that arises naturally because we want to know what eludes us, what can philosophy accomplish? Ortega's response to that question produced instructive insights.

A first step, Ortega asserted, is to recall that philosophy comes into existence in response to the fact that life confronts us with what he called "dramatic questions": "Where does the world come from, whither is it going? What is the definitive power in the cosmos? What is the essential meaning of life?" To that list, others might be added: How can we best respond to the Holocaust and to other genocides? If we fail to respond ethically, what will happen? To answer such questions completely, Ortega explained, requires nothing less than "knowledge of the Universe," and that is how Ortega defined philosophy. But understanding what this definition involves also entails asking whether philosophy is really possible.

Part of Ortega's answer was, "I can't be sure that philosophy is possible." He had several reasons for saying so. No human being, for instance, knows what the Universe is as a whole. Even to speak about the "whole Universe" may hide as much as it explains, because *Universe* means "everything that is." Thus, said Ortega, the philosopher "sets sail for the unknown as such." The future of this voyage is profoundly uncertain; no one knows in advance how far it is possible to answer the questions of philosophy. The dilemma, moreover, is not simply that human intelligence may be too frail to know what is knowable. The origin of philosophy's difficulty lies deeper still. "There is also the chance," Ortega thought, "that the Universe may be unknowable for a reason which the familiar theories of knowledge ignore," namely, because "the world, the state of being, the Universe in itself, in its own texture, may be opaque to thought because in itself it may be irrational." Well researched historically though it is, comprehensible up to a point in terms of cause and effect though it may be, the Holocaust does nothing to lay that uneasiness to rest.

Recognizing that we may not be able to satisfy philosophy's hunger, Ortega nevertheless staunchly believed that we should make the attempt.

We can know that we lack knowledge, Ortega thought, and thus we can at least try the philosophical quest. Philosophy is to that extent possible. As Sophie Amundsen came to understand, joining its adventures is one of the qualities that makes us truly human. Post-Holocaust philosophy, especially when it concentrates on what happened to ethics during and after that catastrophe, confirms that judgment. It will also show that true philosophers, far from giving up in the shadow of Birkenau, extend an invitation to learn, to venture into the future, by joining their efforts to mend the world.

2
Why Study the Holocaust?

> I know the difference between before and after.
> Charlotte Delbo, *Auschwitz and After*

Before losing her life to cancer in 1985, Charlotte Delbo wrote that she knew "the difference between before and after."[1] More than forty years earlier, on January 24, 1943, she had been deported from her native France to Auschwitz, the concentration and death camp where more than a million people were gassed to death during the Holocaust. Of the 230 women in her convoy, most of them—like Delbo herself—non-Jews who had worked in the French Resistance, she was one of only 49 who survived.[2] For Delbo, *after* irrevocably referred to Auschwitz. Its reality, she emphasized, was "so deeply etched in my memory that I cannot forget one moment of it."[3]

To the extent that study and teaching about the Holocaust take place today, that work definitely takes place *after*, and that fact may make us ask, "Why should we learn about the Holocaust?" That event is receding further and further into the past. In addition, we live in the aftermath of the terrorist attacks launched against the United States on September 11, 2001. Ours is also a world with almost daily bloodshed in the Middle East, and we live in the midst of a war on terrorism that will not end even with an American victory in Iraq. Those realities only begin a list of worries that seem to provide more than enough to call fond hopes into question. In the United States alone, one thinks of an erosion of trust in business and religious institutions, massive budget deficits that threaten the quality of education, the awareness that the infliction of torture has called the nation's moral integrity into question, and the destruction inflicted by Hurricane Katrina. If we extend the survey of human darkness beyond American shores, it is clear that we are still living in a world—sixty years after the liberation of Auschwitz—that has been repeatedly revisited by mass murder, ethnic cleansing, and genocide. Add to these disasters the resurgence of antisemitism and the catastrophic tsunami that engulfed so much of Asia in 2004, and it seems that worries about the present and the future deserve attention far more than study of the past.

A long-standing trend in Holocaust education might be summed up as follows: We study the Holocaust because it happened, but not only for that reason. We study and teach about it for ethical reasons—even, it has often been said, to ensure that such things never happen again. Unfortunately, history and current events show that answer to be too easy. On the contrary, one could say, given all that has happened after Auschwitz, especially the wasting of human life that continues to accumulate, why learn about the Holocaust? What good could it do to keep doing, or to start doing, that? So, in spite of the fact that American interest in the Holocaust is at an all-time high in the early twenty-first century, in spite of an outpouring of Holocaust-related films or statistics showing, for example, that more than 22 million people have visited the United States Holocaust Museum since its 1993 opening in Washington, DC, a suspicion nags: whatever their trends, learning about the Holocaust may be a waste of time and resources.

The challenge I am posing is one that I think about a great deal because I have devoted much of my life to learning, teaching, and writing about the Holocaust. Thus, I want to address some of the ethical yearnings and aspirations that stand, I believe, at the core of Holocaust studies. Let us see where such an approach might go.

An immense human failure

In our pluralistic world, where cultural, religious, and philosophical perspectives vary considerably, a widely held belief is that values are so relative to one's time and place that the "truth" of moral claims is much more a result of subjective preference and political power than a function of objective reality and universal reason. That relativistic outlook meets resistance in the Holocaust, for there is a widely shared conviction that the Holocaust was *wrong*. An assault not only against Jewish life but also against goodness itself, the Holocaust should not have happened, and nothing akin to it should ever happen again. Michael Berenbaum puts the point effectively when he emphasizes that the Holocaust has become a "negative absolute." Even if people remain skeptical that rational agreement can be obtained about what is right, just, and good, the Holocaust seems to reestablish conviction that what happened at

Auschwitz and Treblinka was wrong, unjust, and evil—period. More than that, the scale of the wrongdoing, the magnitude of the injustice, and the devastation of the Holocaust's evil are so radical that we can ill afford not to have our ethical sensibilities informed by them. As another Holocaust scholar, Franklin Littell, has stressed, "study of the Holocaust is like pathology in medicine."[4] Pathology seeks to understand the origins and characteristics of disease and the conditions in which it thrives. If such understanding can be obtained, the prospects for resistance against disease, and perhaps even a cure, may be increased.

Unfortunately, to identify the Holocaust as a negative absolute that reinstates confidence in moral absolutes is a step that cannot be taken easily, and no one is advised to rush to judgment that study of the Holocaust can obtain the hopeful results of medical pathology at its best. The fact is that the Holocaust signified an immense human failure. It did harm to ethics by showing how ethical teachings could be overridden or even subverted to serve the interests of genocide.[5] When Berenbaum calls the Holocaust a "negative absolute," the absoluteness involved means that not even ethics itself was immune from failure and, at times, complicity in the pathological conditions and characteristics that nearly destroyed Jewish life and left the world morally scarred forever. The status of ethics after the Holocaust is far from settled. One way to focus that fact further involves two of the Holocaust's victims, Calel Perechodnik, who did not survive, and Jean Améry, who did.

Assault and degradation

On August 20, 1942, Calel Perechodnik, a Polish Jew, returned home. This fact is known because Perechodnik recorded it in writing that he began on May 7, 1943. Sheltered at the time by a Polish woman in Warsaw, the 26-year-old engineer would spend the next 105 days producing a remarkable document that is at once a diary, memoir, and confession rooted in the Holocaust.

Shortly before Perechodnik died in 1944, he entrusted his reflections to a Polish friend. The manuscript survived, but it was forgotten and virtually unknown in the English-speaking world until Frank Fox's translation appeared in 1996.[6] Charged with ethical issues, Perechodnik's testament is of special significance because he was a Jewish ghetto policeman in Otwock, a small Polish town near Warsaw. While that role was not his chosen profession, it was a part that he decided to play in February 1941—not knowing all that would soon be required of him.

Already the German occupiers of his native Poland had forced Perechodnik, his family, and millions of other Polish Jews into wretched ghettos. "Seeing that the war was not coming to an end and in order to be free from the roundup for labor camps," Perechodnik wrote, "I entered the ranks of the Ghetto Polizei."[7] When Perechodnik returned home on August 20, 1942, he knew in ways that can scarcely be imagined how optimistic, mistaken, fateful, and deadly even his most realistic assumptions had been. His decision to join what the Germans called the *Ordnungsdienst* (Order Service) had not only required Perechodnik to assist them in the destruction of the European Jews but also implicated him, however unintentionally, in the deportation of his own wife and child to the gas chambers at Treblinka on August 19, 1942. Perechodnik's testament says that he returned home on August 20, but his words indicate that a genocidal Nazi state meant that "home" could never be a reality for him again. That reality challenges some of humanity's fondest assumptions about moral judgments and ethical norms.

In *The Cunning of History*, Richard Rubenstein underscored some of the challenges when he contended that "the Holocaust bears witness to *the advance of civilization*."[8] To see how that proposition bears on the dilemmas that Calel Perechodnik and his family confronted in wartime Poland, it is crucial to understand that the Nazis' racist antisemitism eventually entailed a destruction process that required and received cooperation from every sector of German society. On the whole, moreover, the Nazi killers and those Germans who aided and abetted them directly—or indirectly as bystanders—were civilized people from a society that was scientifically advanced, technologically competent, culturally sophisticated, efficiently organized, and even religiously devout.[9] Those people were, as Michael Berenbaum has cogently observed, "both ordinary and extraordinary, a cross section of the men and women of Germany, its allies, and their collaborators as well as the best and the brightest."[10]

Some Germans and members of populations allied with the Nazis resisted Hitler and would not belong in the following catalog, but they were still exceptions to prove the rule that there were, for example, pastors and priests who led their churches in welcoming nazification and the segregation of Jews that it entailed.[11] In addition, teachers and writers helped to till the soil where Hitler's racist antisemitism took root. Their students and readers reaped the wasteful harvest. Lawyers drafted and judges enforced the laws that isolated Jews and set them up for the kill. Government and church personnel provided birth and baptismal records that helped to document who was Jewish and who was not. Other workers entered such information into state-of-the-art data processing machines. University administrators curtailed admissions for Jewish students and dismissed Jewish faculty members. Bureaucrats in the Finance

Ministry handled confiscations of Jewish wealth and property. Postal officials delivered mail about definition and expropriation, denaturalization, and deportation.

Driven by their biomedical visions, physicians were among the first to experiment with the gassing of "lives unworthy of life." Scientists performed research and tested their racial theories on those branded subhuman or nonhuman by German science. Business executives found that Nazi concentration camps could provide cheap labor; they worked people to death, turning the Nazi motto, *Arbeit macht frei* (Work makes one free), into a mocking truth. Radio performers were joined by artists such as the gifted film director, Leni Riefenstahl, to broadcast and screen the polished propaganda that made Hitler's policies persuasive to so many. Railroad personnel drove the trains that transported Jews to death, while other officials took charge of the billing arrangements for this service. Factory workers modified trucks so that they became deadly gas vans; policemen became members of squadrons that made mass murder of Jews their specialty. Meanwhile, stockholders made profits from firms that supplied Zyklon B to gas people and that built crematoriums to burn the corpses.

The Holocaust's evil appears to be so overwhelming that it forms an ultimate refutation of moral relativism. No one, it seems, could encounter Auschwitz and deny that there is a fundamental and objective difference between right and wrong. Nevertheless, short of Germany's military defeat by the Allies, no other constraints—social or political, moral or religious—were sufficient to stop the "Final Solution." One might argue that Nazi Germany's defeat shows that right defeated wrong and that goodness subdued evil, thus showing that reality has a fundamentally moral underpinning. The Holocaust, however, is far too awesome for such easy triumphalism.

The Nazis did not win, but they came too close for comfort. Even though the Third Reich was destroyed, it is not so easy to say that its defeat was a clear and decisive triumph for goodness, truth, and justice over evil, falsehood, and corruption. Add to those realizations the fact that the Nazis themselves were idealists, a point to which we shall return in more detail later on. They had positive beliefs about right and wrong, good and evil, duty and irresponsibility. We can even identify something that can be called "the Nazi ethic."[12] The "Final Solution" was a key part, perhaps the essence, of its practice, which took place with a zealous, even apocalyptic, vengeance. It would be too convenient to assume that the Nazi ethic's characteristic blending of loyalty, faith, heroism, and even love for country and cause was simply a passive, mindless obedience. True though the judgment would be, it remains too soothing to say only that the Nazi ethic was really no ethic at all but a deadly perversion of what is truly moral. Most people are unlikely to serve a cause unless that cause makes convincing moral appeals about what is good and worthy of loyalty. Those appeals, of course, can be blind, false, even sinful, and the Nazis' were. Nevertheless, the perceived and persuasive "goodness" of the beliefs that constituted the Nazi ethic—the dedicated SS man embodied them most thoroughly—is essential to acknowledge if we are to understand why so many Germans willfully followed Hitler into genocidal warfare.

Paradoxically, the "Final Solution" threatens the status, practical and theoretical, of moral norms that are contrary to those that characterized the Nazi ethic, whose deadly way failed but still prevailed long enough to call into question many of Western civilization's moral assumptions and religious hopes.[13] This dilemma is underscored by statements from *The Cunning of History* that bring Calel Perechodnik's case to mind again: "there are absolutely no limits to the degradation and assault the managers and technicians of violence can inflict upon men and women who lack the power of effective resistance."[14]

The destruction of trust in the world

In the aftermath of the Holocaust, there has been renewed emphasis on the importance of human rights and on the prohibition of crimes against humanity, which can be positive steps for ethics after the Holocaust. Nevertheless Hans Maier, a contemporary of Perechodnik, would concur with Rubenstein's appraisal, which includes the debatable claim that "*rights do not belong to men by nature*. To the extent that men have rights, they have them only as members of the polis, the political community. ... Outside of the polis there are no inborn restraints on the human exercise of destructive power."[15]

Born on October 31, 1912, the only child of a Catholic mother and a Jewish father, more than anything else Maier thought of himself as Austrian, not least because his father's family had lived in that land since the seventeenth century. Hans Maier, however, lived in the twentieth century, and thus it was that in September 1935 he studied a newspaper in a Viennese coffeehouse. The Nuremberg Laws had just been promulgated in Nazi Germany. Maier's reading made him see unmistakably that, even if he did not think of himself primarily as Jewish, the Nazis' policies meant that the cunning of history had nonetheless given him that identity.

Maier lacked the authority to define social reality in the mid-1930s. Increasingly, however, the Nazi state did possess such power. Its laws made him Jewish even if his consciousness did not. As he confronted that reality, the unavoidability of his being Jewish took on another dimension. By identifying him as a Jew, Maier would write later on, Nazi power made him "a dead man on leave, someone to be murdered, who only by chance was not yet where he properly belonged."[16]

When Nazi Germany occupied Austria in March 1938, Maier drew his conclusions. He fled his native land for Belgium and joined the Resistance after Belgium was occupied by the Germans in 1940. Captured by the Gestapo in 1943, Maier was sent to Auschwitz and Bergen-Belsen, where he was liberated in 1945. Eventually taking the name Jean Améry, by which he is remembered, this philosopher waited twenty years before breaking his silence about the Holocaust. When Améry did decide to write, the result was a series of remarkable essays about his experience. One is simply entitled "Torture." Torture drove Améry to the following observation: "The experience of help, the certainty of help," he wrote, "is indeed one of the fundamental experiences of human beings." Thus, the gravest loss produced by the Holocaust, Améry went on to suggest, was that it destroyed what he called "trust in the world, ... the certainty that by reason of written or unwritten social contracts the other person will spare me—more precisely stated, that he will respect my physical, and with it also my metaphysical being."[17]

Améry doubted that rights belong to people by nature. "Every morning when I get up," he tells his reader, "I can read the Auschwitz number on my forearm. ... Every day anew I lose my trust in the world. ... Declarations of human rights, democratic constitutions, the free world and the free press, nothing can lull me into the slumber of security from which I awoke in 1935."[18] Far from scorning the human dignity that those institutions emphasize, Améry yearned for the right to live, which he equated with dignity itself. His experience, however, taught him that "It is certainly true that dignity can be bestowed only by society, whether it be the dignity of some office, a professional or, very generally speaking, civil dignity; and the merely individual, subjective claim (I am a human being and as such I have my dignity, no matter what you may do or say!) is an empty academic game, or madness."[19] Lucidity, believed Améry, demanded the recognition of this reality, but lucidity did not end there. He thought it also entailed rebellion against power that would make anyone a "dead man on leave." Unfortunately, it must also be acknowledged that Améry's hopes for such protest were less than optimistic. On October 17, 1978, he took leave and became a dead man by his own hand.

The writings that Calel Perechodnik left behind include a poignant and disturbing document composed in Warsaw, Poland, on October 23, 1943. Almost apologetically, Perechodnik states, "I am not a lawyer by profession, and so I cannot write a will that would be entirely in order, and I cannot in the present circumstances ask for help from the outside."[20] Explaining his "present circumstances," Perechodnik observes that, "as a result of the order of German authorities, I and my entire family, as well as all the Jews of Poland, have been sentenced to death."[21] This death sentence, he notes, has claimed almost all of his family, and thus Perechodnik's formal, documentary language is also an understated lamentation that records their fate as best he knows it. He has no personal property, Perechodnik goes on to say, but he is the legal heir to property left by his father, Ussher, and wife, Chana. He makes clear what should be done with it. His last testament is a real will, prepared as carefully and executed as properly as Perechodnik knew how.

Nobody can say how much Perechodnik believed that anybody, let alone any legal system, government, or state, would care one whit about his will. Nevertheless—perhaps with irony and protest as much as hope, perhaps to resist despair by asserting his human dignity, or perhaps with none of those feelings—Perechodnik writes respectfully and specifically asks "the Polish court to make possible the execution of this will according to both the spirit of my wishes as well as the law involved."[22] Perechodnik lists the property to which he is heir and designates those to whom he wants to leave it. Giving addresses and exact locations, he carefully explains that the property exists in Otwock, his hometown. There is the movie house called "Oasis." There are two lots and two villas. The latter contain apartments.

The apartments were homes. Not just people but families—Jewish and Polish, members of Perechodnik's family, Perechodnik himself— returned to those family homes after work, school, or shopping, and after journeys that took them away but brought them back home again. After Perechodnik saw his wife and child deported to Treblinka in August 1942, he said that he returned home, but he did not return there—could not do so—because the Holocaust destroyed not only Perechodnik's physical home, leaving him ghettoized, but senses of *home* that are even more precious and profound than the specific places and times without which those deeper senses of *home* cannot exist.

Returning home?

If we think about the most fundamental human needs and about the most important human values, *home* looms large. *Home* means family, parents and children. *Home* connotes shelter and safety, care and love. It has much to do with the senses of identity, meaning, and purpose that govern our lives, because *home* involves our closest relationships with other people and provides key motivations and reasons for the work we do. Not all particular homes fit such descriptions, which sometimes leads us to speak of "broken homes," a condition that no one chooses as good. Unfortunately, the Holocaust and the devastating world war that provided "cover" for it did more than break homes. It ruined them—physically and metaphysically—because the Nazi assault, driven by a debased yearning for an exclusively German homeland, was so successful in destroying the *trust* on which *home* depends.

The senses of *home* that we identify most with goodness depend on stability, fidelity, communal ties, law, government that encourages mutual respect, a shared ethical responsibility, and, for some but not all persons, religious faith. Phrases about *home*—for example, "going home" or "being at home" or even "leaving home"—reflect those elements. The Holocaust, as the philosopher Jean Améry said, destroyed trust in the world. It showed that without sufficient defense, violent powers can leave people bereft of home, if those powers leave their victims alive at all. True, human resilience may act remarkably to rebuild senses of *home* in the ruins but never without a residue of distrust that is metaphysical and perhaps religious as well as political.

Remembering the Holocaust confers obligations in the present and for the future. Moral indignation, of course, can be largely irrelevant when the powers that be determine that the disappearance of defenseless persons and the prosperity of their persecutors constitute business as usual. After Auschwitz ethics must be concerned with outcomes. Seeking ways to "return home," it must emphasize not only good intentions that persist *in spite of* history but also how to achieve results that increase the trust on which our best senses of *home* depend. So much depends on the human will. That fact means that the relationship between *might* and *right* is crucial. Although might does not make right, relationships between right and might still remain, and they are as important as they are complex. Ethics needs the support of politics, but politics also needs ethics, lest it become inhuman.

Consider why Calel Perechodnik was unable to return home. He could not do so because Nazi power prevented him from doing so. No ultimately sustainable reasons—judgments that could stand full critical scrutiny—could be found to justify that Nazi power, but nevertheless Perechodnik could not return home. Might did not make right in that case, but might had much to do with the functional status of right. The same point can be seen in relationships such as the following: A law that is not obeyed may still be a law, but its functional status depends on obedience and credible sanctions against disobedience. An injunction that is not heeded lacks credibility. When Nazi Germany unleashed the Holocaust, the force of the injunction "Thou shalt not murder" was impugned to the degree that millions of Jews were slaughtered before the violence of a world war crushed the Third Reich. Similarly, if God is not acknowledged, God's existence is not necessarily eliminated but God's authority is curtailed. And if God's authority lacks credibility, then the nature of God's existence is affected too.

Our senses of moral and religious authority have been weakened by the accumulated ruins of history and the depersonalized advances of "civilization" that have taken us from a bloody twentieth century into an even more problematic twenty-first. A moral spirit and religious commitment that have the courage to persist *in spite of* humankind's self-inflicted destructiveness are essential, but the question remains how effective those dispositions can be in a world where power, and especially the power of governments, stands at the heart of that matter. To find ways to affect "the powers that be" so that their tendencies to lay waste to human life are checked, ethics after Auschwitz will need to draw on every resource it can find: appeals to human rights, calls for renewed religious sensitivity, respect and honor for people who save lives and resist tyranny, and attention to the Holocaust's warnings, to name only a few. Those efforts will need to be accompanied by efforts that build these concerns into our educational, religious, business, and political institutions. Moves in those directions can be steps toward home.

People study the Holocaust because it happened, but not only for that reason. We study it, teach about it, and try to learn from it primarily for ethical reasons that are rooted in deep longing for a safer and more humane world. That deep longing has everything to do with remembering. Perhaps especially in the twenty-first century, Holocaust studies aim to give us good memories in spite of all that has happened *before* and *after*. That claim contains a paradox that calls for explanation. Of course, I do not mean that the *content* of those memories is good. With the exception of the cases of rescue that were too few and far between, most of the content of Holocaust-related memories is bereft of goodness. In that sense, the Holocaust scholar Lawrence Langer rightly reminds us that "there is nothing to be learned from a baby torn in two or a woman buried alive."[23] Nor do I mean that the good memories Holocaust education aims to create consist only of figures, dates, and facts, important though those details surely are, because it is through such detail, especially when we focus on what happened to particular people in specific places, that we are helped to learn from the Holocaust.

What I do mean is that, as we learn about and from the Holocaust, our memories will become good in the sense that they will not let us forget what is most important. The Holocaust can and should make us see differently. So quickly and in such devastating ways has the Holocaust swept away good things—basic ones that every person needs, such as a home, safe and secure—that too often are taken for granted.

Fateful decisions

This chapter began by referring to Charlotte Delbo. As it draws to a close, I want to refer again to that woman from the French Resistance. Having endured Auschwitz and Ravensbrück, a Nazi camp for women to which she was eventually transferred, Delbo wrote a trilogy called *Auschwitz and After*. It begins with poetic prose that reflects on the theme "Arrivals, Departures." As she recalls the trains that brought Jews to Auschwitz from every corner of Europe, Delbo indicates that Nazi Germany's "Final Solution" meant that "women and children are made to go first."[24]

Depending on the time and place, it was not literally true that women and children were the first to be murdered during the Holocaust. But Delbo's claim still makes sense, because it contains insights about genocidal intent. Nazi Germany sought to make Europe, if not the entire world, *judenfrei* and *judenrein*. In the vocabulary of that regime's racist antisemitism, those lethal euphemisms meant that Jewish life and tradition must be destroyed. To fulfill its dream of a "Jew-free" society, one that would be "cleansed" of every Jewish "pollution," it was not enough to kill men. All Jews had to go, but even if they were not always the first to be killed, Jewish women and children had to have a very real priority nonetheless, for their ability to perpetuate Jewish life could not be tolerated if a truly final "solution" to the so-called Jewish question was to take place.

Heinrich Himmler, head of the SS, clearly understood this point. "We had to answer the question: What about the women and children?" Himmler remembered in one of his speeches. "Here, too, I had made up my mind. ... I did not feel that I had the right to exterminate the men," he went on to say, "and then allow their children to grow into avengers, threatening our sons and grandsons. A fateful decision had to be made: This people had to vanish from the earth."[25] The result was that one and a half million Jewish children, most of them under the age of 15, lost their lives to the Germans and their collaborators in the major killing centers at Chelmno, Belzec, Sobibor, Treblinka, Majdanek, and Auschwitz, and in the thousands of ghettos and camps that set apart Nazi Germany's map of Europe.

Whether one considers the Armenian genocide that preceded the Holocaust or the Rwandan genocide that followed in its wake, the genocidal mentality—wherever it exists—always has the targeting of children somewhere in view. To the extent that such a mentality is "logical," it must give priority to the elimination of children, one way or another. If outright killing is not the method of choice, and not every form of genocide requires the extreme paths that were taken in the Holocaust, then the elimination can and must be obtained by cultural destruction that renders the continuation of a people's identity problematic, if not impossible. If genocidal impulses are to be kept in check, children should go first, but in a very different sense than Delbo had in mind when she wrote *Auschwitz and After*.

Who goes first? That question was at the core of the Holocaust, and for that reason, it remains crucial today. If genocide is to end, children must go first in the sense of coming first. If there is to be healing after the Holocaust, there is no better place to begin than with the world's children. If humankind cared for its children—all children, not just "mine" and "yours"—not only would genocide be a thing of the past, but arguably many of the world's other ills would be in remission, if not cured. The quality of human life depends on our putting children first. Holocaust education remains an effective, even indispensable, way of doing so. Why learn about the Holocaust? One of the best reasons is because our doing so is a crucial reminder of the importance of putting children first.

The difference between *before* and *after* should make us remember to take nothing good for granted. That point deepens, intensifies, and grips me more and more as the trends in my own Holocaust education continue. Why study the Holocaust, why teach about it as we move further away from the years in which that event took place but seemingly no further away from the wasting of life that human beings inflict on one another? For me, the bottom-line answer to that question is not-so-simply this: *No work that I know does more than study of the Holocaust to make me remember to take nothing good for granted.* Other aspects of the past or current experience may drive home that point as well, but learning about the Holocaust has compelling power to do so. Especially *after*, we fail to learn about the Holocaust not only at our own peril but at our children's as well.

3
Handle with Care

After Treblinka ... / We see differently.
Edward Bond, "How We See"

In chapter 2, the focus was on the question "Why study the Holocaust?" With the epigraph from the British poet Edward Bond offering the reminder that the Holocaust ought to make us see differently, this chapter turns to the topic "How should the Holocaust be studied?" An unpacking of that question reveals some important ethical implications embedded in and entailed by an interdisciplinary approach to Holocaust studies, an approach that is required if study of the Holocaust is itself to be ethically sound. As this chapter shows, those implications exist because of what happened to ethics during and even long before the Holocaust.

My thesis is that "handle with care" is the most basic ethical requirement and implication of interdisciplinary Holocaust studies. To explain what I mean, I will begin with an episode from the Holocaust's history and with a moment from my own teaching. Then I will consider briefly how several angles of vision amplify what it means to handle the Holocaust with care. These illustrative ways of seeing the Holocaust—many other disciplines could be cited—include history, gender studies, literature and the arts, and religious studies.

An episode

On May 4, 1961, Dr. Aharon Peretz, a survivor of the Kovno ghetto, gave testimony in Jerusalem during the postwar trial of the Holocaust perpetrator Adolf Eichmann. Peretz described how the Germans rounded up Lithuanian Jews, including several thousand children who were driven to a killing site and then shot to death. He remembered one moment in particular:

> A mother whose three children had been taken away—she went up to
> this automobile and shouted at the German, "Give me the children,"
> and he said, "You may have one." And she went up into that auto-
> mobile, and all three children looked at her and stretched out their
> hands. Of course, all of them wanted to go with their mother, and the
> mother didn't know which child to select and she went down alone,
> and she left the car.[1]

No single discipline, and arguably no scholarly or pedagogical perspective imaginable, can fully encompass the Holocaust and its legacy,
because that catastrophe included such a vast array of episodes akin
to the one that Peretz recalled. Each of those events differed, because
men, women, and children perished one by one, just as every killer,
bystander, or rescuer was an individual with all the complex relationships and circumstances that such identity includes. Nevertheless, there
is much that can be understood about the Holocaust, provided we take
the limits of understanding seriously, which involves the recognition
that multiple perspectives, ones that skillfully weave different angles of
vision together, give us the best chances to learn *about* and also *from* the
Holocaust.

A moment

I start my Holocaust courses by asking my students to write some information about themselves. For example, I invite them to share with me
what they enjoy doing outside of their academic work. I ask what they
hope to be doing in ten or fifteen years. I also inquire about their major
academic interests. In the next class meeting, I offer feedback with some
interdisciplinary and ethical points in mind.

This opening allows me to note how healthy and active my students
must be, because so many of them enjoy sports, dancing, and working
out. There are runners, hikers, campers, and skiers among them, plus
swimmers, basketball players, and champions of "ultimate frisbee."
There are also those who love music and who are involved in art,
theater, and religious pursuits. I remind my students that Jews who
perished in the Holocaust enjoyed such activities too. So did the
Holocaust's perpetrators. So did people who stood by or those who
risked their lives to rescue others. The Holocaust involved ordinary
people who were alike in many ways but also extraordinarily different in

many others. How to understand that configuration is a puzzle marked "handle with care."

When my students indicate what they hope to be doing in ten or fifteen years, their answers are suggestive in multiple ways. Frequent responses identify a professional role of one kind or another. Some want to manage or own a business; some want to practice law or medicine. Others have journalism in mind. Still others envision themselves as artists or teachers. Sometimes the answers are much more vague: I want to be doing "something I enjoy," or they may say, "I'm not sure." Nearly all of the students, however, indicate that they hope to marry and to become parents. As you can imagine, all of these responses brim with "interdisciplinary" significance but two aspects are especially noteworthy: First, the Holocaust's victims had similar hopes, but for the most part those hopes were stolen from them. Second, those hopes were taken from people by people who were in every one of the professions the students mention and more. Those hopes were stolen from people by people who had wives, husbands, lovers, and children. Many questions trail such relationships. No quick responses to them are likely to be sound.

When the students list their primary areas of academic interest, the spread is again considerable. In one recent class, psychology was the field most often identified, but history and politics, economics and philosophy, gender studies, religious studies, the arts, biology, and even neuroscience were also represented. The students grasp—sometimes more intuitively than academic specialists—not only that all of these fields can contribute to Holocaust studies, but also that our approaches are likely to be inadequate, or at least less rich than they need to be, if they lack a variety of outlooks. At the same time, the students can see that there is no virtue in an interdisciplinary approach that is superficial, lacking in focus and rigor. To paraphrase comments by the Holocaust historian Christopher Browning, it is not only important to survey the landscape but also to study the twigs and bushes and to do so with the distinctive tools and styles of individual disciplines, blending them where and when one can as best one knows how, a challenging task that should also be marked "handle with care."[2]

History: no closure

Historical research is the bedrock discipline for study of the Holocaust and for achieving understanding not only about how and why it happened but also about the ethical issues and insights that flow from such study. Everyone who approaches the Holocaust as a student or teacher owes an immense debt to scholars who do the painstaking work of archival research, where written documents are appropriately the coin of the realm. The Holocaust's documents, of course, come in many shapes and sizes. There are the railroad timetables that Raul Hilberg has shown to be invaluable for grasping how the perpetrators made the Holocaust happen, but there are also the memoirs of Charlotte Delbo and Primo Levi and the testimonies of *Sonderkommandos*—the predominantly Jewish squads in Auschwitz–Birkenau who were forced to man the gas chambers and crematoria—which have been gathered by Gideon Greif.[3]

Much of the Holocaust's documentation has been lost forever. The murdered cannot speak. The Germans destroyed massive amounts of evidence or war's devastation turned it to rubble. The survivors of the Shoah Visual History Foundation has more than 50,000 survivor testimonies in its holdings, but the Holocaust's perpetrators have said comparatively little about what they did.

Historians study the twigs and bushes and they survey the landscape, but it remains the case that the Holocaust and its legacy are so vast that, at best, there can be only selective historical narratives and analyses about it. Done well, they more or less weave together reliable glimpses, documented perspectives, focused but not all-embracing slices from a destruction process that swept through a continent from 1933 to 1945. This melancholy work is done not to achieve an unattainable mastery but, as Hilberg says, "lest all be relinquished and forgotten."[4]

Is the Holocaust "historically explicable," to use Yehuda Bauer's phrase?[5] When Bauer defines that term, he suggests that "the historical craft (history is no science) makes it possible to explain an event in general terms. If the historians are successful, then many, if not most, of its facets can be explained adequately." I do not disagree with such claims, but I think they must be handled with care, for much hinges on the meaning of words such as *general terms* and *adequately* as well as on the meaning of *explanation* itself. To raise questions about such concepts does not lead, at least not necessarily, to what Bauer has called "a postmodernist stance that would deny factual objectivity and deny the possibility, ultimately, of any historical conclusions."[6] What does follow, I believe, is that scholars and teachers should have the modesty to realize that historical inquiry about the Holocaust has an open-ended and, therefore, somewhat inconclusive quality about it

That claim makes sense for at least two reasons: First, new findings may appear and interpretations will vary (sometimes considerably).

Anyone who reads Holocaust historians seriously comes to see that even when basic facts are agreed upon, the historical interpretations do not stay fixed and in one place, nor is it likely that they will do so. Second, history is not all there is. History is part of reality, not the whole of it, and history neither does nor can explain itself. The importance of historical research for grasping how and why the Holocaust happened—and that importance is as huge as the best historical research is reliable—can also make us aware of something else that is equally significant: *No discipline or combination of them "owns" the Holocaust. If history is the foundation, it is not the whole of Holocaust studies. One of the important, if not entirely intended, contributions that history makes to Holocaust studies is to show that other disciplines are needed but that no one of them or all of them together can achieve finality and closure.*

Gender studies: no simplicity

The Holocaust took an immense toll on Jewish children. From the Nazi perspective, their die was cast by the faith of their great-grandparents. No mercy could be shown to boys and girls thus targeted; they were the next generation of the racially threatening population that must be eliminated. So, as Isaiah Trunk argued, "Jewish children had to fend for themselves in a world so base no prior experience could have prepared them for it. ... The percentage of Jewish children who survived this German infanticide is the lowest of any age group to have come out of the Holocaust alive."[7] One and half million Jewish children, most of them under the age of fifteen, lost their lives to the Germans and their collaborators. What about their mothers and grandmothers, their aunts and older sisters? What happened to women during the Holocaust?

Although many Holocaust memoirs written by women have existed for a long time, questions specifically about women, or about gender differences in any respect, got relatively little attention in Holocaust scholarship until the 1990s. In the most basic way, of course, the Holocaust's killing drew no distinctions among Jews: Hitler and his followers intended oblivion for them all—every man, woman, and child. Nevertheless, as pioneering efforts by scholars such as Elizabeth Baer, Myrna Goldenberg, Marion Kaplan, Dalia Ofer, Joan Ringelheim, Carol Rittner, Lenore Weitzman, and others have shown, the hell was the same for Jewish women and men during the Holocaust, but the horrors were frequently different.

Women's experiences during the Holocaust varied immensely. While German women, for instance, were expected to bear children for the

Third Reich, Jewish women had to be prevented from becoming mothers. The Nazis invested considerable time and energy to find the most effective ways to sterilize them, but the "Final Solution" for this "problem" was death. Of course, if they were healthy and neither too old nor too young, Jewish women could be used before they were used up or killed. At Auschwitz, for example, some were "selected" for slave labor; at Ravensbrück, a concentration camp established especially for women, others became objects for the "scientific" experiments that were intended to advance Nazi programs of racial hygiene and purity.

Women could be found among other victim groups during the Holocaust—Roma and Sinti, political prisoners, Jehovah's Witnesses, and the so-called asocials, to name a few. In addition, women were among the neighbors who stood by while Jews were rounded up and deported all over Europe. They were among those who rescued Jews as well. Women could be found in virtually every intersection and intricacy of the Holocaust's web. Such facts make analysis and understanding of the Holocaust far more complex than was the case before attention to gender differences staked an appropriate claim in Holocaust studies. It does not follow, of course, that the perspectives of gender studies automatically produce good scholarship and sound teaching about the Holocaust. Here, too, "handle with care" is an ethical implication that deserves attention, even as gender studies puts forth a fundamental ethical insight of its own, namely, that *study of the Holocaust takes away the comfort of simplicity.*

Literature and the arts: no feelings = no understanding

The Germans sent Primo Levi to Auschwitz from his native Italy in late February 1944. He called his deportation "a journey towards nothingness."[8] Eight months later, Levi knew that autumn's receding light and retreating warmth meant that the devastation of another Auschwitz winter was at hand. "From October to April," he understood, "seven out of ten of us will die. Whoever does not die will suffer minute by minute, all day, every day."[9] *Winter*, insisted Levi, was not the right word for that dreadful season. Nor could *hunger* and *pain* capture the realities of Auschwitz.

If the Holocaust did not last long enough to produce in full the "new, harsh language" to which Levi thought it would give birth, that event continues to leave survivors, historians, philosophers, theologians, novelists, and poets groping for words.[10] Related experiences confront film makers, musicians, and artists who try to use their gifts to ensure that the Holocaust will not be forgotten. Out of those struggles have come remarkable and instructive responses to the Holocaust.

The philosopher Theodor Adorno argued that it would be barbaric to write poetry after the Holocaust. His claim rightly condemns artistic and literary responses that ignore or trivialize the Holocaust, but Adorno's judgment should not be applied to all the literature and art that the Holocaust has evoked. Adorno himself knew as much, for his dialectical thinking challenged his own attack on post-Holocaust poetry. "Perennial suffering has as much right to expression as a tortured man has to scream," he wrote, "hence it may have been wrong to say that after Auschwitz you could no longer write poems."[11]

Not only have artistic and literary responses done much to keep memory of the Holocaust alive, but also the most powerful and authentic expressions of that kind help to drive home a deepened sense of the losses that the Holocaust produced, the warnings that reverberate from them, and the questions that remain. Just as no one history book can fully contain the Holocaust, let alone completely explain it, no film, musical score, painting, memoir, essay, novel, or poem can provide access to more than a sliver of that disaster. Yet when such contributions are well done, memory can be sharpened, feeling sensitized, understanding increased, and memorialization enhanced in ways that we can ill afford to be without. One could sum up these points by underlining another ethical implication embedded in and entailed by interdisciplinary Holocaust education: *Absent the feelings that the best Holocaust-related art and literature evoke, understanding of the Holocaust will be diminished, if it can be said to exist at all.*

Religious studies: exploring the depths of the Holocaust's roots and implications

As Mel Gibson's excruciatingly bloody scourging of Jesus reaches its climax in his controversial blockbuster *The Passion of the Christ*, one of Pontius Pilate's lieutenants intervenes and chastises the Roman soldiers for excessive brutality. "You weren't supposed to beat him to death!" he exclaims. That moment was only one of many that jarred me when I saw Mel Gibson's film two days after it opened in the United States on February 25, 2004. Given the scourging that Gibson created, the judgment of Pilate's lieutenant seemed ludicrous and incredible. After such a beating, scarcely anyone could have remained alive, as Jesus had to be for his crucifixion to follow. Of course, a caveat in that judgment is needed, and this point is no doubt one that Gibson wanted to make: namely, Jesus was not "anyone"; he was the incarnation of God and thus able to take any abuse that human beings could devise and still triumph over it.

At least four Holocaust-related realizations follow from the description I have offered. They can help us to see how the study of religion is crucial for interdisciplinary Holocaust education. First, few events, if any, in human history have had more volatile consequences and potent implications than the ancient Roman execution by crucifixion of a relatively obscure Jewish teacher from Galilee. To employ one of several shorthand equations, which I use to put key issues in bold relief: *No crucifixion of Jesus = No Western civilization as we know it.*

Second, the reason that equation holds is that the crucifixion of Jesus has always played a decisive part in the Christian tradition's understanding of God, the world, and the meaning of our individual lives. These connections are so strong that one may confidently assert another equation: *No crucifixion of Jesus = No Christianity.* Absent Christianity, Western civilization and indeed the world as we know it would be inconceivable.

Taking the New Testament gospels as the historically accurate source, Mel Gibson's film arrived amidst claims that it truthfully portrayed what really happened during the last twelve hours of Jesus' earthly life. However, as many have already pointed out, Gibson's film is authentic neither as history nor as a representation of the gospels, at least as far as the details are concerned. To one watching the film, checking the New Testament texts, and tracking Gibson's use of sources, it is apparent that *The Passion of the Christ* is a highly idiosyncratic interpretation of events whose reality remains elusive. Thus, a third key point emerges: Beyond the barest of outlines, no one today can be very confident that they know precisely what happened in Jerusalem during the last twelve hours of Jesus' life. That Jesus was crucified is not in question, but precisely how and why the crucifixion took place is profoundly contested. Hence, another equation holds: *No crucifixion of Jesus = No Christian–Jewish rivalry.*

Fourth, the Christian–Jewish rivalry had such catastrophic implications that, particularly after the Holocaust, we Christians should be especially careful about how the crucifixion of Jesus is interpreted and portrayed. Nazi Germany's attempt to destroy the Jewish people would have been virtually inconceivable without Christianity's (my tradition's) negative depictions of Jews. That conjunction creates a shameful burden that should shake Christianity to its core. The shame, in turn, should lead not only to repentance about the Christian tradition's long-standing, and only very recently reformed, stance toward Jews but also to fundamental rethinking about what it should and should not mean to be a Christian after Auschwitz. Among the many shortcomings of Gibson's film, therefore, I believe that none is more egregious than its insensitivity about the Holocaust, its failure to acknowledge the equation: *No crucifixion of Jesus = No Holocaust.*

Less than a month after I saw *The Passion of the Christ*, I was teaching my students on an academic travel program in Poland and the Czech Republic. For several days, we worked at the Auschwitz–Birkenau State Museum. Walking through the Auschwitz gate inscribed with the mocking motto *Arbeit Macht Frei*, standing before the crematoria ruins at Birkenau, I thought about the crucifixion of Jesus and about Gibson's interpretation of it. As a Christian, I felt shame and anger—shame for Christianity's complicity in the Holocaust and anger about Mel Gibson's negative portrayals of Jews, which were set forth as if the Holocaust never happened. No post-Holocaust portrayal of the crucifixion can be trustworthy if it fails to link the crucifixion to that twentieth-century catastrophe. Gibson's film forged no links of that kind, but interdisciplinary Holocaust education must not shy away from the resulting ethical challenge, which demands savvy in the area of religious studies. *Among the many contributions that the discipline of religious studies can make—perhaps as no other—is to explore the depths of the Holocaust's roots and implications. Such inquiry goes to the heart of what it means to be human. "Handle with care" should be its hallmark too.*

Antisemitism and the shadow of Birkenau

I do not know if Mel Gibson has ever visited Auschwitz or even encountered the echoes of the Holocaust as they are found, for example, in the United States Holocaust Memorial Museum in Washington, DC. Be that as it may, a visit to such places is a profoundly thought-provoking experience before or after viewing *The Passion of the Christ*, for Christians ought to view Gibson's film—even if he did not—with the following ethical question in mind: How are the Holocaust and Christianity linked together?

In the Holocaust Memorial Museum, biblical words from the prophet Isaiah—"You are my witnesses"—are inscribed on a wall where it is difficult for visitors to miss them.[12] Whenever I visit the Museum, I stop for a moment to read that ancient text, which at once expresses an expectation, a commandment, and a fact. Those simple but immensely challenging words make me think about my Christian identity, and after February 2004, they are likely to make me think again about *The Passion of the Christ* in particular. Specifically, Isaiah's words require me to reflect on Christianity's relationship to the Holocaust and to wrestle with the implications of that event for my religious tradition.

Most of my academic life has been devoted to studying the Holocaust. Frequently people wonder how I became involved in that work, which has been my passion for more than thirty years. Sometimes people ask, "Are you Jewish?" perhaps assuming, mistakenly, that dedicated attention to Holocaust history is something that only Jews are likely to pursue. To the question "Are you Jewish?" I would be glad and proud to answer "Yes," but my identity is different. It is precisely because of my Christian identity that I have immersed myself in the study of the Holocaust, for I believe that my identity (as indeed anyone's identity as a Christian) is linked to that catastrophe. As I explain what I mean, I also want to suggest how we Christians might reidentify ourselves in a post-Holocaust situation and how we might do so in ways that would give our tradition greater integrity, an integrity that depends in so many ways on solidarity with Jewish tradition and the Jewish people. Meanwhile, the tragedy of Mel Gibson's film is that it subverts and undercuts the very solidarity that Christianity needs to reclaim in order to redeem itself.

To develop these ideas with Gibson's film in mind, follow me from the entry hall in the United States Holocaust Memorial Museum, where Isaiah's words are inscribed, to a smaller but even more solemn place within the Museum, a circular space called the Hall of Remembrance. The names of Nazi killing centers, such as Auschwitz and Treblinka, where Jews were gassed, can be found around the perimeter of this hall. The Hall of Remembrance also includes places for memorial candles to be lit in honor and memory of the six million Jewish children, women, and men who were killed, one by one, in those camps of death and destruction. Opposite the entry to this circular hall, an eternal flame burns in a place where soil from camps in Poland, Germany, and other countries has been deposited.

Biblical words appear on the circular walls of the Hall of Remembrance. Shared by Jews and Christians, the three passages from the Hebrew Bible can be read in different sequences, depending on how one's eyes follow the arc that contains them. Consider those three passages (one from Genesis, the other two from Deuteronomy) as guideposts for deepening reflection about identity, integrity, and being a witness, especially as those ideas relate to Christian life after the Holocaust and after Mel Gibson's *Passion* has gone from theaters.

The first biblical quotation says this: "And the Lord said, 'What have you done? Listen; your brother's blood is crying out to me from the ground.' "[13] Those words remind one that witnesses are those who have seen or heard something. They are people who are called to testify. They furnish evidence. Often, they sign their names to documents to certify an event's occurrence or a statement's truth. So, when one reads that verse from the Genesis story of Cain and Abel, God's question calls for testimony and for bearing witness.

A Christian who reads those words (What have you done?) in the United States Holocaust Memorial Museum setting must do some soul-searching about identity and integrity, for the Holocaust's history testifies to a disturbing fact, namely, that while Christianity was not a sufficient condition for the Holocaust, Christianity was a necessary condition for that disaster. That statement does not mean that Christianity caused the Holocaust.[14] Nevertheless, the Holocaust that actually happened is scarcely imaginable apart from Christianity because Nazi Germany's targeting of the Jewish people cannot be explained apart from the anti-Jewish images ("Christ-killers," willful blasphemers, unrepentant sons and daughters of the Devil, to name only a few) that have been rooted deeply in Christian practices—and, ominously, reappear in Gibson's film.

Especially after Christianity came to dominate the Roman world in the fourth century of the Common Era, Christian images and institutions that vilified and demonized Jews started laying the groundwork for an increasingly multifaceted antisemitism. Frequently inspired by the New Testament's crucifixion narratives and the interpretations evoked by those texts, these ideas came decisively to define and govern many of Western civilization's most influential worldviews. Well before the Nazi Party struggled its way into existence in the aftermath of World War I, antisemitism was so axiomatic in Christian-dominated cultures that, with few exceptions, Jews could be fully included within Western civilization's fundamentally Christian-defined boundaries of moral obligation only if they first rejected their Jewishness. Understandably, most Jews chose not to do so.

There can be no credible doubt about it: what we can call Christian antisemitism provided essential background, preparation, and motivation for the Holocaust that happened when Germans and their collaborators carried out the "Final Solution" of the so-called Jewish question. "What have you done?"—God's question to Cain—is a question put to Christians, too, and it is put to us Christians in a crucial way after the Holocaust, a reminder that *The Passion of the Christ* might have underscored, but, unfortunately, did not.

The second biblical quotation in the Hall of Remembrance at the United States Holocaust Memorial Museum says this: "Keep these words that I am commanding you today in your heart. Recite them to your children and talk about them when you are at home and when you are away, when you lie down and when you rise."[15] They are inscribed above the eternal flame that burns in the Hall of Remembrance near the spot where soil from the Nazi death camps has been deposited. In that place, standing before those words should make deep impressions on Christians, and, at least for me, they do. Those impressions involve, once again, identity, integrity, and being a witness.

The words inscribed from Deuteronomy are calls to living witness, which entails not only personal and communal experience but also memory of it, so that one's witnessing has specific content that can be passed from one generation to another. Such calls are crucial because the Jewish saying is true when it proclaims that in remembering and bearing witness lie the redemption of the world. That outlook, of course, is not referring to just any kind of bearing witness. Its particularity argues that bearing witness should keep ourselves and our children close to God and on the right path.

Bearing witness is hard and often painful work, but it can remind us of other qualities. More importantly, bearing witness, from generation to generation, calls us post-Holocaust Christians back to our roots in ways that remind us about who we are and who we ought to be when we are at our best. Here I can clarify my meaning by emphasizing that what drew me to study the Holocaust included a growing conflict between two features of my experience. On the one hand, although not without qualification, I have experienced Christianity as something good. On the other hand, I know that Christianity, my tradition, has not been good for everyone; the Holocaust bears witness to that. Thus, I found myself wanting to know where things had gone so badly wrong, especially insofar as Christians and Jews are concerned. In the process of self-definition, I came to believe that we Christians have lost sight of our close and essential ties to Jewish tradition.

Very few people anywhere—American or not—would be among the world's two billion Christians if it were not for a centuries-old Christian mission whose history includes Holocaust-related hostility to Jews and Judaism, even if many Christians are not as aware of this fact as we ought to be. Lest I be misunderstood, my point is not that anti-Judaism was or is the underlying force behind the evangelism that made Christianity a global religion, but Christians need to come to terms with the fact that antipathy toward Jews and Judaism has been embedded persistently in the Christian tradition that has been spread far and wide. It is neither sufficient nor indeed historically accurate to say that Christians who have harbored anti-Jewish sentiments or even antisemitism have not been real Christians. This revisionism is reflected in post-Holocaust teachings that antisemitism is a sin, but Christians need to face the fact that our tradition has not sustained that approach for very long. In fact, the mainstream of Christianity long has been anti-Jewish, if not antisemitic, including the greatest leaders of the Christian churches, such as Augustine of Hippo and Martin Luther, to cite but two. It is for this reason that post-Holocaust reform of the Christian tradition continues to be necessary.

Many contemporary Christians—like those of us who live in the United States and flocked to see Mel Gibson's film—may wonder why we need to remember Christianity's role in the Holocaust. After all, we might argue, that involvement took place long ago and far away. It was part of Europe's "Old World" corruption. In our country, we twenty-first-century Americans may be tempted to say, things have been different; we made a new beginning and we broke away from fallen European ways. The Holocaust was not, could not have been, any responsibility of ours, especially if, like me, we live in Mel Gibson's California, which is about as far away from Auschwitz as one can get.

The problem is that Gibson's film has much more in common with pre-Holocaust Christian animosity toward Jews than it does with post-Holocaust reconciliation between Christianity and Judaism. Judging by polls that differentiate between Americans who have seen the film and those who have not,[16] *The Passion* leaves no doubt that Jews were the instigators and unrelenting advocates of that gruesome death. To be sure, Gibson and his supporters have claimed that all of humanity, not any group in particular, is responsible for the crucifixion of Jesus and the suffering of God. However, such universalizing is too easy, too convenient, as a way out of the dilemmas that attend narratives that are unavoidably particular and specific. Christianity, like Judaism, does not regard God primarily as a universalizing, cosmic metaphysician but as One who acts in very specific and concrete ways within history. If the responsibility is universal, and therefore everyone's but no one's in particular, then Gibson's authority for saying that his account is faithful to the New Testament is in double jeopardy: once for going far beyond the texts, and twice for not taking them seriously enough. And if Gibson wanted to advance an account of universal human responsibility for the crucifixion, his film does a very poor job of making that case.

The problem with it is that it relies too much on emotion, and not enough on accuracy.

Let us return to the words from Deuteronomy inscribed above the eternal flame in the Hall of Remembrance at the Holocaust Museum. The commandment to bear witness contained in the words from Deuteronomy immediately follows other words that say, "Hear, O Israel: The Lord is our God, the Lord is One. You shall love the Lord your God with all your heart, with all your soul, and with all your might."[17] When the Christian New Testament reports that Jesus was asked which commandment was the first of all, he paraphrased those words in reply, adding in true Jewish fashion that the second is to love your neighbor as yourself.[18] Then, when Jesus was asked to define one's neighbor, he told the parable of the Good Samaritan,[19] a figure who epitomizes what it ought to mean to be a Christian. The key point here, however, is that we Christians have our identity because the workings of history put before us a relationship with God that can be understood neither apart from Jewish history nor (and this is very important) apart from the ongoing vitality of Jewish life.

We Christians came to know God through the Jewish tradition as Jesus and his followers made that tradition accessible to us and grafted us into it.[20] As time passed, changes distorted those connections, and, tragically, the full price of those distorted connections would not be exacted or known until the Holocaust scarred the earth. Nevertheless, the basic point was there to be recognized all along: if Christians are the followers of Jesus, a faithful Jew, then our responsibility is to love God and to love our neighbors—most emphatically including Jesus' Jewish people—as ourselves. As we Christians interpret the identity of Jesus, the bottom line comes back to those words from Deuteronomy that are inscribed above the eternal flame in the Hall of Remembrance, including the way in which they point to God. Christian reidentification after the Holocaust, I believe, can lead to a deepened integrity for Christian life just to the extent that there is a Christian *teshuvah*, a repentant returning to a love of our rootedness in Jewish tradition.

This returning needs to emphasize something very different from the negative pictures of Jews highlighted by Mel Gibson's *Passion*. That is, Jews are not indebted to Christians; rather, we Christians are indebted to them. As Clark Williamson, a thoughtful Christian theologian, has put it, we Christians should think of ourselves as guests in the house of Israel and behave accordingly.[21] Mel Gibson's filmmaking in *The Passion of the Christ* does not fit that description.

Finally, as my eyes follow the Hall of Remembrance's arc from left to right, from words that question "What have you done?" to words, illuminated by an eternal flame, that encourage one to live and bear witness, a third inscription requires attention as well. Its words, attributed to Moses, say this: "I have set before you life and death ... Choose life so that you and your descendants may live."[22] As I think about those words, I am reminded of Pope John Paul II's special concert at the Vatican in April 1994 to commemorate the Holocaust.[23] It was a night of "firsts," although not entirely a cause for celebration because the "firsts" were so late in coming.

On that occasion, for example, the chief rabbi of Rome was invited for the first time to co-officiate at a public function in the Vatican. (In 1994, Rav Elio Toaff held that position.) For the first time, a Jewish cantor sang in the Vatican. For the first time, a 500-year-old Vatican choir sang a Hebrew text in performance—Leonard Bernstein's *Chichester Psalms*. Late though these "firsts" turned out to be, the music at the Vatican's interfaith concert was moving, and the pope's concluding words went to the heart of the matter when he asked the concert's listeners to observe silence and to "hear once more the plea, 'Do not forget us,' " a plea rising from the Holocaust's victims, the dead and the living. Calling it "powerful, agonizing, heartrending," Pope John Paul II also suggested that no memory can be worthy of that plea unless remembering leads people to resist what he called "the specter of racism, exclusion, alienation, slavery, and xenophobia" and to act so that "evil does not prevail over good," as it did for millions of Jews during the Holocaust.

The music, the pope's words, and particularly the *Chichester Psalms* accented a very important point: the value of beliefs (Christian or Jewish) must be measured by the justice or injustice, the good or evil, they inspire. Therefore, we must measure our Christian beliefs— including beliefs surrounding the Passion of Jesus—against both their contributions to the Holocaust *and* their responsiveness to it. Such a test leaves Christianity wanting in ways that should make my religious tradition much less triumphalist and much more modest than it has been in the past and still often is. More than ever, Christianity requires honesty, candor, and atonement—indeed, living witness that protests against injustice and that tries its best to protect those who fall prey to evil.

The post-Holocaust condition that is most necessary for us Christians is a spiritual and ethical turning, a soul-searching (personal and communal) that leads us to ask: What should it mean for me, for us, to be Christian after Auschwitz? Sound Christian responses to that question are still taking time to form. Christianity will have the identity and integrity that it needs only to the extent that these responses are formed well. Those responses should focus on three points:

1. Our answer to the question, "What have you done?"
2. Our acknowledgment that Christians are followers of the Jew named Jesus; and
3. Our responsibility to choose life.

Thinking and acting well with regard to these points will qualify Christians to respond authentically to the Deuteronomic charge that we bear witness in everything that we do. Only to the extent that we post-Holocaust Christians make that response an honest one will our identity and integrity become what they ought to be.

My identity—perhaps the identity of each of us—is in its own way inseparable from Christianity, but that proposition does not mean that either our personal identities or the nature of Christianity is set in concrete. I could abandon Christianity, but I choose not to do so because Christianity includes affirmations that I value, and it does so in the ways that are most familiar to me. The passion and resurrection of Jesus are key parts of that tradition. Nevertheless, we must rethink, reform, and at times reject the ways that the narratives about those events have been understood in the past and are presented here and now. It is in that spirit that I suggest that we reject Mel Gibson's *Passion* precisely because it fails the tests I describe above.

As the twenty-first century unfolds, we Christians most definitely do not need a version of Jesus' crucifixion that imputes guilt and responsibility unfairly and that implies Christian triumphalism after the Holocaust. Instead, we need a narrative that shows how Christians can affirm Jews as Jews, and that opens a way for Jews to find that the cross and the crucified Jesus are neither alien nor threatening. This can occur only when those who claim to follow Jesus as Lord practice with persistence and humility what he preached: that we should love God and love our neighbors as ourselves. Were such a story real and then told again in film, it still might not get the hype and the huge box office receipts heaped on the Gibson movie. But such a film, especially if it were informed by deep awareness of the Holocaust, would help to show that *The Passion* has gone because it would have been eclipsed by something far more deserving of attention.

A postscript

"There now, it's finished: there's no more to be done," wrote Primo Levi in a poem called "The Work," which concludes with the question "What to do now?"[24] As these reflections on some ethical implications of interdisciplinary Holocaust education draw to a close, they also suggest that after Treblinka we must see differently and that much still remains to be done in Holocaust studies.

We need penetrating historical research that encourages study of the twigs and bushes as well as the landscape of which they are a part but also a style of historical research that discourages misleading quests for closure and finality. We need gender analysis that alerts us to the Holocaust's complexity. We need art and literature to sensitize the feelings without which Holocaust understanding is impoverished. We need sound religious studies to plumb the depths of the Holocaust's roots and implications. We need determination to heal and restore ethics, which the Holocaust left so badly wounded.

The ethical study of the Holocaust should not only be a particular discipline, but it should also penetrate the heart of every other discipline—from education to science, from history to theology, from the arts to philosophy, from politics and law to daily life. In short, as we continue to develop interdisciplinary Holocaust education, which is the only education that can begin to do justice to the awesome event it approaches, we need to remember to handle it all with care.

4
Raul Hilberg's Ethics

> In all of my work I have never begun by asking the big questions, because I was always afraid that I would come up with small answers.
>
> Raul Hilberg

In *The Politics of Memory*, an autobiographical account of the journey that made him preeminent among Holocaust scholars, Raul Hilberg recalls boyhood railroad trips with his parents in the 1930s. "The train," he says, "opened the world to me".[1] As events unfolded, trains provided not only Hilberg's "awakening to space" but also one of his most penetrating perspectives for analyzing "the so-called Final Solution, which entailed the transfer of Jews from all parts of Europe to death camps or shooting sites."[2]

Owing to this research, the French film maker Claude Lanzmann tracked Hilberg down at his Burlington, Vermont, home during a winter several years before *Shoah*, Lanzmann's epic film about the Holocaust, appeared in 1985. Lanzmann showed him a Holocaust-related railway document, which, Hilberg says, he seized "like an addict to explain the hieroglyphic contents."[3] Seizing, in turn, on Hilberg's gift of explanation, Lanzmann got Hilberg to repeat for the camera his decoding of the German timetable. The result was that a miniature version of Hilberg's magisterial study, *The Destruction of the European Jews*, and other aspects of his scholarship, particularly Hilberg's work on *The Diary of Adam Czerniakow*, became a central informing thread in Lanzmann's film.

One of Lanzmann's key decisions was how to introduce Hilberg in *Shoah*, a film that featured survivors, perpetrators, and bystanders or "neighbors" who played parts large and small in the destruction process, but not scholars, let alone the "talking heads" of conventional documentaries. Lanzmann's intelligent strategy determined that Hilberg's first words would not deal with German railroads or even with the Holocaust directly. Instead they compactly identified Hilberg's methods and standards as a Holocaust scholar. "In all of my work," Hilberg states in his opening line:

> I have never begun by asking the big questions, because I was always afraid that I would come up with small answers; and I have preferred to address these things which are minutiae or details in order that I might then be able to put together in a gestalt a picture, which, if not an explanation, is at least a description, a more full description, of what transpired.[4]

One sentence could not be enough to guarantee Hilberg's credibility to an audience that had never laid eyes on him. A few words of that kind did not ensure that Hilberg's analysis would be instantly embraced by people who had never studied his writings. In *Shoah's* context, however, Hilberg's "entry" could scarcely have been more compelling. For me, and I expect for many others, the effectiveness of his opening statement emerged from the sense it conveyed that there was *something* ethical—not really stated but still profound—about this scholar's commitment and approach to study of the Holocaust.

Not only in the Lanzmann's film but also long before and after, Hilberg's appeal, his authority one could say has never been exclusively found in the fact that he knows more than anyone else about the Holocaust and the German destruction process in particular. His appeal and authority reside in a combination of extensive knowledge plus a style of inquiry, an expression of feeling (often muted or understated), and a determination to keep going in spite of frustration, melancholy, and despair. As an observer and a student of Hilberg for more than thirty years, I think that his contribution to analysis of the Holocaust, not only its history but also its consequences and implications, cannot be sufficiently grasped unless one consciously detects Raul Hilberg's ethics. More than that, and as this chapter shows, detecting Hilberg's ethics also produces important insights about ethics during and after the Holocaust.

Detecting Hilberg's ethics

For several reasons, I refer to detecting Hilberg's ethics, a task that takes careful work. First, one needs to refine the scope and limitations of the concept *Hilberg's ethics*. The detective work I have in mind is not to offer a biographical account, let alone an appraisal, of Hilberg's personal or professional life, except insofar as his scholarship and analysis of the Holocaust involve reflection that has ethical content and insight. The two elements are intertwined and, at times, inseparable, but the emphasis here is less on Hilberg's conduct than on what can be called his moral philosophy. Arguably every person lives more-or-less consistently but imperfectly with respect to his or her ideals. No one lacks ethical shortcomings. Hilberg is no exception to that rule. What concerns me, however, is an exploration of the ethical insights embedded in his study of and reflection about the Holocaust. I believe that Hilberg practices well what his insights reveal, but my analysis will fall on the latter, leaving the work of biography to others.

A second reason why it is appropriate to speak of detecting Hilberg's ethics and why the detection requires careful work is that he does not think of himself as a philosopher and even less does he want to be considered a theologian. He is known as an historian of the Holocaust, but he frequently reminds his readers and audiences that he is a political scientist, which goes far toward explaining his interest in bureaucracy, decision-making, the ways in which documents contain information, reflect and communicate decisions that have been made, and his judgment that sheets of paper, "artifacts of the administrative machinery itself," can constitute "a form of action."[5] Repeatedly and in depth, Hilberg's scholarship deals with human choices and decisions, with human responsibility for their implementation and their consequences, which are all key factors in ethics. Nevertheless, Hilberg's main interest has been to find out how decisions were made, what led them to go one way or another, and how a web of decision-making and responsibility took the shape of a process of destruction. He is always on the edge of overt ethical reflection, but he holds it back, or at least in reserve, so that he can keep the focus on the process more than on the ethical appraisal of it. The result is that only occasionally does Hilberg speak overtly and explicitly about ethics, and yet ethical concerns are always nearby, awaiting exploration, beckoning to his readers and listeners because Hilberg, the historian and political scientist, concentrates on an unprecedented moral disaster.

Hilberg's writings and lectures do not offer more than fragments of what could be called an ethical theory. Nevertheless, it is difficult to read or to hear Hilberg without sensing that ethical impulses and passions run deep in his scholarship. Sometimes they dwell "between the lines," beneath the surface of his understated prose; sometimes they are implied in the tenacity that the clarity of his expression reveals as it seeks to leave a lasting record of how a catastrophe took place. Thus, Hilberg's written and oral expression points toward a third reason why it is appropriate to speak of detecting Hilberg's ethics and to recognize the complexity involved in such work. Hilberg's language is spare, lean, unembellished, and therefore robust. Clarity and precision, characterized not only by attention to organizational structures but also by understatement that conveys a keen sense of irony as well as a melancholy mood, are among the hallmarks of his expression. His skill as a speaker and a writer is to master and communicate a vast amount of detail and then to communicate his findings in ways that show how an exploration of twigs and bushes enables the landscape they comprise to stand out in bold relief.[6] But if one is looking for Hilberg's ethics in the projects that have occupied his life, the task is a complex one of detection because there is a need to consider not only what he says overtly and explicitly but also what is not said but still conveyed, what is left in silence but nonetheless voiced, what is pointed at but not directly because to divert attention in that way would be to deflect attention from the details that have to be identified and related so as to obtain the "picture which, if not an explanation, is at least a description, a more full description, of what transpired." Since one has to detect Hilberg's ethics to put his perspective into words, the task is complicated because one could get things wrong. One risk leads to another, for in this case Hilberg may do what he often does with precision, namely, identify the errors of one's ways. His interpreters must try and hope for the best.

Hilberg stresses that documents, especially written documents from the days, months, and years of the Holocaust itself, are the gold standard for understanding how and why the Holocaust took place. Although their content may be elusive when it comes to detecting Hilberg's ethics, the written documents—in this case Hilberg's books, essays, lectures—are the documentary source. That source, however, creates problems even as it remains indispensable for identifying Hilberg's ethical perspectives. Thus, a fourth problem encountered by an interpreter of Hilberg's ethics can be stated as follows: The question that governs such an inquiry—What is Hilberg's ethics?—may be one of those "big questions" that would make Hilberg cautious, if not skeptical, about answering for fear that the answers, which would have to be made with the Holocaust to test them, might be small. When the Holocaust is the context and the testing ground for ethical thinking, careful thought hesitates because ethical statements may end up being abstract, superficial, inadequate, or, in some other way unpersuasive. Such caution rightly carries over to any attempt to put Hilberg's ethics into words.

The sources of Hilberg's moral insight

Giving these reservations and cautionary notes their due, it is neverthe-less instructive to identify and reflect upon Hilberg's ethical insights. Again, several reasons loom large. First, arguably no one has thought longer and with greater care about the Holocaust than Hilberg. He wit-nessed the *Anschluss* in his native Austria, fled by train with his parents to France in the spring of 1939, and then by ship to Cuba before he reached Miami, Florida, on September 1, 1939, the day that Hitler invaded Poland and World War II began. Eventually reunited with his parents, New York became the family home. After graduating col-lege, Hilberg, still in his teens, returned to Europe with the US Army. By 1948, while a graduate student in the Department of Public Law and Government at Columbia University, he was doing work that would lead to the first edition of *The Destruction of the European Jews*, which appeared in 1961. Hilberg has spent a lifetime studying, researching, writing, and rewriting about the Holocaust. How is such a commitment to be understood? What insights about ethics does this work focus for Hilberg? Such questions are important, for Hilberg's life and work have positioned him to have angles of vision that no one else could have.

Second, because Hilberg has studied the Holocaust for so long and in such depth, devoting himself especially to understanding how the destruction process worked, he knows that the Holocaust reveals an immense moral failure. The dimensions of that failure are made all the more extensive because of Hilberg's scholarship, which shows again and again how the steps that led to Nazi Germany's genocide against the Jews were carried out by ordinary people who were not bloodthirsty killers but willing nonetheless to make choices and take decisions that were genocidal. Hilberg is a witness of a distinctive kind. Having immersed himself in this history for such a long time, any insights that Hilberg has about the implications, warnings, and even lessons that might be drawn from the Holocaust are ones that humankind can ill afford to miss.

Third, the ways in which Hilberg has done his Holocaust research may be an important source for thinking about ethics in a post-Holocaust context. Not only has Hilberg spent a lifetime trying to find out what happened during the Holocaust, how that catastrophe happened, and why, but also he has reflected deeply and repeatedly on how that research is best carried out, what pitfalls need to be avoided, and how one should proceed in a field where evidence is both vast and incomplete and where the perpetual threat of error requires vigilance and a willingness to admit and correct mistakes. One could easily overlook the broader implications of Hilberg's methodological reflections, but his hard-won insights in this area turn out to be among the richest veins to mine in detecting not only Hilberg's ethics but also the ways in which his insights can and should inform ethics generally after Auschwitz.

An ethical perspective's ingredients

To detect Hilberg's ethics, one has to consider at least five questions that are fundamental for identifying an ethic's perspective, content, texture, type, and significance: (1) What moods are echoed in, constitutive of, and promoted by a thinker's reflection? (2) What principles, maxims, injunctions, or imperatives are central for the ethic's content? (3) What virtues or characteristics are most highly valued? (4) On what foundations do the ethical principles and virtues rest, or, if the ethical perspective neither articulates nor assumes a single grounding of some kind, then how are those ingredients derived and on what basis is the outlook's credibility commended? (5) Then, as one takes stock of the appropriate responses to the first four questions, what appraisal should be made with regard to the strengths and weaknesses of the ethical perspective in question? Some further detail about these questions can contextualize the analysis of Hilberg's ethics that follows.

Ethics does not and cannot exist without distinctions between *right* and *wrong*, between what *ought* and *ought not* to be done. These distinctions both imply and advance a vision about what is good and what is not. Neither the distinctions nor the visions are unencumbered by history and a thinker's experience of and within it. That experience is thick with feelings, emotions, memories, and particularities that affect people deeply. When thinking turns, implicitly or explicitly, to consider how well or poorly life is unfolding—not only one's own but also the lives of others with whom one shares the world—the place of what can be called *moods* becomes significant. These moods reveal much about what could be called one's sense of things overall. Hence, we can detect whether a thinker is basically optimistic or pessimistic, hopeful or gripped by senses of tragedy and despair. Ethical outlooks vary in style and substance depending on the moods embedded in and projected by them. In Hilberg's case, his moods are among the richest sources of his ethical insights.

Next, when one notes that ethics does not and cannot exist without distinctions between *right* and *wrong*, between what *ought* and *ought not* to be done, or without a vision of the good, it is important to underscore that these elements of ethics are typically expressed in the form of principles or imperatives, or in judgments that imply a maxim or an injunction. "Do unto others as you would have them do unto you" would be an example of such an ethical principle or imperative. "It is important to study the Holocaust" could be a judgment that implies a maxim or an injunction to remember so that one does not live blindly in the present or take decisions lightly with regard to the future. In detecting Hilberg's ethics, one needs to identify his imperatives and the judgments that may entail them, even if the latter do not explicitly mark such principles.

Ethics is neither completed by nor reducible to moods, imperatives about right and wrong, or visions of the good. It also involves habits of mind, qualities of judgment, characteristics of will, dispositions to act, and senses of responsibility. When such elements of personality and behavior are positive and desirable, one thinks of them as *virtues* (thoughtfulness, wisdom, determination, courage, caring, etc.). When negative and undesirable, they are often called *vices* (blindness, imprudence, arrogance, rigidity, unaccountability, etc.). In detecting Hilberg's ethics, one needs to identify the virtues that he takes to be most important and the vices that he most wants to avoid.

If there are ethical principles and imperatives that ought to be followed, what is their source? What "grounds" them? At the end of the day, why is virtue better than vice? Can the sources and grounds of ethics be located? What makes an account of virtue persuasive and a discussion of vice convincing? Philosophical approaches to ethics include questions such as these. Sometimes these approaches are referred to as *metaethics* because they come after ethical judgments have been made, and they seek to understand more fully how those judgments work as well as what limits they face and problems they entail. Meanwhile, it does not follow that the responses to philosophical probing about ethics will be in agreement, which raises the additional question of what to do about the variety and disagreement that seem to be unavoidable in ethical and metaethical reflection.

Where the issue is about the sources or the groundings for ethics, a variety of positions, sometimes mutually supportive and sometimes at odds with one another, have traditionally been advanced, explored, and criticized. The sources and grounds might be found in appeals, for example, to divinity, reason, intuition, conscience, social evolution, or individual subjectivity and feeling, to name a few. When the issue is about priorities among virtues and vices, similar justifying "mindscapes" present themselves. As one identifies and reflects on Hilberg's ethics, it will be helpful to consider these traditional sources of moral authority, for

Hilberg is well aware that some or even all of these sources have been wounded or shattered by the Holocaust. His position about the grounding of ethics, which is implied but also explicit on at least some counts, has been formed with awareness of, indeed in spite of, the Holocaust's harm to ethics.

One of the complexities that ethical reflection includes is that the identification of a person's ethical outlook does not ensure that the ethic can withstand criticisms that may be brought against it. On the other hand, it does not follow that there is some neutral, purely objective, context-free Archimedean point from which such criticisms flow and appraisals derive. Recognition of that situation can produce skepticism about humanity's ability to discriminate rationally among different ethical outlooks, at least if the assumption is that one or more of them can rightly be called *true* while others are *false*. If that skepticism escalates, the result is moral relativism, which holds that it is difficult, to the point of impossibility, to discriminate rationally between competing ethical viewpoints.

According to the relativist's outlook, discrimination can and does take place but it hinges much more on matters of taste, culture, historical context, privilege, or power than on objectivity, rationality, and truth. Persuasive though it may look at first glance, the relativist's outlook has its own problems. One of the most telling is that, unless moral relativism lays claim to objectivity, rationality, and truth, it cannot reasonably occupy the privileged position it tries to maintain. On the other hand, that recognition does not banish the corrosive effects of skepticism, at least not entirely. It is unlikely, though not impossible, that any particular ethical perspective will be able to defend itself perfectly against every reasonable criticism that can be brought against it. Thus, ethical pluralism, which is not the same as ethical relativism, is likely to remain. No single view will trump every other outlook. Universal agreement about ethical matters will be less, probably far less, than complete. In the process of detecting Hilberg's ethics, one will eventually face the question: How sound, ethically, is Hilberg's ethics? What will be important to discern is whether Hilberg's ethics may contain insights that can help one to cope with the dilemmas of objectivity, skepticism, and relativism that are embedded in a post-Holocaust question of that kind.

Moods

In Lanzmann's film *Shoah*, Hilberg interprets *Fahrplananordnung* 587, a German railroad timetable that routed Polish Jews to the gas chambers at Treblinka in the autumn of 1942. Summing up what the document reveals, he tells Lanzmann that the timetable refers to four different transports, each one doomed. "We may be talking about ten thousand dead Jews on this one *Fahrplananordnung* here," he states, but having followed the calculations closely, Lanzmann insists, "More than ten thousand." Hilberg counters: "Well," he says, "we will be conservative here."

Letting Hilberg's judgment stand, Lanzmann moves to another question. Why, he asks, does Hilberg find the timetable so fascinating. "When I hold a document in my hand, particularly if it's an original document," Hilberg replies, "then I hold something which is actually something that the original bureaucrat held in his hand. It's an artifact. It's a leftover. It's the only leftover there is. The dead are not around."[7]

My description of this exchange cannot do it justice, but I believe that Hilberg's expression—the intense look on his face, the measured cadences and focused inflection of his voice, as well as the words caught by Lanzmann's sound track—reveal that *anger*, at times close to seething but controlled rage, is a dominant mood in Hilberg's ethics. How could it not be? Writing twenty years later in his preface to the third edition of *The Destruction of the European Jews,* Hilberg noted that his research on the Holocaust was destined to end because exhaustion, if not death, would overtake him. Nevertheless, as that edition appeared in 2003, he remarked that he had not yet "come to an end, and I knew that no topic was more important to me than this one."

Perhaps the answer is obvious without asking the question, but why is study of the Holocaust and of the German destruction process in particular so important to him? There is no evidence to suggest that a credible answer could be found in any fame or fortune that such work could produce. Nor would routine or even the history's vast and lethal scope be fully adequate to explain Hilberg's passionate commitment. Closer to the truth of the matter is recognition that in Hilberg's view the destruction of the European Jews was immensely devastating and utterly wrong. It could have been prevented; it might have been stopped before the worst took place, but "the dead are not around," and to a large extent the murderers got away with their crime. In my judgment, it is this moral anger that accounts for Hilberg's impassioned/dispassionate scholarly commitment to study of the Holocaust. His outraged sense of justice, moreover, beats within the heart of his ethics.

Righteous anger, however, is not the only mood that governs Hilberg's moral outlook. It blends with melancholy and sadness. In *The Politics of Memory,* Hilberg recalls a September Sunday in Boston.

The year was 1992. His book *Perpetrators Victims Bystanders* had just been published, but a *New York Times* review was less favorable than he had hoped, and when Hilberg visited a large Barnes & Noble store, his new book was not to be found. As he took his lunch that day in a hotel dining room above a street-level restaurant called The Last Hurrah, Hilberg reports feeling "an indescribable sadness."[8] Alone in that moment, he felt that he was saying goodbye to his life.

Many writers have received ungenerous reviews. Even more have been disappointed when their writings are absent from bookstore shelves. One could read Hilberg's lament as self-indulgence, but his sadness and melancholy are not simply or best explained by his feeling slighted. I think that the sadness, the melancholy, were most importantly prompted by his awareness that the history he cared about so much, the moral failure that angered him so deeply, the loss of the dead who are not around might be receding toward oblivion no matter how hard he tried to stem the tide of forgetfulness and ignorance.

One senses a related disposition in Hilberg's 2001 study, *Sources of Holocaust Research*, which speaks about the researcher's ideal of accessing and preserving "the past in its pristine state" but ends by acknowledging that "the reality of the events is elusive, as it must be" and by suggesting that the researcher's work goes forward not so much to achieve mastery as to prevent the past, and awareness of the Holocaust's destruction process in particular, from being "relinquished and forgotten."[9]

About two months after that Sunday in Boston when Hilberg felt his indescribable sadness, he returned to Vienna, the city of his boyhood, which he had not visited since 1976. There a woman named Evelyn Adunka interviewed Hilberg, calling his attention to a letter she had found in an archive. Its author was H. G. Adler, a survivor of the Theresienstadt ghetto, who had written an important book about that place. Dated March 6, 1962, the letter contained a commentary about *The Destruction of the European Jews*, whose first edition had appeared in the previous year. Adler praised Hilberg's book. "It is not likely to be surpassed very soon," he observed, "even though it is by far not yet the final portrayal. No one until now has seen and formulated the total horrible process so clearly."

What was especially moving about *The Destruction of the European Jews*, Adler went on to say, was "the hopelessness of the author ... . At the end nothing remains but despair and doubt about everything, because for Hilberg there is only recognition, perhaps also a grasp, but certainly no understanding."[10] Upon reading these comments, Hilberg observed that Adler "had peered directly into the core of my being."[11]

Impassioned anger, melancholy, sadness—these elements are part of Hilberg's mood but not the whole of it. At least two other feelings affect his ethical outlook. Paradoxically, the passion of Hilberg's anger is both masked and muted but also revealed and communicated through prose and description that are matter-of-fact to the point of being *cool*. In his introduction to *The Warsaw Diary of Adam Czerniakow*, for example, one finds a vintage "Hilbergian" sentence: "Almost a half-million Jews had lived in the Warsaw ghetto," he writes. "By the time the war was over, 99 percent of them were dead."[12] Such sentences—short, unembellished, understated, overtly dispassionate, matter-of-fact—characterize Hilberg's expression and abound in his writing.

Hilberg's writing is far from emotionless, I believe, but feeling is controlled and condensed, at times repressed, so that he can report as straightforwardly as possible what took place. The cool prose, moreover, is supported as thoroughly as possible by documentation that undermines disconfirmation and short-circuits disbelief. The Holocaust precludes the possibility that justice can prevail. Nevertheless, Hilberg's cool analysis brings the case against the perpetrators, bystanders, and to some extent against the victims too. On the latter score, Hilberg assesses responsibility wherever he must, but with empathy for the constraints and pressures that faced a Jewish leader such as Czerniakow, who led the Jewish Council in the Warsaw ghetto.

Hilberg reports that, figuratively, he "spent about six years with Czerniakow" while working on the diary of a man who took his own life upon learning that there was no reprieve for the Jews of Warsaw when the Germans ordered deportations from the ghetto to begin on July 22, 1942. Czerniakow's diary was filled with short statements and factual descriptions. Hilberg pays a kind of tribute to him by writing about Czerniakow in a similar vein. "When the deportations began," Hilberg remarks as he considers Czerniakow's final hours, "he wanted to save the Jewish orphans, and when he could not secure even their safety, he killed himself."[13] In *Shoah*, Lanzmann's film, Hilberg's last words are about Czerniakow. They refer to reports that after Czerniakow had closed his diary for the last time, he wrote a note in which he said: "They want me to kill the children with my own hands."[14] After Lanzmann had heard Hilberg speak about Czerniakow, again capturing his commentary for his film, he said of Hilberg, "You were Czerniakow."[15] Lanzmann could well have been referring to Hilberg's understated expression, a kind of mood that conveys rage and despair with authority and power.

At times, especially when Hilberg writes or speaks about the perpetrators, notes of irony and of a dark humor in particular enter to affect the mood that provides the backdrop for his ethics. As the so-called Final Solution unfolded and unprecedented decisions were taken, Hilberg's analysis frequently points out that bureaucrats had to become initiators and other perpetrators had to become innovators and inventors. Such terms are often part of a vocabulary of "progress," where they signal "virtues" of one kind or another. The "Final Solution" was a kind of "progress," and it demanded and received creative thinking so bent on destruction that it produced what Hilberg calls "a turning point in history."[16] In Hilberg's irony there are ethical warnings to which we will soon return.

Meanwhile, Hilberg's irony sometimes takes the form of dark humor contained in anecdotes that he recounts in his typically understated way. In 1976, for example, Hilberg was doing archival research in Germany when a group of lawyers invited him to a party. They were investigating and prosecuting "National Socialist Crimes."[17] Confessing that he had published comments about Adolf Hitler's role in the Holocaust that were not entirely accurate, Hilberg asked the deputy chief of the prosecutors' office what he thought about Hitler as the Holocaust's chief perpetrator. The deputy chief replied that the prosecutors had "often fantasized about drawing up an indictment against Adolf Hitler" for the Holocaust. But then, the German lawyer added, it dawned upon them that "we didn't have the evidence." Hilberg's direct comment on this story consists of three words referring to the lawyer: "And he laughed." Hilberg does not say that he did likewise, but one can sense a wry, ironic smile as the prelude to the task of holding Hitler and his followers accountable, which has been Hilberg's passion.

Toward the end of *The Destruction of the European Jews*, Hilberg includes a twenty-two page list of Holocaust perpetrators, which identifies their role in the Nazi regime, the outcome of any legal proceedings that may have been brought against them, and, in some cases, their postwar careers and ultimate fate. "An all-encompassing roster of perpetrators," notes Hilberg, "would fill a multivolume directory. ... For the large majority there is no postwar report. ... By the law they had not lived. By the law they did not die."[18] One of the entries in Hilberg's catalog refers to Hermann Pook, an official in the SS *Wirtschafts-Verwaltungshauptamt* (WVHA, Economic-Administrative Main Office) who "had salvaged the gold from the mouths of the gassed." Without commentary, Hilberg simply states a fragment of absurdity from the defense—Hilberg calls it "unique"—that Pook's lawyer offered on behalf of his client: "The corpse has no more rights of any sort, but no one has any right to the corpse either. The body, so to speak, from a legal point of view, floats between heaven and earth." This less-than-convincing defense brought the convicted Pook a five-year sentence from a US military tribunal. Hilberg notes, however, that the sentence was reduced to time served. With its darkly humorous twists and turns, the Holocaust's irony multiplies irony. Its nuances affect Hilberg's mood by making him do all that he can to ensure that men such as Pook are not rehabilitated by obscurity and oblivion.

Imperatives

In 1971, Hilberg published a book called *Documents of Destruction: Germany and Jewry 1933–1945*. This edited volume, which contained Hilberg's commentary, includes documents from German and Jewish sources that recorded and constituted actions in the destruction of the European Jews. The book's front matter contains two epigraphs that highlight the most important imperative in Hilberg's ethics.[19] The first comes from Heinrich Himmler's speech to his SS and police leaders in October 1943. Himmler praises his men for remaining decent and for having been "hardened" under the stress and strain resulting from having "gone through this"—Himmler's non-specific way of referring to mass killing. What has been accomplished, Himmler states, "is a page of glory in our history," but also one "never written and never to be written."

In juxtaposition to Himmler's injunction that silence must cover the "page of glory," Hilberg sets the following words from a Jewish survivor named Jacob Celemenski: "Today I am one of the survivors. For twenty years I have constantly heard within my mind the very cry of the murdered: Tell it to the world!"

The contrast between these two passages is of fundamental importance in Hilberg's ethics. Himmler refers to a "page of glory," but it is significant that he counsels silence about it. Celemenski breaks the silence in multiple ways. He unmasks the "glory" by indicating that it refers to mass murder. Himmler may want the "page of glory" to be unwritten, but the absence of dead Jews resounds in the cries that reverberate in Celemenski's mind. Those cries, moreover, have a specificity, which insists upon remembrance and testimony: Tell it to the world! This is Hilberg's most important ethical imperative.

Ethical imperatives direct attention and guide action, but their meaning is not always self-evident. If, for example, one important imperative is to love one's neighbor as oneself, then questions such as "Who is my neighbor?" and "What is and is not involved in loving oneself?" have their place. The same can be said of Celemenski's "Tell it to the world!" What is one to tell and how should the telling be done? One can even reflect on what "telling" does and does not involve. Hilberg's work sheds light on his most crucial imperative by illustrating what it means and what is entailed by it.

The *it* that must be told has at least three dimensions. First, paramount importance must be given to telling what has happened, to do so as thoroughly, honestly, and persistently as possible. To do so, one has to reckon with both Himmler and Celemenski, with who they were, what they did, and what they said. Himmler and Celemenski, of course, are not only particular persons but they are also emblematic of countless others who played their parts in the destruction of the European Jews. It is this recognition that takes Hilberg on his quest for what he calls the "minutiae" that constitute the immensity of the Holocaust.

Second, recording and telling the history of the Holocaust is both an end in itself and the means to something more than that. "Telling it to the world" may be the best that one can do to remember the dead, to mourn the loss, and to hold accountable those who perpetrated the Holocaust but have eluded justice. Such telling has value that is not reducible to instrumentality. Among other things, it is distinctive for its power to differentiate between *right* and *wrong*. It may not be universally impossible but it would certainly be difficult to read the epigraphs in Hilberg's edition of documents, to study those items, and then to return to the difference between the statements of Himmler and Celemenski without feeling that what took place was wrong.

Third, when "telling it to the world" arouses and deepens feelings about the difference between right and wrong, the juncture is reached when the telling becomes more than an end in itself. If wrong has been done, then it ought to be set right as far as possible, and, at the very least the wrong ought not to be repeated. "Telling it to the world" means persistent, on-going, and ever-more detailed and firmly documented reporting so that forgetfulness does not make it easier for others to create more never-to-be-written pages of "glory." Commenting on Himmler's speech of October 1943, Hilberg puts forth the point as follows: "There are some things that can be done only so long as they are not discussed, for once they are discussed they can no longer be done."[20]

Hilberg knows that "telling it to the world" is an imperative that strives for more than it can achieve. Just as "an all-encompassing roster of perpetrators would fill a multivolume directory," there is no way to remember every victim or to appraise the conduct of every neighbor and bystander.[21] "All that has gone on in the world," says Hilberg, "can be preserved only in fragments, and these leftovers constitute our material . ... Empirical historiography is by definition salvage. It cannot be more."[22] Completeness, finality, closure—these are not qualities that pertain to "telling it to the world." The absence and impossibility are what require the telling to continue in spite of the melancholy and sadness that such awareness evokes.

Factors of this kind help to explain the high esteem in which Hilberg holds a relatively obscure book by the sociologist John K. Dickinson. First published in 1967, *German & Jew: The Life and Death of Sigmund Stein* focused on a single German Jew—his real name was Hermann Reis—a lawyer of "obscure prominence" in Marburg before the Nazis' rise to power ruined his career, destroyed his family, and left him dead, probably at a satellite camp of Auschwitz that Dickinson identifies as Golleschau.[23]

In his introduction to the 2001 reissue of this book, Hilberg both praises the work as unique and laments the fact that it is. Although Hilberg's reservations about oral testimony are well known, he credits Dickinson for interviewing 172 people who knew Stein/Reis. Taking his notes carefully, Dickinson sifted and sorted findings critically and turned them into a narrative that shed light not only on the fate of one Jew during the Holocaust but also on those who knew him, including, as Hilberg observes, "some of [Stein/Reis's] German acquaintances as they distanced themselves from him, and as they coveted during his last hours in Marburg some of his possessions for 'safekeeping.' "[24]

Hilberg wonders why the 1967 appearance of Dickinson's book did not inspire other studies of a similar kind. While there was still time to do so, studies focused on bystanders and neighbors might have revealed much of importance about the context in which the Holocaust unfolded. In a melancholy mood, Hilberg observes that there was a time "when many people, who as grown men and women had watched the fate of their Jewish neighbors at close range, could still have related in abundant detail what they had seen. But hardly anyone wanted to hear much from such observers, and now the ideal moment for questioning them is gone."[25] Telling it to the world entails small deeds, such as writing an introduction to an unusual but scarcely popular book that one hopes may still attract at least a few readers.[26] Telling it to the world is work for a lifetime as well. In that imperative and the principles that flow from it, the core of Hilberg's ethics is found.

Virtues

Putting an ethical outlook into practice depends on the cultivation of virtues, which are those habits of thought and action that turn ideas and ideals into realities. The virtues highlighted and required in Hilberg's ethics are primarily those of scholarship, but those qualities have transferability that reaches well beyond the classroom, library, archive, and writing desk.

Students who studied with Hilberg during his thirty-five years of teaching at the University of Vermont report his saying that one must "know what you're looking at. Study it. Never take anything at face value." Telling it to the world depends on finding out what is true, right, and good. That work cannot be done without study, questioning, and inquiry, all of which refuse to take things as they appear at first glance.

As the epigraph for his autobiographical work *The Politics of Memory*, Hilberg selected a sentence from H. G. Adler, the Holocaust survivor who had observed Hilberg's despair and doubt, even his hopelessness, upon reading the first edition of *The Destruction of the European Jews*. "History without tragedy does not exist," wrote Adler, "and knowledge is better and more wholesome than ignorance." In a world so laced with devastation, loss, and grief, ignorance might be bliss, but not if the imperative is to "tell it to the world." Knowledge is indispensable for that moral task, no matter how hard it is to acquire or difficult to bear.

"Advances of knowledge," cautions Hilberg, "are not automatic. They become possible when someone steps out of a habitual framework of thought to recognize complications or connections not seen before, or when fortuitously a missing fact is found, or when patient sifting in large collections of records allows glances at life as it was lived."[27] Moreover, "researchers do not wait until all the archives are open to them," says Hilberg. "They begin with whatever is at hand."[28] It takes discipline and curiosity, patience but not passivity, courage, determina tion, and always attention to detail to acquire and bear the knowledge on which the chance depends for something better and more wholesome than the ruined world that the Holocaust left in its wake. Clear-sightedness and every effort to avoid delusion, mystification, and forgetfulness loom large. One should never conclude that there is nothing more that can and should be done.

Hilberg's *Perpetrators Victims Bystanders* ends with a paragraph devoted to Bernhard Lichtenberg, the Roman Catholic priest who served as Prior of St. Hedwig's Cathedral in Berlin during the time of the Third Reich. After the *Kristallnacht* pogrom in November 1938, he prayed publicly each day for non-Aryan Christians and Jews. On August 21, 1941, he was denounced to the Gestapo. His arrest followed on October 23. He offered to join Jews who were being deported to the Lodz ghetto in Poland, but instead he was sent to prison for endangering the public peace.

Imprisoned on May 29, 1942, he was released on October 23, 1943, but only to be sent to Dachau. Taken ill on the way, he was hospitalized and died, after last rites, in the early morning of November 3, 1943. In his brief account of Lichtenberg, Hilberg highlights two brief reminders that he found in Lichtenberg's writings. Marginalia in those documents sometimes said "Do not delude yourselves" and "This must be said."[29]

Truth-seeking and truth-telling, courage and curiosity, realistic senses of limitation and fallibility and yet a willingness to break new ground, refusal to give up and a life-long commitment to telling it to the world in spite of hopelessness, despair, and doubt—these qualities are among the cardinal virtues in Hilberg's ethics.

Groundings

Hilberg is a self-identified atheist. If one asks about the foundations or groundings for his ethics, he will not and cannot locate them in any divine source. Equally clear is the fact that Hilberg is not an ethical relativist. He does not think that might makes right. Nor does he follow Nietzsche in claiming that the human will alone is the source of our values and evaluations. I make these claims because there is an important lecture that Hilberg delivered when he spoke at a conference on ethics after the Holocaust at the University of Oregon in 1996.[30] Explaining, as he has done more than once, that he does not consider himself a philosopher or a theologian, Hilberg asserted that ethics is the same today as it was yesterday and even the day before yesterday; it is the same after Auschwitz as it was before and during the lethal operations at that place. Especially with regard to needless and wanton killing, he emphasized, ethics is the same for everyone, everywhere. Hilberg left no unclarity. Such killing is wrong. We know that, "in our bones," he said, for such knowledge is the heritage of many years.

Hilberg's denial that he is a philosopher notwithstanding, the position reflected in such statements is philosophically provocative and bold. It is provocative because one has to consider what Hilberg's unelaborated propositions mean. It is bold because of what they imply. First, how should one understand the tantalizing idea that ethical sensibilities are "in our bones," especially if something such as "the heritage of many years," which implies a social formation of the ethical, has put them there? In addition, how would that outlook square with the idea that ethics is the same today as it was yesterday and even the day before yesterday?

It is not clear how the three elements—I would call them intuition or conscience, tradition, and a kind of timelessness—fit together coherently, if they do, but I think that Hilberg's ethic does locate its grounding in the view that social history or evolution produces a deep-seated ethical consciousness that has universal and, in that sense, timeless qualities. Ethical outlooks do have a history, and they are socially formed. Those elements can fuse to make ethical outlooks, at least some of them, so widely accepted that at least the appearance of universality and time-lessness attaches to them. But those relationships, even if they are coherent, scarcely put to rest all of the questions about the grounding of ethics.

It can be argued that ethical injunctions against needless and wanton killing, for example, obtain normative status because collective experience shows them to have social utility. Such killing is wrong, on such a view, because it threatens individual and social well-being. Over time this lesson is experienced, taught, and driven home so that the ethical norm becomes embedded "in our bones." But what if individuals or social groups do not understand wanton and needless killing in the same way? Himmler and his followers could agree that wanton and needless killing was wrong, but they did not think that the destruction of the European Jews fit that description. Rightly, they should be held accountable for ethical wrongdoing of the most devastating kind, but their deviation from the norm raises suspicion about ethical groundings of the kind that Hilberg's ethics includes. If the grounding is as Hilberg has it, then why did the Nazis do what they did? Why was the heritage of many years, the timelessness of the ethical, as well as the embedding of moral insight in German bones, so obviously insufficient to prevent Himmler and his followers from staining their unwritten pages of "glory" with so much blood? Such questions gnaw at Hilberg: "No obstruction stopped the German machine of destruction," he writes. "No moral problem proved insurmountable. ... The old moral order did not break through anywhere along the line. This is a phenomenon of the greatest magnitude."[31]

These vexing questions double in complexity because Hilberg's position commits him, I believe, to the view that the Nazis and their collaborators knew that what they were doing to the European Jews was wrong. This issue is a crucial one for consideration of ethics during and after the Holocaust, and Hilberg's analysis in *The Destruction of the European Jews* dwells on it at some length. One cannot be sure, of course, that the Nazis and their collaborators knew with certainty that their policies toward the Jews were ethically wrong. To have clinching evidence about that fact, trustworthy confessions would be needed, including some explanation of why the perpetrators violated their own ethical sensibilities.

Such confessions and explanations we do not have, at least not for the most part from the perpetrators who were most responsible for the Holocaust.[32] Hilberg, however, points to less direct and more circumstantial evidence to make a case that the perpetrators acted in spite of "knowing better."

Hilberg acknowledges that the destruction process "had meaning to its perpetrators," but he argues that the meaning had to vie with what he thinks was a "growing uneasiness that pervaded the bureaucracy from the lowest strata to the highest. That uneasiness was the product of moral scruples that were the lingering effect of two thousand years of Western morality and ethics. A Western bureaucracy had never before faced such a chasm between moral precepts and administrative action; an administrative machine had never been burdened with such a drastic task."[33] Rising to the occasion, the German bureaucrats, according to Hilberg, took into account "that at crucial junctures every individual makes decisions, and that every decision is individual," and thus they developed a two-pronged approach that could trump, if not entirely assuage, bad conscience: repression and rationalization.[34]

Illustrated well in Himmler's previously mentioned speech, repression included hiding the truth about mass murder and limiting the flow of information about it; making sure that those who knew were also directly involved in some aspect of the killing; prohibiting criticism; urging perpetrators not to talk about their work; and making no direct mention of killing in reports. Repression was insufficient to do the job of neutralizing conscience, however, and thus rationalizations were provided as well. Two were especially important. First, the destruction of the European Jews was a defensive measure or a preventive countermeasure. Second, it was acknowledged that the individual's role was difficult but also that the hard and dirty work was both necessary and excusable, all the more so with respect to excusability because the anti-Jewish actions were not being taken out of any personal vindictiveness. According to the Nazi ideology, the Jews were conspiratorial, criminal, and inferior. Not only their actions but also their very existence threatened German interests. Thus, orders against the Jews had to be followed, but if there were those who were not up to any particular task, opportunities to step aside were available. Furthermore, the division of labor in the destruction process made it possible for one to say that someone might be doing unethical deeds—outright killing, for instance—but I was not unethical because I was simply doing my duty at this desk or in that office. There was always a receding moral horizon that provided safety for one's conscience, but if one was in the thick of going "through this," as Himmler put it, then there was what Hilberg calls "the jungle theory," a last-ditch defense emphasizing that life is a struggle and those who refused to do what was necessary to preserve their way of life would lose it.

If Hilberg is right when he says that, from the German perspective, "the most important problems of the destruction process were not administrative but psychological"—would *ethical* be a term at least as apt as *psychological?*—then it is also crucial to see that those problems, too, were solved, at least long enough for the "Final Solution" to sustain itself until Nazi Germany was crushed by the Allies' superior military might. If ethics is in our bones, they are precariously fragile. If ethics is the result of the heritage of many years, that heritage guarantees very little. If ethics is the same today as it was yesterday and even the day before yesterday, its status remains as vulnerable and problematic as it is fundamental and important.

A conclusion without closure

"Within the ranks of the perpetrators," Hilberg contends, "the one premise that shaped all the orders, letters, and reports from 1933 to 1945 was the maxim that the Jews must be removed from German spheres of life."[35] In one of his compact, understated, and yet emotionally charged sentences, Hilberg identifies the imperative that governed much of the Nazi ethic and the "conscience" of Himmler and his men in particular. Even with the philosophical problems that remain unresolved in Hilberg's ethics, it offers itself as at least part of a post-Holocaust response that is needed to strengthen the ethical impulses against ethnic cleansing, genocide, and the many other human rights abuses that plague our twenty-first century world.

The third edition of *The Destruction of the European Jews* ends, significantly, with a discussion of the Rwandan genocide in 1994. "The disaster of the Tutsis took place in the full view of the world. ... History had repeated itself."[36] As Hilberg knows, history does not, could not, repeat itself exactly, but its repetitions question optimistic assumptions about progress and continue to be warnings if they do not paralyze us with the despair that study of the Holocaust and genocide is bound to produce. What Hilberg's ethics shows is that there is a way to respond to despair that could help to prevent or check at least some of the conditions and circumstances that cause it. By no means is it a small answer to big questions. If Hilberg's ethics can get under our skins, it may find its way not only into our bones but also into our hearts and minds. The world would be a better place if it did.

On November 5, 2004, I presented a version of this chapter at Lessons and Legacies, a Holocaust studies conference held at Brown University, which included a panel of papers devoted to Raul Hilberg's distinguished scholarly career. After the papers were presented, Hilberg responded. Four aspects of his response remain particularly vivid in my mind.[37]

First, Hilberg's moral anger and his impassioned emphasis on the importance of truth-telling were evident as he spoke about the Holocaust's perpetrators. Second, those moods were evident because Hilberg remained convinced that, for the most part, the perpetrators knew that their murderous policies and actions had crossed a moral dividing line. Third, Hilberg's attention riveted on key questions. Why did the perpetrators do what they did, especially if they knew that their policies and actions crossed a moral dividing line? Why did they do these things so easily and persistently? Coupled with those questions were others pertaining especially to civilian bystanders who witnessed the Nazi onslaught against the Jews. Realistically, what could have been expected of them? Finally, there was Hilberg's conclusion, which again put the emphasis on questions. For those who live after the Holocaust, he urged, we have to keep asking self-critically whether our own policies and decisions are right. We have to keep pressing the issue: How can the imperative "Never again!" be credible?

As I listened to Hilberg's response, I recalled the University of Oregon lecture he delivered several years before. Its melancholy moments had referred to an observation made by Sigmund Freud in 1915, while World War I was raging. Hilberg recalled Freud's remarking that one should not be too disappointed about humanity's fallen condition, for civilization's moral progress had never been as great as most people assumed, believed, or hoped.

Like Freud, Hilberg has continued to wonder if anything more than such melancholy deserves to remain. As his passionate insistence bears witness when he insists that we must keep asking "Is it right?" and "How can 'Never again!' be credible?" the future of civilization is in our post-Holocaust hands.

5
Gray Zones and Double-Binds: Holocaust Challenges to Ethics

> Not every being with a human face is human.
>
> Carl Schmitt

This book's subtitle uses a phrase by Elie Wiesel, who suggests that Birkenau, the killing center at Auschwitz, which was the Holocaust's most lethal site, calls everything into question. In particular, he says, the shadow of Birkenau requires reconsideration of traditions, theories, assumptions, and hopes. It should make us think more than twice about many things.

What should I do?

Especially because this chapter will both raise significant Holocaust challenges to ethics and attempt to respond to them credibly, it will be helpful to recall that the German philosopher Immanuel Kant, one of the most important thinkers in Western civilization, suggested that three questions define philosophy: What can I know? What should I do? What may I hope? Much hinges on whether people can rightly claim to possess knowledge. Scarcely an hour passes without our wondering whether we ought to do some things and not others. Those issues keep people thinking and hoping about the future. Questions about the meaning and destiny of our lives—individual and collective—are never far behind.

Ethics or moral philosophy revolves around Kant's second question: What should I do? This means that ethics is as old as human existence and also as new as today's dilemmas and tomorrow's possibilities. Thus, ethics is both the same and different as experience unfolds and history develops. Among the defining characteristics of human life are our

75

abilities to think, make judgments, and remember. Human beings are also identified by a web of social relationships. We are members of families and societies. As history has developed, we have become partic- ipants in political and religious traditions, and we are citizens of coun- tries too. Enriched and complicated by memory of past actions and their consequences, these characteristics and relationships require us to make evaluations. With its structure and environment necessitating that we have to make choices and live or die with the consequences of our deci- sions, human life is unavoidably inseparable from distinctions between what is right and wrong, just and unjust, good and evil.

We human beings deal constantly with factual matters, but we also make value judgments, issue prescriptive statements, and formulate normative appraisals. In short, we try to figure out what we ought to do. Few of us are always and entirely content with the way events happen to turn out. How *should* they come out, we ask. There is nothing new about these realities. They have been with humanity from its beginnings.

Whenever concepts such as *should* and *ought, right* and *wrong, good* and *evil* are employed, ethics comes into play, but what it means to say so requires a closer look. Many factors enter into the evaluations that people make. They include our cultural backgrounds, religious training or lack of it, the influence of parents, teachers, and friends, to mention but a few. Ethics can refer simply to the value judgments that people make and to their beliefs—individual and collective—about what is right and wrong, good and evil, precious and worthless, beautiful and ugly, or sacred and profane. Value judgments affect everything we do: from the ways that individuals spend their money to the interests that nations defend. Taken in this sense, it can be argued that every person, community, and nation is ethical. All of them have normative beliefs and make evaluative judgments.

Ethics, however, involves much more than a primarily descriptive use of that term suggests. For example, ethics also refers to the study of value judgments and the ways in which they influence—and are influenced by—institutions. Such study has historical dimensions; it may concen- trate, for instance, on how a society's values have changed or developed over time. In one way or another, work of this sort has also been going on for centuries. Its roots are in the earliest human awareness that groups and persons are not identical, that they think and act differently.

How important is wealth? Is religion desirable? What kind of education should the young receive? Versions of these questions are ancient, and responses to them both reflect and depend upon the value commit- ments that people make. Historically, people have taken varied positions on ethical issues, even as they have exhibited widespread continuity about some fundamental convictions such as those, for instance, that condemn murder. If ethics is inseparable from human existence, however, the manifestations of that fact are many and varied. Arguably, study of ethical beliefs and practices throughout human history is likely to confirm that their variety is more pronounced than their commonality.

Ethics does not end with either description or study of human belief and action. The core of ethics, in fact, lies elsewhere. People make value judgments when they say, for example, that "abortion is wrong" or that "the death penalty is right." Does the variety of values, and especially the arguments that conflicting value judgments can produce, mean that value judgments are culturally relative and even personally subjective? Or are at least some value judgments objectively grounded and true for everyone? For centuries, philosophers and religious teachers have debated such questions, which are crucial parts of ethics as normative inquiry. Agreement about how to answer those questions is not universal, but ethics would not be *ethics* if it failed to emphasize the importance of critical inquiry about the values that people hold. For example, much can be learned by asking, "Is this value judgment true, and, if so, why?" Much can also be learned by asking, "What makes some values positive (e.g., courage, honesty, and trust) and what makes others negative (e.g., hatred, selfishness, or infidelity)?"

In the form of critical inquiry about values, ethics contends that nothing is truly good or right simply because someone desires or values it. In fact, to say that something is good or right simply because someone values it would contradict one of our most fundamental experiences: The differences between what is valuable and what is not depend on more than an individual's feelings or a culture's preferences. We know this because our value judgments can be *mistaken*. We often criticize, change, or even reject them because we learn that they are wrong. Thus, while people may not agree about values, the questions that critical inquiry raises—for example, how should we evaluate the values we hold, and which values matter most?—are at the heart of ethics. Again, such insights are not new. Buddha and Confucius, Moses and Jesus, Socrates and Plato brought them to life long ago, and even those ethical pioneers had predecessors in earlier history.

Ethics is as old as human existence itself. Its basic questions, concerns, and fundamental vocabulary have exhibited considerable continuity amidst the accompanying diversity. One of the reasons is that another feature of human life also remains deeply entrenched, namely, that human beings so often make bad judgments, inflict harm, lay waste to things that are good, treat each other brutally, rob, rape, and kill. At its best, ethics attempts to check and correct those tendencies by urging us to make human life more caring and humane and by showing how it can be more just and promising.

Unfortunately, our abuse of human life is often so great that ethics seems too fragile, weak, or subject to subversion to do what we hope, at least in our better moments, it can accomplish. Ethical theory and teaching have a long history, but it is hard to say with clarity and confidence that humankind has been forever making moral progress. Sometimes, in fact, the vocabulary of ethics has been used to legitimate immense harm. Such was the case during the Nazi years and the Holocaust that ensued. Arguably the twentieth century was the most murderous in human history. There is no assurance that the twenty-first will be an improvement in spite of the fact that there may be more talk than ever about the need for ethics. Human life is full of discouragement, cynicism, and despair produced by human folly, miscalculation, and wrongdoing. Undeniably, the importance of ethics looms large because the issue remains: Will human beings take their ethical responsibilities seriously enough?

Concerns of this kind lead philosophers to offer new approaches to ethical reflection. Having lost much of his family in the Holocaust, the Jewish philosopher Emmanuel Levinas (1906–95) argued that ethical theory had failed to concentrate on something as obvious and profound as the human face. By paying close and careful attention to the face of the other person, he affirmed, there could be a reorientation not only of ethics but also of human life itself, for our seeing of the other person's face would drive home how closely human beings are connected and how much the existence of the other person confers responsibility upon us.

Working in a different but related way, the American philosopher John Rawls (1921–2002) proposed a form of ethical deliberation that could make human life more just. He suggested that we consider ourselves placed behind what he called a "veil of ignorance." In that position, we would not know our exact status or role in the world, but we could deliberate constructively about the rights and rules that we would all find reasonable to implement. Rawls thought that such deliberation would place a high priority on liberty and equality. Much of his work in *A Theory of Justice* and other influential writings was devoted to considering how those values could best be mutually supportive. Rawls did not conclude that deliberation from behind the veil of ignorance would lead reasonable persons to expect that everyone should be treated exactly alike. Inequality of the right kind could be beneficial for everyone, but for that condition to hold, caring attention would always have to be paid to those who are the least well-off.

By no means were Levinas and Rawls the only recent innovators in ethical theory. Nor is it true that Levinas and Rawls developed their ideas independently of previous traditions in ethics. Levinas took seriously the ancient Jewish teaching that human beings are created in the image of God. The face of the other person, therefore, has at least traces of the divine within it and deserves respect accordingly. Rawls reinvented the idea of the social contract, which thinkers such as Thomas Hobbes and John Locke developed in the seventeenth century. Levinas and Rawls help to show how one can move beyond previous outlooks as they try to encourage humankind to respond to the ethical dilemmas of our time.

Arguably critical ethical reflection would not exist—there would be no need for it—if human beings knew everything, understood all the consequences of their actions, never made mistakes, always agreed with one another about what to do, and put exactly the right policies into practice. Human experience, however, is not that clear or simple. Our knowledge is incomplete. We do make mistakes; we do disagree. Often, human life is full of conflict because we do not see eye to eye about what is true and right. Thus, human life simmers, boils, and at times erupts in controversies, debates, and disputes. All too often, issues intensify and escalate into violence, war, and even genocide.

Fortunately, those destructive responses are not the only ones that human beings can make. Ethical reflection may prove insufficient to save the day; nevertheless it remains crucial, and it can be ignored only at our peril. Done well, ethical thinking can focus a community's attention helpfully and stimulate constructive activity—education, cooperation, better understanding, caring, and beneficial political and economic action. It can assist people to understand contemporary life better and to make their own thoughtful responses to the ethical issues that require attention both now and in the future.

The gray zone

The foregoing description of ethics or moral philosophy emphasizes clarity and understanding as the aims of inquiry. Life's complexities and confusions make it difficult to obtain those outcomes, but the philosophical quest typically assumes that clarity and understanding are obtainable. If reason works long and hard enough, it is possible, at least in principle, to "get things right." Primo Levi, the Auschwitz survivor who explored what he called "the gray zone," makes one reconsider that assumption. Although Levi has not obtained Kant's canonical status, and in spite of the fact that he said of philosophy, "no, it's not for me," I regard him as a very important philosopher.[1] He, too, sought clarity and understanding but in a way that diverged significantly from philosophy's conventional path and assumptions.

If clarity and understanding were to be obtained, Levi contended that they would have to reckon with "the gray zone." As he experienced and explored that Auschwitz region, Levi stressed that it contained surprises and shocks that revealed a "world" that was not only "terrible … but also indecipherable: it did not conform to any model."[2] His brilliant chapter on "The Gray Zone" in *The Drowned and the Saved* helped to make the region decipherable, at least in part, but his honesty made it impossible—at least for him—to remove completely the ambiguity and compromise that blocked the hope that full clarity and understanding could be obtained, even in principle. Rejecting the speculative claim that Holocaust studies sometimes evoke—"in my depths there lurks a murderer"—Levi did not hesitate to say that "I was a guiltless victim and I was not a murderer."[3] Nor did Levi mince words about the fact that the Holocaust epitomized wrongdoing, and never moreso, in his judgment, than when the Germans created the *Sonderkommando*, those units of predominantly Jewish prisoners whose task it was to man the Auschwitz crematoria. "Conceiving and organizing [those] squads," he said, "was National Socialism's most demonic crime."[4] Those clear and distinct moral judgments, however, mixed and mingled with two other dimensions of awareness that make Levi a much more complicated and profound ethical thinker.

First, Levi saw both that gray-zone behavior could not be neatly analyzed in terms of right and wrong, at least not as most traditions of philosophical ethics might try to do. Arguably, those traditions could still be used to judge the National Socialist perpetrators of the Holocaust, but no Kantian categorical imperative, Aristotelian theory of virtue, or utilitarian calculations about consequences were of much relevance for judging those who were conscripted into the *Sonderkommando*, let alone for determining what those hapless men should do, condemned as they were to a fate of choiceless choices, before they too were murdered.

Next, Levi saw how the gray zone revealed a tragic dysfunctionality for ethics. That dysfunctionality had at least two parts. First, traces of idealism about treating one's neighbor as oneself or of refusing to steal might remain in the gray zone, but within that region of experience such teachings lost their appeal. As Levi put the point: "The physiological reserves of the organism were consumed in two or three months, and death by hunger, or by diseases induced by hunger, was the prisoner's normal destiny, avoidable only with additional food. Obtaining that extra nourishment required a privilege—large or small, granted or conquered, astute or violent, licit or illicit—whatever it took to lift oneself above the norm."[5] Second, if the most basic ethical teachings lost their appeal in the gray zone, then that fact scarcely inspired confidence—then or now—that the world has a fundamental moral structure that can be trusted. True, Levi thought that, "At least sometimes, at least in part, historical crimes are punished," and that the Nazi project had been suicidal.[6] But Levi's book *The Drowned and the Saved* was written, overall, in a minor key, and its chapter on the gray zone ends as follows: "Willingly or not we come to terms with power, forgetting that we are all in the ghetto, that the ghetto is walled in, that outside the ghetto reign the lords of death, and that close by the train is waiting."[7]

Levi knew that a kind of "logic" governed Nazi thinking. He did not unpack, however, something implied by his insight, something that others have underscored in ways that not only are consistent with Levi's outlook but also create additional worries about and for ethics, especially after the Holocaust. In 1988, Peter J. Haas sparked a controversy when he identified what he called "the Nazi ethic."[8] Fifteen years later, the historian Claudia Koonz has also ignited debate by writing about "the Nazi conscience." Anticipating or responding to critics, real or potential, she contends that this concept "is not an oxymoron." On the contrary, Koonz argues persuasively, "The popularizers of antisemitism and the planners of genocide followed a coherent set of severe ethical maxims derived from broad philosophical concepts."[9]

Typically, criticism brought against Haas and Koonz argues that references to the Nazi ethic or conscience are confusing, discouraging, or sensationalistic. According to these outlooks, confusion results by linking Nazism with ethics and conscience because the former was antithetical to the latter. Discouragement follows from the confusion, for if one links Nazi ways with ethics and conscience, then it would seem that anything and everything could be ethical or a matter of conscience, and the doors to moral relativism become wide open and inviting. Or, the criticism could say, Haas and Koonz are being sensationalistic. They are causing a stir, but where these serious matters are concerned, cleverness ought to be avoided. In my view, such criticism would be justified if Haas and Koonz were saying, without qualification, that the Nazi ethic and the Nazi conscience were truly moral. However, I do not take them to be making that claim. I think they are saying that Nazism functioned as a value system that deeply motivated and governed its followers—it was an ethic in that descriptive sense of the term—and Nazism did so because it took advantage of concepts and virtues that definitely had moral content. It does not follow that the Nazi ethic and its conscience were right, true, and good. On the contrary, they were wrong, false, and evil, and yet one can speak of the Nazi ethic and the Nazi conscience nonetheless. Far from being sensationalistic, it is important to do so if we are to understand how Nazi ways seemed attractive, good, and compelling to so many Germans.

Both Haas and Koonz help to show that value systems—ethics and ethical reasoning in that sense—can take forms that are not only multiple but at lethal odds with one another. Koonz makes the point by referring to the German political theorist Carl Schmitt, who rejected universal human rights and argued in May 1933 that, in Koonz's translation, "Not every being with a human face is human."[10] One can and must argue that such reasoning is false and wrong, but arguments do not guarantee the triumph of rationality, especially when what counts as rational is not only arguable but also a factor in struggles for power and political control. Neither philosophy nor ethics can take much comfort from saying, after its devastation was wreaked, that the Holocaust was wrong.

What happened to ethics?

As the existence of Primo Levi's gray zone helps to show, the Holocaust signifies an immense human failure. That failure leaves ethics gray-zoned, for the Holocaust did enormous harm to ethics by showing how ethical teachings could be made ambiguous, how they could be overridden, rendered dysfunctional, or even subverted to serve the interests of genocide.

The Holocaust years and our own times have been far from devoid of morality. An important example can be found in the booklet *Ethics for the Marine Lieutenant*, published by the US Naval Academy's Center for the Study of Professional Military Ethics. It begins by citing Title 10 of the US Code, whose Section 5947 deals with the requirement of exemplary conduct. Its words are worth quoting.

All commanding officers and others in authority in the naval service are required to show in themselves a good example of virtue, honor, patriotism, and subordination; to be vigilant in inspecting the conduct of all persons who are placed under their command; to guard against and suppress all dissolute and immoral practices, and to correct, according to the laws and regulations of the Navy, all persons who are guilty of them; and to take all necessary and proper measures, under the laws, regulations, and customs of the naval service, to promote and safeguard the morale, the physical well-being, and the general welfare of the officers and enlisted persons under their command or charge.[11]

I will revisit that text, but first note some of the questions that come into play when one reflects on what happened to ethics during the Holocaust and considers some of the implications for our own time. Here are some of the most important ones that are on my mind. (1) During and after the Holocaust why have ethical traditions, such as those found in religion (Judaism and Christianity) and in philosophy, been so unable to withstand powers and policies that were antithetical to them? (2) How has ethics itself contributed to the appeal and legitimation of those same powers and policies? (3) Does the shadow of Birkenau make clearer what ethics must be and do, or does it leave ethics in a "gray zone" that undermines confidence in the traditional sources and underpinnings of ethical claims (religion, reason, philosophy, intuition, conscience, and even feeling)? (4) Is the Holocaust, as some have argued, a *negative absolute*? Or is the Holocaust's negativity so great that it calls into question all prescriptive absolutes, except as assertions of will? And if the later outcome is the one that results, then does might make right so that ethics, problematically, becomes a matter of "the triumph of the will"?

My concern, you see, is not only about how the Holocaust, how the shadow of Birkenau, might lead us to advocate certain things as right and good and other things as wrong and evil. My concern is not only about strategies for "mobilizing morality." My concern also pertains to how the Holocaust, how the shadow of Birkenau, does and should affect our understanding of the foundations—or lack of them—for ethics and its most fundamental content.

The role of conscience

How do we know the difference between right and wrong, justice and injustice, good and evil? Possible answers to that question are numerous. We may refer to authorities of one kind or another: parents, teachers, traditions, religion, God. We can appeal to reason, to our ability to think and to think things through. These paths could put us in contact with important ethical theories in philosophy such as those developed by Aristotle and his views about virtue, Immanuel Kant and his views about the categorical imperative, and John Stuart Mill and his emphasis on calculations that serve the greatest good for the greatest number. We may also appeal to conscience—an ethical capacity, sense, or intuition— that acts compass-like to guide us in the direction of morality's "true north" if only we consult it thoughtfully and consistently. All of these ingredients operate in ethical deliberation and choice-making. Each has considerable power. None, however, is free of problems, as exploration of the Nazi conscience and its ethic helps to show.

If Claudia Koonz is correct when she says that it is no oxymoron to speak of the Nazi conscience—and I believe she is correct—then that possibility suggests something that we might prefer not to consider, namely, that neither the moral capacity we call *conscience* nor its content is universal or generically human, at least not in any way that can give us much moral comfort. Conscience and its contents are real, but there may not be a "one size fits all" quality about them, except that the capacity to think unavoidably includes value discriminations and judgments. Beyond those general characteristics, conscience and its contents—including theories about them—may be socially constructed in ways that go "all the way down" so that no Archimedean point is reached from which one can say with purely rational certainty that one version of conscience and its contents is absolutely true—period.

That result, however, does not mean that appeals to conscience are irrational or that relativism prevails. Nor does it follow that might alone makes right. Reasons, arguments, and criticisms can still be offered to promote or defend one ethical outlook over another. Judgments of better and worse, right and wrong, can still be made. Recognitions of error and falsity may still take place. But will, choice, and the particularity of experience will have infused the moral situation much as a soup is irretrievably flavored when Tabasco sauce seasons it. One result is that ethical views can be at lethal odds with each other. In fact, their confrontation is likely to be intensified just because conscience is involved, for appeals to conscience are less likely to result in agreement than they are to be expressions of the fact that moral collisions are in the making if they have not already taken place.

Ten commandments

Was there a Nazi conscience and a Nazi ethic? I believe that the answer to that empirical question is clearly yes. Of course, one could say that this ethic was really not an ethic, or that the Nazi conscience was really not conscience, but those judgments would be too easy and convenient. They would overlook how most citizens of the Third Reich lived, how they acted and thought. They were not mindlessly obedient; they acted in terms of what they came to regard as right and good. To do the latter, they may have had to suppress or override some moral inhibitions, but they could do so without feeling that they were irrational or morally unjustified in doing so. The outcomes of those decisions were abhorrent and ethically wrong. We can and must say that decisively and with confidence, but we still ignore at our peril the need to figure out how the Nazi conscience worked and why its version of ethics was appealing to so many, even unto death.

The devil is in the details. Turn, then, to a specific example that reveals some key features of the Nazi conscience and its ethic. In 2004–05, the United States Holocaust Memorial Museum featured a special exhibit called "Deadly Medicine." It documented how Nazi Germany's programs of so-called racial science and hygiene emerged from nineteenth- and early-twentieth-century forms of genetic engineering called *eugenics* and eventually led to decisions, policies, gas chambers, and crematoria that killed tens of thousands of the physically disabled and mentally handicapped and murdered millions of Jews. During visits to the "Deadly Medicine" exhibit, a particular document riveted my attention. The exhibit identified its source as a book issued by a Berlin publisher in 1935. Its author, Dr. Hermann Böhm, titled this book *Darf ich meine Base heiraten?* (May I marry my cousin?).

Before noting the content of the document from this book about marriage, some glimpses of its author are instructive.[12] His fate is unknown to me, but Böhm, who was born in 1884, was a German university professor and research institute director who specialized in genetics and racial science. In 1936, shortly after Böhm's book appeared, Dr. Gerhard Wagner, founder of the National Socialist German Physicians' League in 1929 and subsequently the Reich Physicians' Führer (*Reichsärzteführer*), entrusted Böhm, his fellow Nazi, with an important educational assignment: he would teach National Socialist views on genetics and race to German physicians. Specifically, he would do so at an important training center, the SS Doctors' Führer School, an arm of the Physicians' League. The school's six-week courses supplemented traditional medical training by "character building" activities—"manual, mental, and moral," to use Robert Proctor's words—whose purpose was to impress upon young and promising doctors, nurses, and midwives their importance as leaders in promoting the Third Reich's program of racial hygiene. Under

Böhm's tutelage, the emphasis was less on curing illnesses among the living and more on preventive measures to protect the health and purity of "German genetic streams." At the Doctors' School, Böhm created an Institute for Genetics. Its library and laboratory facilities advanced teaching and its research put German racial purity at the forefront of a worldview that blended science, medicine, and politics in ways that both reflected and extended the Nazi conscience and its ethic, both of which were deeply antisemitic and ultimately genocidal.

Returning to Böhm's book about marriage, its best-known part was called *Zehn Gebote für die Gattenwahl* (Ten commandments for choosing a spouse). A prefatory paragraph indicates that the commandments were promulgated by "The Reich Committee for the National Health Service together with the Reich Ministry of the Interior, the Reich Office of Health, and the NSDAP Office for Racial Policy." Böhm's book not only indicated his support for them but also added his scientific prestige to their credibility. Meanwhile, the commandments were widely distributed in an attractive poster format by the Reich Committee for Public Health.[13]

These *Zehn Gebote* definitely have ethical content ("You should keep your mind and spirit pure!" "Marry only for love." "You should wish for as many children as possible"). But what is particularly interesting and disturbing is the way in which this document drew upon traditional ethical forms, categories, and content to promote policies and to legitimate powers whose "logic" eventually led to Birkenau.

Two instances, obvious ones, illustrate what I mean. First, these Nazi commandments were intended to be a kind of Decalogue; they hearkened back to the form of the biblical Ten Commandments. That form was used to give them authority, to enhance their normative power. Second, there is a striking contrast between the biblical Decalogue and the one that Böhm supported. It might not have been fully conscious to German readers in 1935, and it might be even less so today, but there are still resonances and echoes that deserve comment: The first commandment in the Nazi list is "Remember that you are a German." At least as the Hebrew text is often construed, the first commandment in the biblical Decalogue is "I am the Lord your God, who brought you out of the land of Egypt, out of the house of slavery; you shall have no other gods before me" (Exodus 20:2). Böhm, I am confident, knew that the Nazi commandments in his book drew on a biblical form. Whether he sensed any dissonance between the first Nazi commandment and the one that Moses communicated to his people is a harder call to make, but one worth pondering when the question is what happened to ethics during and after the Holocaust.

Meanwhile, consider in more detail how the version of the ten commandments in Böhm's book contains Nazi ethics in Peter Haas's sense of "a complete and coherent system of convictions, values, and ideas that provides a grid within which some sorts of actions can be classified as evil, and so to be avoided, while other sorts of actions can be classified as good, and so to be tolerated or even pursued"[14] and reflects Nazi conscience in terms of what Claudia Koonz calls "an inner voice that admonishes 'Thou shalt' and 'Thou shalt not.' "[15]

What was the Nazi conscience?

The Nazi conscience and its ethic were epitomized in the first of the commandments about marriage featured in Hermann Böhm's book: "Gedenke, dass du ein Deutscher bist" (Remember that you are a German).[16] In Böhm's context, that imperative contains three key themes. First, Germans are different from and better than other human groups. Second, one's existence as a German is dependent on the *Volk* and its heritage, whose continued vitality, including one's own posterity, depends on commitment to its purity. Third, one's actions should be guided by national interests. Germany's good comes before self-interest.

At first glance, such thinking might not seem ominous, but if one reconsiders those propositions in the shadow of Birkenau, the situation looks different, for they are gray-zoned ideas that contain a dangerously tempting vision of the good, demanding virtues to implement it, and a form of conscience to match. Koonz rightly identifies the latter as an "ethnic conscience" based on four assumptions whose credibility and appeal in Nazi Germany has by no means been completely discredited in our twenty-first-century world.[17]

Those assumptions may be stated as follows: (1) A people's life is organic; it involves a cycle of development. If a nation does not progress and exert its influence, decline threatens and death follows. (2) Communities are not identical; they have their own values, which evolve over time. Protection of those values and their development is fundamental for communal vitality. (3) Those who do not share a community's values—especially those who cannot share them because they are judged to be fundamentally different, not "us" but other-than-us—are threats to *our* way of life. Enemies exist. Aggression against them, especially where national interest is at stake, is justifiable and even necessary for self-defense. (4) Threats and enemies do not exist entirely beyond national borders; they may dwell within as well. If so, they deserve neither assimilation nor legal protection. The nation is better off rid of them.

From these assumptions, it was not much of a stretch for the Nazi propagandist Joseph Goebbels to argue persuasively that the Nazi conscience would say, "Love Germany above all else and your ethnic comrade [*Volksgenosse*] as your self!"[18] That teaching, Goebbel's Nazi version of the Jewish and Christian commandments to "love the Lord your God with all your heart, and with all your soul, and with all your might" and "love your neighbor as yourself," (see Deuteronomy 6:5 and Leviticus 19:18), took the Nazi ethic in two complementary directions.

One of those directions involved understanding the boundaries of obligation and, in particular, the identities of the outsiders, threats, and enemies. So-called racial science was crucial in Nazism's drawing of these boundaries. Far from dissenting against such thinking and classification, far from being intimidated and coerced into accepting racial classifications and discriminations as pivotal, Germans under Hitler widely embraced a worldview that made an *us* versus *them* mentality dominant. First and foremost, that outlook targeted Jews as undesirable and unwanted, as inferior to the point of being sub- or even nonhuman, and yet as threatening as lethal bacilli or cancers on the body politic. Such thinking led first to segregation and the destruction of Jewish civil liberties, including opportunities to earn a living, then to expropriation of property and deportation, and ultimately to ghettoization, shooting squadrons, and killing centers aimed at destroying Jewish life root and branch.

Difficult and even loathsome though the so-called Final Solution's ethnic cleansing turned out to be, Koonz is correct when she says that "the road to Auschwitz was paved with righteousness."[19] That claim points in a second direction taken by the Nazi ethic. It consisted of an emphasis on and an appeal to *virtue*, which played a key part in the Nazi ethic. Virtues are distinctive qualities of thought and character. They can be compared to habits, and in that case, the reference to habit points toward forms of ethical conduct that are not only noble and good but also deeply rooted in one's life.

Integrity, communal solidarity, self-sacrifice, loyalty, courage, patriotism—these virtues, along with *hardness*, a mixture of discipline and refusal to succumb to sentimental or humanitarian concern for those who were regarded as one's enemies, were a key part of the Nazi ethic and, in Koonz's words, "a conscience that kept to a minimum the psychic stress [Germans] might experience when murdering Jews—'undesirables' who had no place on the perpetrators' moral map."[20] In fact, one could say, the Nazi conscience, because it emphasized these virtues and because of the particular way in which that emphasis was driven home, made it a matter of conscience to murder Jews for the sake of Germany and its posterity. Absent the Nazi ethic and its conscience, it is scarcely conceivable that the Holocaust could have happened.

An ethics of ethics

Not only is ethics fragile and easily overridden. Not only is it subject to subversion. It can be an immense force for evil as well as good, and that description fits because the very nature of good and evil are not crystal clear to everyone but profoundly contested. In that sense, the Holocaust shows us that ethics is not simply a solution for social and political ills. It is also a problem and even a contributor to them. It does not follow, however, that ethics should be trashed or that we can get along very well without ethics. What has to be reconsidered might be called *the ethics of ethics*.

Earlier, I quoted a passage from *Ethics for the Marine Lieutenant*. When it speaks about "honor, patriotism, and subordination," when it urges vigilance to "guard against and suppress all dissolute and immoral practices," we trust and hope that there is no connection between that ethic and the Nazi ethic, between an American conscience, for example, and a Nazi conscience. To ensure that there is never any transferability of that kind, we have to make sure that our ethics are indeed ethical. A key step in that direction depends on critical thinking that raises a key question in the shadow of Birkenau, namely, what deserves attention, what matters most?

If the first thing to remember, even if the context is something as particular as whom one should marry, is *not* "I am a German," then what is more deserving of memory and where should one's priorities be found and why? Is the answer, "I am an American"? Is the answer, "I am a human being"? Is the answer, "I am a child of God"? It could be that all three of those responses are part of the puzzle that we need to work in ethics after the Holocaust, especially if the sense of "I" is relational, by which I mean that it implies an Other whose very existence confers responsibility upon me, a responsibility that is never fulfilled or completed as long as my life and yours go on.

We study the Holocaust because it happened but not only for that reason. We study it for ethical reasons as well. There are pitfalls in making that claim. One of them involves the attempt to derive *lessons* from Holocaust studies, especially ethical lessons. I think that there are senses in which lessons can and should be drawn from the Holocaust and from study about that event, but this matter must be handled with care.

Two dangers are especially acute, and they keep bearing down on a project such as mine. First, one must try hard to avoid triviality and banality, which always threaten to intrude where normative ethical reflection takes place. In this area, the need is to avoid *clichés*. Second, one must try equally hard not to preempt the Holocaust, to use Lawrence Langer's phrase. Instead one has to let the Holocaust in, one has to admit it, so that the ethical analysis does not attain credibility at the expense of the Holocaust but rather obtains credibility by its faithfulness to the historical record. In this area the need is to avoid ethical judgments and prescriptions that cannot pass the test of being called into question by the shadow of Birkenau. With that last point in mind, I turn to a Holocaust survivor, the philosopher Sarah Kofman (1934–94).

Knotted words

What can words say? What can they do? Words can be put to many uses. They can make statements and ask questions. They can mystify and deconstruct; they can be used against themselves. Speeches, propaganda, orders, laws—these are only a few of the ways in which language can advance mass murder. Testimonies, memoirs, poems, stories—these are only a few of the ways in which language can bear witness to atrocity. Words can kill. They are also memory's voice. Without words, there could have been no Holocaust. Words, however, cannot do everything. One reason is that words can be smothered or, as Sarah Kofman sometimes said, words can be knotted. The Holocaust produced knotted words, especially for the survivors, because such words, Kofman suggests, are "demanded and yet forbidden, because for too long they have been internalized and withheld." Knotted words, she went on to say, "stick in your throat and cause you to suffocate, to lose your breath"; they "asphyxiate you, taking away the possibility of even beginning."[21]

Kofman understood all too well what she was saying, for this French philosopher was a Holocaust survivor. Like four other important writers who also endured that catastrophe—Jean Améry (1912–78), Tadeusz Borowski (1922–51), Paul Celan (1920–70), and Primo Levi (1919–87)—she took her own life. Kofman left behind a rich collection of philosophical works, among them significant writings on Sigmund Freud and Friedrich Nietzsche—especially the latter's outlook affects in varied ways Kofman's moral philosophy—as well as major contributions to feminist theory. Her voice, which was often heard on French radio and in political debate, earned its prominence in an influential generation of French philosophers that has included Jacques Derrida, Emmanuel Levinas, and

Jean-Luc Nancy, who said of Kofman that "Fidelity was for her the very course of life. Not 'truth' but fidelity, the truth of fidelity, which has no final sense but the sense of its very course. Truth that returns to life and not the converse."[22]

Kofman is better known in many philosophical and literary circles than the other survivor-suicides mentioned above, but in the field of Holocaust studies it has thus far been her fate to be overlooked and too little appreciated. True, she wrote less—or at least less directly—about the Holocaust than some survivors, including Charlotte Delbo (1913–85), arguably the woman who has written the most impressively in French about the Holocaust.[23] Kofman's explicit works about the Holocaust consist primarily of two small books, *Paroles suffoquées* (1987), a reflection focused on her father, Berek Kofman, a Parisian rabbi who was deported to Auschwitz in 1942, and *Rue Ordener, Rue Labat* (1994), her memoir about antisemitism, family separation, and hiding during the German occupation of her native France.[24]

Ann Smock, one of her translators, notes that Kofman began writing *Rue Ordener, Rue Labat* during the winter of 1992–93. She was almost sixty at the time. The memoir takes its title from two Parisian streets, which, Kofman observes, were separated by one Métro stop.[25] The family home had been on Rue Ordener, but everything changed when Kofman's father was caught in the roundup of some thirteen thousand Parisian Jews that took place on July 16–17, 1942.[26] Subsequently Sarah's mother, who survived the Holocaust, had to find hiding places for the children. Kofman's turned out to be on the Rue Labat with a Christian widow named Mémé.[27]

Meanwhile Kofman never saw her father again. In *Smothered Words*, Kofman sums up the bare facts of her father's fate as follows:

> My father: Berek Kofman, born on October 10, 1900, in Sobin (Poland), taken to Drancy on July 16, 1942. Was in convoy no. 12, dated July 29, 1942, a convoy comprising 1,000 deportees, 270 men and 730 women (aged 36–54); 270 men registered 54,153 to 54,422; 514 women selected for work, registered 13, 320 to 13, 833; 216 other women gassed immediately.[28]

The ending of the five-page chapter that contains those words mentions the memorial register created by Serge Klarsfeld, a French historian of the Holocaust and a hunter of Nazi war criminals. Kofman reproduces a portion of its double-columned, alphabetized list of the French deportees. There, in the left-hand column between the names of Simone Klempen and Grange Kohn, one finds Berek Kofman. Klarsfeld's memorial list, with "its endless columns of names ... takes your breath away," says Kofman. "Its 'neutral' voice summons you obliquely; in its extreme restraint, it is the very voice of affliction, of this event in which all possibility vanished, and which inflicted on the whole of humanity 'the decisive blow which left nothing intact.' This voice leaves you without a voice, makes you doubt your common sense and all sense, makes you suffocate in silence: 'silence like a cry without words; mute, although crying endlessly.' "[29]

Her father's death suffocated Kofman, stifled her words. It did so, however, not simply because it was her father's death, grievous enough though a father's death can be for anyone. "Because he was a Jew," as her stifled voice expresses it, "my father died in Auschwitz."[30] Kofman's emphasis on smothered words, moreover, shows that it was inseparable from the memory of how her father died in Auschwitz. "My father, a rabbi," she writes, "was killed because he tried to observe the Sabbath in the death camps; buried alive with a shovel for having—or so the witnesses reported—refused to work on that day, in order to celebrate the Sabbath, to pray to God for them all, victims and executioners, reestablishing, in this situation of extreme powerlessness and violence, a relation beyond all power. And they could not bear that a Jew, that vermin, even in the camps, did not lose faith in God."[31]

"Because he was a Jew, my father died in Auschwitz." Her father's suffocation and her own produce the double-binding questions that follow: "How can it not be said? And how can it be said?"[32] Not just a father's death but a particular Jewish father's death in its Auschwitz specificity—that event, which Kofman calls "my absolute," made the suffocating difference. When Kofman says that her father's death is her absolute, her claim is significant and suggestive. Moral absolutes may exist, I believe she is saying, but they are neither best construed nor most credible as propositional truths or universal imperatives. Instead they may be found in frail but determined particularities, which could be different for different people in their particularity but also understood to be broadly applicable within the human condition. For Kofman, taking her father's death to be her absolute meant that it is wrong, everywhere and always, for anyone's life to be taken in circumstances and ways like those that destroyed Berek Kofman. She held that conviction because she took her father's death in the way she did. Her moral judgment was deeply rooted in, emergent from, and governed by the most deeply personal of experiences. Far from being merely "subjective" factors that lead to moral relativism, such experiences are the source of the most profoundly human ethical insights.

Kofman elaborated these hints by suggesting further that "death in Auschwitz was worse than death."[33] Her point was not restricted to the brutality of that place or even to the systematic, assembly-line character of the mass murder that took place in Birkenau's gas chambers and crematoria. When she says that an Auschwitz death was worse than death, she is not mystifying death, let alone denying that death is death. She points instead to the tragic smothering, even the death, of words such as *human* and *humanity*. After Auschwitz, Kofman claims, people "do not really die" because death itself—in the sense that the death of every man, woman, and child is the death of a human being—was degraded and mocked by Nazi Germany's "Final Solution." Auschwitz meant that people died *differently* in the sense that the Nazi extermination camps, whose mass killing went on for months and years, was a devastating assault on the very idea of a shared humanity that puts us all on a common ground of rights and responsibilities, of dignity and respect.

This tragic insight is not solely a lament about the loss of humanity conceived generically, universally, or in terms of some fixed philosophical essence, for, in the words of the philosopher Richard Rorty, "most people—especially people relatively untouched by the European Enlightenment—simply do not think of themselves as, first and foremost, a human being."[34] The loss of humanity involves a destruction of particularity, difference, and the potential for personal development—ingredients without which humanity is an abstraction. Not simply wanton but calculated and intended again and again by Nazi Germany and its collaborators, the destruction of Berek Kofman—a particular Jewish rabbi with a distinctive social identity, a specific name and a singular face whose difference is definitive of his humanity—constitutes the assault on humanity that is also the death of human death. There was, could be, only one Berek Kofman. The Nazi assault on humanity was systematic, extensive, and devastating. It could only be what it was by destruction that murdered particularity and difference—social and personal—as it destroyed children, women, and men *en masse* but also one by one by one.

Kofman thought that cost for such insights had been huge. In fact, the price was still being paid, and perhaps it would prove to be too much. Post-Holocaust people, Kofman indicated ironically and tragically, have survived death only to discover, if they will, that reviving suffocated *humanity* is a task that puts us, and perhaps philosophers and ethicists in particular, in "a strange *double bind*: an infinite claim to speak, *a duty to speak infinitely*, imposing itself with irrepressible force, and at the same time, an almost physical impossibility to speak, a *choking* feeling."[35]

A significant version of the dilemma that Kofman identified definitely remains in effect. The Holocaust does create a duty to speak, an obligation to make ethics stronger and less subject to overriding, dysfunctionality, or subversion, an insistence not only to drive home the difference between right and wrong but also to influence action accordingly. Yet such an obligation can also produce a choking feeling, a sense that too much harm has been done for a good recovery to be made, a suspicion that ethics may be overwhelmed by the challenges it faces. The bind is double, for the sense of ethical responsibility, real though it is, remains hopelessly optimistic and naïve unless it grapples with the despair that encounters with the Holocaust are bound to produce. To be touched by that despair, however, scarcely encourages one to believe that ethical responsibilities will be accepted and met. Caught between the post-Holocaust need to speak for ethics and above all to speak ethically and boldly, on the one hand, and the feeling that the key elements of ethics—words, arguments, appeals to reason, persuasion through the example of moral action—may be inadequate, on the other, the question persists: Given what happened to ethics during the Holocaust, what can and should be made of ethics after Auschwitz?

Power to choose

All she has left of her father, Kofman observes at the beginning of *Rue Ordener, Rue Labat*, is his fountain pen. "Patched up with Scotch tape," it can produce words no more, but "right in front of me on my desk," she says, that mute pen "makes me write, write."[36] As she penned those words, Kofman was trying to do what she had not done overtly very much before. "Maybe all my books," she observed, "have been the detours required to bring me to write about 'that.' "[37] *That* included her father's death, the Holocaust, the loss of humanity, the death of death. Kofman had written about some of these matters already and in ways many and diverse, but a direct encounter with the Holocaust, unavoidably including the particularity of her father's death and her own identity in relation to that disaster, created in her something akin to the predicament felt by Robert Antelme, a member of the French Resistance, who was arrested by the Germans in June 1944, sent to Buchenwald, and eventually liberated at Dachau. In his philosophical memoir, *The Human Species*, which was originally published in French as *L'Espèce humaine* (1957), he wrote that his "liberation" from Dachau left him to see that "it was impossible to bridge the gap we discovered opening up between the words at our disposal and that experience which, in the case of most of us, was still going forward within our bodies. How were we to resign ourselves to not trying to explain how we had got to the state we were in? For we were yet in that state. And even so, it was impossible. No sooner would we begin to tell our story than we would be choking over it."[38]

Confronting this double bind, but not paralyzed—at least not completely—by it, Antelme told his story, and Kofman examined the message that she took from it. Antelme saw that the more Adolf Hitler and his followers tried to destroy an inclusive sense of *humanity* through their genocidal antisemitism and racism, the more undeniable the "indestructible unity" of humanity became, or, as Antelme himself put it, "there is only one human race." The SS, continued Antelme, "can kill a man, but he can't change him into something else."[39] Kofman seems to share what she calls Antelme's "pleasure in tearing the Nazis' power to shreds and overturning their mastery," but as much as she admires his resistance, his determination not to permit the Nazis or even his own devastating experience to choke his words completely, Kofman appears to find Antelme's affirmative understanding of the persistence of a single humanity less than sufficient and therefore not entirely convincing.[40] It is not that she denies the unity but that Antelme may not have emphasized enough how Nazism wreaked havoc on *community*.

Her father's death never far from her consciousness, Kofman starts to draw out what remained only implicit in Antelme's *The Human Race*. The value of a shared sense of humanity, of our belonging to a human species, depends on whether that belonging binds us together in mutual respect and caring, whether it draws people together in community. As Kofman sizes up the situation, however, the connections between the unity implied by the word *humanity* and the senses of community that may or may not follow are tenuous and even problematic. First, she points out, "No community is possible with the SS."[41] With a vengeance, Nazi ideology rejected the idea of an inclusively shared humanity. Regarding difference—especially alleged racial difference—as profoundly threatening, its genocidal impulses took the world to Treblinka and Auschwitz. Nazi Germany, of course, took pride in its own sense of community, which underscores that community is not necessarily humanity's ally, especially if *humanity* is understood to be pluralistic and diverse. So Kofman makes a second point: It is crucial to support "the community (of those) without community."[42]

Those without community are outsiders, but Kofman's thinking does not stop with a call to defend and protect those who are threatened and harmed because they are left out. More radically and fundamentally, she rejects all senses of community that are based on "any specific difference or on a shared essence" such as reason.[43] The right forms of community, she seems to be saying, are those that consciously accept a double-bind. This bind acknowledges that every community is particular, different, finite, even exclusive in one way or another, but no community should rest on assumptions about immutable superiority or inferiority. On the contrary, the particularity of one community ought to affirm, protect, and encourage the particularity of others. At its best, she contends, community depends on "a shared power to choose, to make incompatible though correlative choices, the power to kill *and* the power to respect and safeguard the incommensurable distance, the relation without relation."[44]

Here Kofman's words are not smothered or knotted, but they remain less than fully expressed. They remain hints, allusions, or signposts pointing to an ethical outlook that would not be the same as old humanisms that appealed to human nature, to the essence of humanity, or to reason as humankind's most decisive characteristic. Instead, she suggests everyday realities and actions—things such as choices and keeping or betraying one's word—reveal our humanity and make all the difference. The Holocaust reaffirmed that all of those caught in it—perpetrators, victims, bystanders, and more—were human. In some sense, humanity survived the Holocaust, if only to testify, as the French philosopher Maurice Blanchot put it, how human indestructibility reveals "that there is no limit to the destruction of man."[45] But if humanity is to mean more than that, if humanity is to be what Kofman thinks it ought to become, then the destruction of old humanisms may make possible the willful reconstitution of a "new kind of 'we,' " even "a new 'humanism' one might say, if it were still acceptable to use this trite and idyllic word."[46] Kofman was cautious but tenacious about that view: "In spite of everything that makes this word [humanism] unacceptable for us today—after 'the death of God' and the end of man that is its correlate—I nonetheless want to conserve it, while giving it a completely different meaning, displacing and transforming it. I keep it because what other, new 'word' could have as much hold on the old humanism?"[47]

The Holocaust's double binds, Kofman's smothered and knotted words, her sense that "after Auschwitz there is no word tinged from on high ... that has any right unless it has undergone a transformation"— each and all, her hard-earned perspectives underscore that nothing human, natural, or divine guarantees respect for the values that human beings hold most dear when we are at our best.[48] Nothing, though, is more important than our commitment to defend them, for they remain as fundamental as they are fragile, as precious as they are endangered. These insights are among those made clearer by Primo Levi's gray zone, the "Nazi ethic," and by Sarah Kofman's guarded hope, her hint of "community (of those) without community," and her glimpses of the possibility of a new humanism, power to choose, and an ethics—new in some ways, old in others—that can and should emerge from the Holocaust's gray zones.

6

Post-Holocaust Restitution of a Different Kind

> The Holocaust remains a highly combustible issue.
>
> Stuart Eizenstat, *Imperfect Justice*

The Holocaust was in the news on January 27, 2005, as death camp survivors and a few of their Russian liberators joined heads of state and Jewish leaders at a snow-covered Auschwitz–Birkenau to observe the sixtieth anniversary of that camp's liberation by the Red Army. The aging and dying of the survivors and liberators meant that such a gathering is not likely to take place again.

Earlier in that month, at least three other Holocaust-related episodes created a context of concern for the commemoration at Birkenau. Costume-party photographs of Prince Harry, third in line to the British throne, not only pictured him in a Nazi uniform but also raised questions about the success or failure of Holocaust education. In Germany, far-right legislators walked out when a minute of silence was observed in memory of the victims of Nazism, which raised questions about the future of Holocaust memory and memorialization.[1] On January 5, the US Department of State issued its Report on Global Anti-Semitism, which documented and analyzed what the report designated as "the increasing frequency and severity of anti-Semitic incidents since the start of the 21st century."[2]

The speeches at the Auschwitz–Birkenau commemoration underscored two themes repeatedly: First, the mass murder of Jews at that place was a warning—not only for Jews but also for all humankind. Second, never again should humanity permit such atrocities. Even as those words were uttered, however, awareness of more recent genocides, such as the 1994 slaughter in Rwanda and the devastation in the Darfur region of Sudan were on the minds of many who heard them.

Meanwhile, during the preceding night, January 26, the American Public Broadcasting System (PBS) aired the first two parts of a six-hour documentary on the history of Auschwitz. Each segment included discussion with Holocaust scholars, one of whom was Melvin Jules Bukiet, whose parents survived the Holocaust. "I think we learn nothing from it," Bukiet said of the Holocaust. "We have to recognize [the Holocaust]," he added, and yet he insisted "it has nothing to teach us."[3]

I disagree with Bukiet's claim that the Holocaust has nothing to teach us, although I take his point that we must be careful not to trivialize that catastrophe by turning it into a means for "moral education" in such a way that the Holocaust is somehow justified or regarded as having a silver lining. Nothing could sensibly justify the Holocaust. Auschwitz, I believe, cannot be interpreted as the means to some greater good. It does not follow, however, that the Holocaust has nothing to teach us. What is more to the point is whether people have learned, really learned, what that disaster can and must teach us.

One might have thought, for example, that awareness of the Holocaust, education about it, would have a significant ethical impact that, in particular, would reduce if not eliminate antisemitism. Such hopes may not be entirely wrong, but unfortunately they have been far too optimistic. In fact, Holocaust educators currently have to deal with an ironic development, namely, that teaching about the Holocaust may inflame antisemitism in some quarters because anti-Jewish/anti-Israeli interpreters (1) indict Holocaust education as special pleading to cover up or to justify Israel's alleged human rights abuses, a strategy that is often accompanied by Holocaust minimalization or denial; (2) seize and spin Holocaust images to portray Palestinians and other non-Jews as victims; and (3) depict Israelis and other Jews as akin to Nazi perpetrators.

Antisemitism has aptly been called the longest hatred, but it is more than hatred of Jews. As the French president Jacques Chirac stated in his January 25, 2005, address on the occasion of the opening of a Holocaust memorial in Paris, "antisemitism is not an opinion. It is a perversion ... rooted in the depths of evil."[4] Antisemitism's intensity has waxed and waned, but as the State Department's Report on Global Anti-Semitism testifies, its frequency and severity have been on the rise again. The report identifies four main sources for this upsurge. First, traditional anti-Jewish prejudice never went away entirely. It enjoys new popularity among ultra-nationalists, especially in Europe, who, as the report put it, "assert that the Jewish community controls governments, the media, international business, and the financial world." Second, inflamed by the Israeli-Palestinian conflict and reaching far beyond objective criticism of some Israeli policies, there is demonization of Israel and vilification of Israeli leaders. Third, in both Europe and the Middle East, specifically in Muslim communities, opposition to "developments in Israel and the occupied territories" intensifies anti-Jewish feelings. Fourth, there is "criticism of both the United States and globalization that spills over to Israel, and to Jews in general who are identified with both."[5]

In the twenty-first century, antisemitism is widely and easily communicated by diverse media outlets, including the Internet. Many governments, the State Department report found, have spoken out against antisemitism, but law enforcement against hate crimes and protection for their targets has been "uneven," to use the report's understated word.[6] Noting that antisemitism is "an intolerable burden" in our "increasingly interdependent world," the report saw Holocaust education as "a potential long-term solution to anti-Semitism" but acknowledged that "the problem is still rapidly outpacing the solution."[7]

In one sense, then, the answer to the question "Why has antisemitism surged in the twenty-first century?" is neither surprising nor difficult to locate: Despite the Holocaust, antisemitism never went away. Current developments in the Middle East intensified it, advances in communication technologies facilitated its spread, and responses have not been sufficient to thwart, let alone eliminate, the threat. Thus, restitution for antisemitism remains a priority item for ethical reflection focused on the Holocaust and its aftermath.

Rough justice

As the twentieth century drew to a close and the twenty-first got under way, the Holocaust remained both combustible and newsworthy. Many reports covered the struggle for financial reparations for Jewish survivors of the Holocaust and their heirs as well as for non-Jewish slave laborers who suffered under Nazi tyranny. Other accounts emphasized the restitution of Jewish property, including art looted from the Holocaust's victims. Tension-filled negotiations—national and international—with governments, corporations, insurance firms, art museums, law offices, and numerous other agencies and agents eventually produced a modicum of what Stuart Eizenstat has aptly called "rough justice."[8] While these post-Holocaust bargains and settlements about bank accounts and insurance policies, financial settlements and property claims, took place with widespread public attention focused upon them, a less publicized but immensely important and still unresolved issue about restitution remained another key part of ethics during and after the Holocaust: namely, the debt that Christianity owes to Jews and Judaism for centuries of anti-Jewish hostility that foreshadowed the Holocaust and still exists in some quarters after the Holocaust.

In a post-Holocaust world, which unfortunately remains one where human beings fall prey to terror, mass murder, and genocide, how far can and should restitution try to go? With that question in mind, reflect on restitution in the context of Christian–Jewish relations. As this chapter will show, many of the post-Holocaust issues surrounding what I call *restitution of a different kind* form minefields that, arguably, are even more difficult to traverse and disarm than those that have made the recent material claims settlements so volatile. Restitution issues within Christian–Jewish relations must be handled with care lest hasty inquiry, insensitive judgment, or premature closure set off explosions that enlarge harm's way.

A terrible darkness

Adolf Hitler and his Nazi regime intended the annihilation of Jewish life to signify the destruction of the very idea of a common humanity that all people share. Jean Améry, who noted that the Nazis "hated the word 'humanity,' " amplified such points when he stated: "Torture was no invention of National Socialism. But it was its apotheosis."[9] Améry meant that the Third Reich aimed to produce men, women, and children whose hardness would transcend humanity in favor of a racially pure and culturally superior form of life that could still appropriately be called Aryan or German but not merely "human." Insofar as *humanity* referred to universal equality, suggested a shared and even divine source of life, or implied any of the other trappings of weakness and sentimentality that Hitler and his most dedicated followers attributed to such concepts, National Socialism intentionally went beyond humanity. Such steps entailed more than killing so-called inferior forms of life that were thought to threaten German superiority. Moving beyond humanity made it essential to inflict torture—not only to show that "humanity" or "sub-humanity" deserved no respect in and of itself but also to ensure that those who had moved beyond humanity, and thus were recognizing the respect deserved only by Germans or Aryans, had really done so.

Jonathan Glover echoed these strains of Nazi "logic" in his important 1999 study, *Humanity: A Moral History of the Twentieth Century*. Convinced that "the Nazi genocide has a terrible darkness all its own," he locates it in the Nazis' "views about cruelty and hardness, and the appalling new Nazi moral identity." Reflected in pedagogy that would train the Nazi young to show cruelty to racial and cultural "inferiors" without dismay, that new moral identity, Glover makes clear, took its goals to include demolishing the idea that Germans, Slavs, and Jews shared the same humanity. Joseph Stalin and Mao Zedong took more lives than Hitler, but Glover thinks that Stalin and Mao defended "hardness and inhumanity," however implausibly, "as the supposed means to a more humane world." By contrast, the Nazis's "twisted deontology" made those qualities desirable in themselves, for they were key characteristics of a National Socialist identity that had moved beyond humanity.[10]

If Améry and Glover are right, and I think they are, then National Socialism entailed that not only Jews but also Judaism and every aspect of Jewish life must disappear, including the insights and imperatives of Jewish ethics that so much undergird the best aspects of human ethics generally.[11] Hitler and his Nazi followers did not succeed completely in implementing their antisemitism, but they went far enough in establishing as a principle what Améry aptly called "the rule of the antiman" that none of our fondest hopes about humanity can be taken for granted.[12] Such understanding entails recognition that Jews inhabit the post-Holocaust world in a distinctive way. To the extent that they confront the Holocaust, their consciousness includes memory that is qualitatively different from any other. Here I want to choose my words carefully, because debates continue about whether the Nazis clearly and distinctly intended that other nationalities or ethnic groups should also disappear root and branch (e.g., Sinti and Roma). So I will make my point as follows: Jewish post-Holocaust consciousness is different from every other because it involves the awareness, beyond doubt or question, that one is part of a people who were targeted for utter elimination—every trace, root and branch—from existence anywhere and everywhere.[13]

Such consciousness means that restitution for antisemitism and the Holocaust can never be a matter of finance or material property alone. A cautious civility may make honesty difficult, but post-Holocaust Jewish consciousness can scarcely be without anger that justifiably borders on rage. I do not presume to speak for Jews on this subject, nor do I assume that there is a single Jewish voice on the matter, but I can speak as an individual post-Holocaust Christian philosopher. That identity leads me to confess: Long before and during the Holocaust, we Christians typically and intentionally kept Jews in harm's way. We could and should have done far better. The Holocaust will always keep Christians and Jews at some distance, if not at odds. How could it not?

The anger and rage to which I have alluded spring from particularities that general references to the Holocaust cannot encompass. What must be faced is not only that Jews were left in harm's way but also how *in detail* they were put and left in that condition. Crucial to that perspective is awareness that the Holocaust's details—such as the specific torture that Améry experienced at the hands of Gestapo agents in a prison at Fort Breendonk, Belgium, in July 1943—show that Jews were abandoned to *useless experience*, whose particularities are as diverse as its wreckage is vast.

Useless experience

In *The Drowned and the Saved*, the Auschwitz survivor Primo Levi's exploration of useless experience concentrated on the Holocaust's "useless violence," which was characterized by the infliction of pain that was "always redundant, always disproportionate." Levi probes deeply precisely because he does not dwell on the obvious—beatings, hangings, or even gassings, for example. Instead his catalog of useless violence recalls the cattle cars that shipped Jews to Auschwitz. Their "total bareness" revealed a "gratuitous viciousness" that left people neither privacy nor dignity when they had to relieve themselves. Or, he observed, the loot collected from the arrivals at Auschwitz meant that there were tens of thousands of spoons in that place. None were given to prisoners; they had to fend as best they could, which might mean spending precious food from the camp's starvation diet to buy a spoon on the camp's black market. There were plenty of ways to identify prisoners, but at Auschwitz the Nazis implemented "the violence of the tattoo," which Levi describes as "an end in itself, pure offense."[14]

Levi's list continues. Its detail corroborates both Améry's judgment that "torture was not an accidental quality of this Third Reich, but its essence" and Glover's claim that "hardness over compassion was central to the Nazi outlook."[15] In turn, Levi's account resonates with theirs when he concludes by acknowledging that National Socialism's useless violence did have one unredeeming element of utility: "Before dying," Levi observed, "the victim must be degraded, so that the murderer will be less burdened by guilt. This is an explanation not devoid of logic but it shouts to heaven: it is the sole usefulness of useless violence."[16] Levi did not go on to say so, but he might have added that the Nazi goal was not simply to lessen guilt's burden but to create practitioners of useless violence who would feel no guilt at all.

Useless violence entails useless suffering, a topic that the Jewish philosopher Emmanuel Levinas explored in an influential post-Holocaust essay that he published on the latter theme in 1982. As a French prisoner of war, Levinas did forced labor under the Nazis, and almost all of his

Lithuanian family perished in the Holocaust. It made a profound impact upon him. Calling the twentieth century one of "unutterable suffering," he wrote that "the Holocaust of the Jewish people under the reign of Hitler seems to me the paradigm of gratuitous human suffering, in which evil appears in its diabolical form." Suffering of the kind that the Nazis and their collaborators wreaked on European Jewry is "for nothing." To try to justify it religiously, ethically, politically—as the Nazis did when they made the practice of useless violence essential to the German "superiority" that they envisioned—was what Levinas called "the source of all immorality."[17]

When Levinas said that the useless suffering administered during the Holocaust was "for nothing," he did not overlook Nazi "logic" and what it meant. To the contrary, he saw that National Socialism was ultimately about destruction, including the annihilation of Judaism and Jewish ethics, its grandiose rhetoric about the creation of a thousand-year Reich notwithstanding. The chief element in National Socialism's destructive arrogance was that regime's resolve to deface the human face—not in some abstract way but by useless suffering visited upon Jewish women, children, and men—with remorseless determination that made its anti-semitic prerogatives dominant until overwhelming force stopped them for doing more of their worst.

At least for those who survive such disasters or contemplate them at second-hand, useless violence and useless suffering entail useless knowledge. Hence it is worth noting that Charlotte Delbo was not Jewish, but her arrest for resisting the Nazi occupation of her native France made her experience the Holocaust when she was deported to Auschwitz in January 1943. Witnessing what happened to European Jewry, Delbo survived the Nazi onslaught. In 1946, she began to write the trilogy that came to be called *Auschwitz and After*. Her work's anguished visual descriptions, profound reflections on memory, and diverse writing styles make it an unrivaled Holocaust testimony.

Delbo called the second part of her trilogy *Useless Knowledge*. Normally we think that knowledge is useful, and it certainly can be, but Delbo showed how the Holocaust produced knowledge about hunger and disease, brutality and suffering, degradation and death that did nothing to unify, edify, or dignify life. "The sound of fifty blows on a man's back is interminable," she recounted. "Fifty strokes of a club on a man's back is an endless number."[18] This was only one example of what Delbo called useless knowledge. Its vast accumulation drove home her point: for the most part, what happened in the Holocaust divided, besieged, and diminished life forever.

Illustrated by Levi, Levinas, and Delbo, useless experience particularizes the Holocaust's ongoing devastation. It remains to be seen how far-reaching that devastation will be, and that is where restitution-in-spite-of-the-Holocaust comes back into play. Primo Levi concluded *The Drowned and the Saved* by contending that "there are no problems that cannot be solved around a table, provided there is good will and reciprocal trust."[19] Emmanuel Levinas thought that awareness of the other's useless suffering could evoke responses, intensely meaningful ones, to try to relieve that suffering. If there is to be post-Holocaust reconciliation between Christians and Jews, it will require a courage that refuses to let skepticism dismiss the hopes of Levi and Levinas too easily. At the hands of non-Jews, including Christians who stood by or aided and abetted the perpetrators of the Holocaust—if only by uncritical participation in a tradition whose millennia-long hostility toward Jews helped to set them up for the Nazi kill—Jewish life was abandoned to, and nearly destroyed by, useless experience that did not have to be. No honesty can or should remove entirely the raw edges of memory that remain, but Charlotte Delbo joins Levi and Levinas to urge that the post-Holocaust situation should not be left there alone. "Do something," she wrote, "something to justify your existence / ... because it would be too senseless / after all / for so many to have died / while you live / doing nothing with your life."[20] No false conciliatoriness could fulfill Delbo's sensibly impassioned imperative, but the courage to keep trying for reconciliation in spite of the Holocaust, which includes doing as much as Christians and Jews can to relieve the useless suffering of others, would help.

Moral reckonings

Daniel Jonah Goldhagen would argue that the steps noted above are only the beginning of a long restitution journey that is required for reconciliation between Christians and Jews. For reconciliation to go deep down, restitution is required, because restitution entails more than words that express repentance. Restitution requires concrete actions to make amends, to compensate people who have been unjustly harmed. It is an understatement to say that Holocaust-related restitution can only be partial at best, but restitution remains important because, without it, reconciliation between Christians and Jews may never escape the false conciliatoriness that Jean Améry especially and rightly despised. I turn to Goldhagen because his book *A Moral Reckoning: The Role of the Catholic Church in the Holocaust and Its Unfulfilled Duty of Repair* not only emphasizes restitution more than most discussions about post-Holocaust Christian–Jewish relations but also contains a restitution agenda that arguably surpasses any other in its ambition and long-term significance.

Critics have often dismissed Goldhagen's book as historically inaccurate, excessively critical of Christianity, and extreme in its recommendations. Nevertheless, the restitution challenges that it poses for Christians deserve consideration and certainly have their place in the broad context of post-Holocaust restitution studies. Goldhagen argues that Roman Catholics and Christians generally should provide what I am calling post-Holocaust restitution of a different kind. As we shall see, the restitution he has in mind is not of the material sort that grabbed so many headlines in recent years. Goldhagen's call for restitution is more fundamental than that. Whether it will help or hinder Christian–Jewish reconciliation is a good question. Cut to the chase and see why.

According to Goldhagen, the wartime pontiff Pius XII was an antisemite, the Roman Catholic Church was "more a collaborator than a victim of Nazism," and the New Testament's "libelous and hate-inducing passages about Jews" must go.[21] In short, he calls for a radical reformation to remove from Christianity the antisemitism that implicated it in the Holocaust and still leaves that tradition immorally mired in deception and hypocrisy.

Unpretentious, indecisive, moderate, and patient are not words that come to mind when reading Goldhagen. Insisting that it is high time to "call a spade a spade," his post-Holocaust moral reckoning with Christianity and the Roman Catholic Church in particular pulls few punches and guarantees a hard-hitting bout over history, ethics, and theology. Goldhagen's book is unlikely to leave its readers indifferent.[22] Its significance, however, depends less on immediate reactions and more on what happens ten, twenty, or even a hundred years after its appearance. Goldhagen may be helping to create a new Christianity. It will take time to tell.

Goldhagen's first book, *Hitler's Willing Executioners* (1996), was widely criticized on the grounds that its views were oversimplified, empirically questionable, and arrogantly argued; the latter complaint was incited by his petulant tendency to think that no scholar before him got much of anything right about the Holocaust. As time passed, and especially owing to the book's favorable reception in Germany, Goldhagen's work withstood much of the criticism. *A Moral Reckoning* has not fared as well, perhaps because it chides scholars of all persuasions. The defenders of Pope Pius XII, for example, have created a "moral blackout" regarding the Vatican's antisemitism. With recent exceptions such as James

Carroll, the author of *Constantine's Sword*, Goldhagen thinks that even most of the post-Holocaust critics of the Roman Catholic Church fail to go far enough; they have barely begun to press the issues of repentance and restitution. If Goldhagen is to be believed, his scholarship and, considerably important here, his moral judgment trump the field. This single-mindedness may not be good public relations, but it would be foolish to dismiss him on those grounds. His case is carefully argued.

Goldhagen's reckoning begins in two places. First, he believes that the Roman Catholic Church, the Vatican, and the wartime popes, Pius XI and especially Pius XII, should be judged no differently than any other institutions or persons—with one qualification: the Church, its members, and particularly its leaders should also be held accountable to the highest ethical standards of justice and love that they profess as Christians.[23] Second, Goldhagen identifies the antisemitism that lies at the heart of his indictment. Deeply rooted in falsehoods about Jews— none worse than the New Testament's allegation that the Jews are Christ-killers or even the offspring of Satan—antisemitism's many varieties reflect and inflame hostility against Jews "simply because they are Jews."[24] It follows, Goldhagen contends, that an antisemite is one who falsely accuses Jews of "noxious qualities or malfeasance," regarding those qualities or behaviors as the result of Jewishness and focusing "criticism disproportionately or exclusively on Jews."[25]

In Goldhagen's judgment, any Christian who believes or advances the tradition's falsehoods about Jews should be identified as an antisemite. Goldhagen finds that such falsehoods abound in Christianity. Correctly referring to what he calls "the Christian Bible's assault on Jews," Goldhagen sums it up as follows: "The Jews killed the son of God who is God. All Jews are guilty for this crime. Because Jews do not hear Jesus, they do not hear God. For their rejection of Jesus, they are to be punished. Jews, the willful spurners of Jesus, cannot gain salvation, cannot go to heaven. And their religion, which cannot bring them to salvation, has been made invalid, superseded, replaced by Christianity."[26]

Goldhagen acknowledges that the post-Holocaust Church has gradually repudiated the allegations of Jewish responsibility for the killing of Jesus. It has also rejected collective Jewish guilt and punishment for that crime. It has also called antisemitism a sin. Before and during the Holocaust, however, such repudiations by Christians—Protestants as well as Catholics— were few and far between. On the contrary, Goldhagen documents that the Church's antisemitism was institutional. As the Church's anti-Jewish teachings were transmitted from one generation to another, Western civilization became increasingly drenched in antisemitism's poison.

The antisemitism that Christianity embodied, inspired, and inflamed was "eliminationist." Clarifying a point central to controversy that swirled when *Hitler's Willing Executioners* appeared, Goldhagen underscores that eliminationist antisemitism "does not necessarily mean killing" and that "the Catholic Church was doctrinally opposed to, and itself did not advocate, killing Jews."[27] That said, Goldhagen adds that the lack of persistent and public Church protest against the Third Reich's slaughter of European Jewry scarcely inspires confidence that the Church was completely opposed to the mass annihilation.

Goldhagen rejects the apologetics that excuse the lack of public protest against the persecution and murder of Jews. He finds it morally incredible to hold that Nazi threats were too severe for stands to be taken in defense of Jews. He utterly rejects any reasoning that tries to excuse Pope Pius XII in particular on the grounds that if he had spoken out more forthrightly in their favor, then the Jews would have suffered even more under Hitler. Cutting in the opposite direction, his analysis of the evidence points to a devastating conclusion: The Church found that "letting Jews die was preferable to intervening on their behalf."[28] Goldhagen does not go so far as to say so, but his analysis leaves a nagging suspicion. Despite deplorably bloody tactics in which the Church would not involve itself directly, did its leaders feel, without ever saying so, that it would be beneficial to be rid of the Jews, one way or another?

Regarding Jews as dire threats, Christian antisemitism had long harbored eliminationist attitudes about them. Christianity's tendencies were to restrict and isolate Jews or to insist on their assimilation or conversion. If they did not advocate physical elimination, many Christians sought the social or religious elimination of Jews for reasons that were rooted in antisemitic stereotypes or allegations. In a fundamental disagreement with "We Remember," the Roman Catholic Church's official statement on the Holocaust, which in 1998 acknowledged that Christian conduct during the Holocaust "was not that which might have been expected from Christ's followers," Goldhagen finds the Church speaking nonsense when it asserts that the Nazis' racial antisemitism "had its roots outside of Christianity."[29] He argues persuasively that "the Church's accusations against Jews were often virtually indistinguishable from those of the racist antisemites."[30] At the time of the Holocaust, for example, Nazi and Catholic antisemitism agreed that the Jews were increasingly linked to Communism, an ideology that Pope Pius XII and many other Catholic leaders loathed. In sum, Goldhagen shows that "examples of the Church's incitement to radical anti-Jewish action are legion."[31] Absent the seedbed and support provided by Christian antisemitism, the

Nazis' racist antisemitism could not have been so powerfully credible to the Germans and their allies, who eventually attempted the total elimination of the Jews in the Holocaust.

Other critics have made similar points long before Goldhagen reiterated them, but he goes further than most in holding the Church accountable. Accountability requires truth telling and restitution. The Church, Goldhagen appropriately contends, has not told the whole truth and nothing but the truth about its antisemitism and its failure during the Holocaust. A moral reckoning requires it to do so, but that step would not be sufficient. The Church, Goldhagen adds, must make amends to Jews and reform itself.

Goldhagen uses the word "must" frequently and unabashedly. His list of "musts" for the Roman Catholic Church is as challenging as it is long. Especially after the Holocaust, three types of restitution are crucial: material, political, and moral. Wherever the Church was implicated in exploiting Jews or in expropriating their property, it must work to set every account straight. Goldhagen notes that Germany's Catholic Church has taken steps in that direction, and he gives credit where it is due, as he does throughout his book. Political restitution is more complicated because Goldhagen links it to the state of Israel. At the very least, he insists, the Church will fail in its moral responsibility toward Jews if it acts to "weaken the foundation of Israel" or takes measures that "might imperil its existence or the lives of many of its citizens."[32] If those arguably vague criteria create a minefield, moral restitution does so even more.

The most basic task of moral restitution sounds simple—eradicate antisemitism from Christianity—but it is not. By Goldhagen's reckoning, conciliatory language, good will, apologies, even the most heartfelt expressions of sorrow, regret, and contrition are not enough. Nothing less than fundamental reform will do. The changes must go deep down because antisemitism lies at the very roots of Christianity. What, then, should the Church do, and how must it change?

For starters, Goldhagen prods the Church to name names. It should identify the individual leaders who came up short during the Holocaust and repudiate them, including "all relevant Popes, bishops, and priests."[33] It should halt immediately the canonization of any person— read Pius XII specifically—who aided and abetted the persecution of Jews. The Church should develop memorials that bear witness to the Holocaust-related suffering and death in which it is implicated. A lengthy papal encyclical should be forthcoming; it should detail the history of the Church's antisemitism, denouncing that history, and any perpetuation of it, as sinful. These steps, however, only begin to deal with Goldhagen's list.

Antisemitism, Goldhagen believes, is inseparable from the Church's authoritarian and imperialistic pretensions. Therefore, the Church must abandon papal infallibility, dissolve the Vatican as a political state, embrace religious pluralism to make clear that salvation does not come through the Church alone, and revise its official *Catechism* to make unmistakable that any teaching smacking of antisemitism is "wrong, null, and void."[34] The biggest issue, however, is the Church's "Bible problem."[35]

Goldhagen's reading of the New Testament leaves him with two striking impressions: First, Christianity is "a religion of love that teaches its members the highest moral principles for acting well. Love your neighbor. Seek peace. Help those in need. Sympathize with and raise up the oppressed. Do to others as you would have them do to you."[36] Second, the New Testament's "relentless and withering assault on Jews and Judaism" is not incidental because it portrays the Jews as "the ontological enemy" of Jesus, goodness, and God.[37]

The "Bible problem," moreover, is not just that two apparently contradictory perspectives collide, but that the collision takes place in texts that are regarded as sacred and divinely inspired. The need, Goldhagen contends, is for Christians to rewrite the New Testament, to expunge antisemitism from it, but he recognizes how difficult, perhaps insurmountable, that task may be. Nevertheless, Goldhagen does not despair. He thinks that the Christian tradition can be self-corrective, resilient, and revitalized if Christians find the will to be true to their tradition's best teachings about love and justice.

Wisely, Goldhagen does not presume to rewrite the New Testament. Nor does he venture to define everything that a truly post-Holocaust Church should be. His book contains touches of modesty after all. Meanwhile, if the Roman Catholic Church, and by implication all churches, moved in his direction, it would not be the first time that a Jewish teacher has shown Christians the way. Goldhagen seems to be betting that Christianity can gain new life by letting its old one die. How many Christians will welcome such prospects remains unknown, but hope of that kind should be familiar to them. It would be good for post-Holocaust followers of Jesus to embrace it. Doing so would advance restitution and reconciliation, two of the after-words on which sound ethics after the Holocaust and, in particular, increasingly good relations between post-Holocaust Christians and Jews so much depend.

Habemus Papam

At 5:50 p.m. local time on the evening of April 19, 2005, a Latin announcement in Rome—Habemus papam! (We have a pope!)—declared that the successor to Pope John Paul II, whose 26–year reign ended with his death at the age of 84 on April 2, had been elected by the Roman Catholic Church's College of Cardinals. An hour later, the 265th pope— the 78-year-old German Cardinal Joseph Ratzinger— appeared on the balcony of St. Peter's Basilica. Taking the name Benedict XVI, he would ascend to the papacy, to leadership of 1.1 billion Roman Catholics, a role that makes him the world's most visible Christian. He took office after his inaugural Mass on April 24 not only as the oldest man to become pontiff in 275 years but also as a hard-line theologian who served for more than two decades as head of the Church's Congregation for the Doctrine of the Faith, the Vatican's guardian of orthodoxy. In that role he was undoubtedly conservative, and surely he will remain that way. As the Lutheran theologian and historian Martin Marty put it in his Internet column "Sightings" on April 25, 2005, "the issue is not 'how conservative will he be?' but 'how will he be conservative?' " As far as Jewish–Christian relations are concerned, Benedict XVI's reign will be very important because it remains to be seen how he will build upon or perhaps step back from the significant interfaith accomplishments of his highly respected predecessor.

By no means did John Paul II satisfy Daniel Goldhagen. He did not write, for example, the papal encyclical on antisemitism that Goldhagen wanted. Nevertheless, no pope in history was more successful in healing the Roman Catholic Church's relations with Jews and Judaism. Owing to his Polish identity, John Paul II was well aware of Nazi tyranny, antisemitism, and the Holocaust. Early in his reign, in 1979, he visited Auschwitz–Birkenau. In 1986 he became the first pope to go to the ancient Jewish synagogue in Rome. Later in his reign, in 1993, the Vatican established diplomatic relations with Israel. In 2000, he traveled to Israel, where he went to Yad Vashem, the Israeli memorial to the Holocaust, and then to the Western Wall, the site of the historic temple in Jerusalem, where he contritely placed his handwritten confession of long-standing Christian sin against the Jewish people.

Benedict XVI also has reason to be well aware of Nazi tyranny, antisemitism, and the Holocaust. Ratzinger's German citizenship took him, reluctantly at age 14, into the Hitler Youth in 1941, and then in 1943 he and fellow seminarians were drafted into the army of the

Third Reich. Ratzinger deserted, became a prisoner of war in American captivity, returned to seminary and was ordained a priest in 1951. Highly regarded for his theological and academic abilities, he rapidly rose to prominence in the Church's hierarchy, elevated by Pope Paul VI to be cardinal of Munich in 1977 and then summoned to Rome four years later, where he was highly valued and trusted by John Paul II.

Many Jewish leaders have given Benedict XVI high marks for honesty about his German past and for the ways in which his influence advanced John Paul II's fence-mending between Catholics and Jews. They believe that the new pope is likely to have a strong commitment to Christian–Jewish relations.[38] Numerous Jews and Christians—Catholic and Protestant alike—are less sanguine. With the Holocaust in mind, some have questioned why the cardinals did not find someone other than a German of Cardinal Ratzinger's generation to be worthy to serve as pontiff; others have suggested that his elevation constitutes a final and not entirely fortunate step in Germany's post-Nazi rehabilitation. An additional sticking point is *Dominus Jesus*, a declaration "On the Unicity and Salvific Universality of Jesus Christ and the Church" issued on September 5, 2000, by the Church's Congregation for the Doctrine of the Faith, which was headed by Cardinal Ratzinger at the time. Despite claims from the Vatican and John Paul II that the declaration was often misinterpreted and misunderstood, controversy about the document remains widespread.

Urging repeatedly that the Church's teachings in this declaration must be "firmly believed," *Dominus Jesus* contained at least two claims that stand at the controversy's core. One is that "the salvation of all" comes uniquely, singularly, exclusively, universally, and absolutely through Jesus Christ. The other asserts that the Church is intended by God to be "the instrument for the salvation of *all* humanity," a condition entailing that "the followers of other religions," even if they may receive a kind of divine grace, remain "in a gravely deficient situation" compared to those who are fully within the Church.

Dominus Jesus claimed that its absolutist teachings about Jesus Christ and the Church express no disrespect for "the religions of the world." Subsequent Vatican commentary urged that the declaration was intended primarily to guide Catholic theologians and the Catholic faithful. Nevertheless, *Dominus Jesus* affirmed that the Vatican's version of Christianity should and does supersede every other religious tradition. In an increasingly pluralistic religious world, that stance is problematic to say the least. As Rabbi Michael Lerner, editor of *Tikkun*, a progressive Jewish magazine, put the point on his Web site soon after Cardinal

Ratzinger's elevation, the posture of *Dominus Jesus* "is a slippery slope toward anti-Semitism and a return to the chauvinistic and triumphalist views that led the Church, when it had the power to do so, to develop its infamous crusades and inquisitions."

In his homily at a Mass in St. Peter's Basilica shortly before the conclave that elected him pope, Cardinal Ratzinger, the conservative absolutist, inveighed against "a dictatorship of relativism which does not recognize anything as definitive and has as its highest value one's own ego and one's own desires."[39] A crucial issue is to determine what the loaded phrase "dictatorship of relativism" does and does not, will and will not, mean to Benedict XVI. Not without reason, Daniel Goldhagen suspects that Benedict XVI's understanding of relativism renders false the idea that religions other than Christianity can ultimately be fully valid and truthful paths to God.[40] If so, the new pope is likely to take relativism to include not only (1) pernicious claims that deny the possibility of rational judgments that accurately distinguish between truth and falsity, right and wrong but also (2) reasonable claims that would reject infallibility and find no human judgment sufficient to say that some particular set of beliefs is absolutely true and right to the exclusion of every other. The latter position is one of pluralism and fallibility but by no means one of relativism, and yet one suspects that ultimately, deep down, Pope Benedict XVI is not and cannot be a genuine friend of pluralism or fallibility no matter how much he may gesture toward dialogue that is civil, open, and sincere and insist that respect must be shown for the equality and dignity of the dialogue partners. At the end of the day, Benedict XVI's rejection of relativism is likely to entail reluctant acknowledgment or condescending toleration of, if not attacks against, views that do not accord with his understanding of absolute truth. Meanwhile, absolutisms of any kind tend to be worse than the problems they purport to solve.

In his inaugural Mass, Benedict XVI emphasized conciliatory themes. Vowing "not to pursue my own ideas, but to listen, together with the whole church, to the word and the will of the Lord," he greeted "brothers and sisters of the Jewish people, to whom we are joined by a great shared spiritual heritage" and offered assurance that "like a wave gathering force, my thoughts go out to all men and women of today, to believers and nonbelievers alike."[41] None of that rhetoric, however, is at odds with the judgment that the new pope can rightly be called a neo-supersessionist. He can scarcely avoid his role responsibility, which involves thinking and acting upon the conviction that his tradition fundamentally embodies the Truth exclusively and that it ultimately trumps every other outlook. Furthermore, the new pope has not spoken very explicitly or emphatically about Christianity's and his Church's serious shortcomings during the Nazi years. An example of his vague if not convoluted diction on that point can be found in a 2000 column in the Vatican daily *L'Osservatore Romano* in which Cardinal Ratzinger wrote of the Christian response to the Holocaust as follows: "It cannot be denied that a certain insufficient resistance on the part of Christians can be explained by an inherited anti-Judaism present in the hearts of not a few Christians."[42] Given that cautious and guarded "Vaticanese" about the Church's immense ethical failure, it seems unlikely that Benedict XVI will go very far toward advancing restitution of the kind that Christians still need to make ethically after the Holocaust, namely, to take the steps that remain necessary to rid Christianity and the world—to the extent that Christians have the power to do so—of antisemitism. Those steps include rejection of the claim that any tradition or outlook—political, philosophical, or religious and including Christianity and definitely the judgments made in this book—possesses absolute truth infallibly and without qualification.

Benedict XVI may do better on that score than this forecast predicts. Stranger things have happened. Encouragement from Christians and Jews to promote that outcome is an important ethical step to take after the Holocaust. In addition, Benedict XVI himself took some important steps in the right direction on August 19, 2005, when his first trip abroad as pope took him to Cologne, Germany, where he became only the second pontiff to visit a Jewish synagogue. In that place, which was rebuilt in the 1950s after being destroyed in the notorious November pogrom (often called *Kristallnacht*) in 1938, he denounced antisemitism and what he called "the insane racist ideology" of Nazism.

While the pope's synagogue remarks emphasized that he "would encourage sincere and trustful dialogue between Jews and Christians, for only in this way will it be possible to arrive at shared interpretation of disputed historical questions," he did not speak explicitly about, let alone apologize for, the Catholic church's much-criticized policies regarding Nazi Germany and Jewish plight during World War II and the Holocaust. Speaking about Christian–Jewish relations, Benedict XVI noted that "much more remains to be done. We must come to know one another much more and much better."[43] Such words are good. Nevertheless, those who hope for Benedict XVI to break much new ground in Christian–Jewish relations are likely to be disappointed during the papal reign that began in April 2005. I hope that I am wrong, but I think that they will have to wait—at least until "Habemus papam!" resounds from St. Peter's the next time.

7
Duped by Morality?

> Everyone will readily agree that it is of the highest importance
> to know whether we are not duped by morality.
>
> Emmanuel Levinas, *Totality and Infinity*

We human beings are often deceived or fooled. Our own plans, dispositions, and actions account for much of that result. Typically, however,
we do not think that morality dupes us. At least if we consider ethical
reasoning, we tend to think that it is not misleading but trustworthy
instead. Such reasoning provides the guidelines and insights that can
keep us on track or warn us that we have gone in wrong directions. As
this line of thought would have it, we will sooner or later be duped if we
fail to follow where ethical reasoning leads, but ethical reasoning itself
is not deceptive. If it were deceptive, that condition would exist only to
the extent that ethical reasoning had not been done well or carried out
sufficiently. Unfortunately, this chapter's epigraph—the words with
which Levinas begins *Totality and Infinity*—suggests a more radical and
tragic alternative as far as ethics during and after the Holocaust is
concerned: namely, that deception may be hard to eliminate if not
inseparable from ethical reasoning.[1]

No event did more than the Holocaust to show that humanity has
been duped by morality. As noted previously, the fact that we can identify what Peter Haas has called the Nazi ethic and what Claudia Koonz
has more recently named the Nazi conscience scarcely gives comfort
regarding the non-deceptive quality of ethical reasoning.[2] Instead, their
studies show how reasoning can produce lethal rivalries, which under-
cut confidence about the philosophical and religious foundations, as
well as the actual content, of moral traditions that were at odds with
Nazism and yet apparently unable to check Nazi power until millions

were slaughtered. After that catastrophe, as discussed in chapter 2, the Holocaust has also been called a "negative absolute," to use Michael Berenbaum's phrase, but that status, warranted as it is, may also be deceptive, for the threat and practice of genocide—to name only one of the evils besieging the world—has not abated and may grow worse.

The Israeli–Palestinian struggle

With the Holocaust reverberating within it, the Israeli–Palestinian struggle adds to the dilemmas that characterize our being duped by morality. Consider four ways in which that claim has validity.

1. The post-Holocaust cry, "Never again!" is an ethical imperative whose meaning is problematic and whose credibility is lacking. On the one hand, it expresses determination to resist the destruction of one's people, including the destruction of the state of Israel. On the other hand, no people has exclusive claim to that imperative; Palestinians can have a version of it too. Embedded within ethical reasoning, "Never again!" is deceptively reassuring.

2. "The killing will stop," it is sometimes said, "when people have had enough of it." This claim contains an ethical hope, namely, that human beings will not keep killing because we value life too much for that. The Israeli–Palestinian struggle, whose latest tragic chapter has been going on for four-and-a-half-years at the time of this writing in 2005, reveals that we may be duped twice if we place too much hope in our valuing of human life. First, weariness about killing is not identical with "enough of it." Second, even the early 2005 breakthroughs of hope, which included handshakes between the Israeli prime minister Ariel Sharon and Mahmoud Abbas, the Palestinian leader who was elected to succeed the late Yasir Arafat as president of the Palestinian Authority, do not offer much empirical reassurance that all will turn out well this time around the negotiating table. Despite the prospect of new and ultimately successful Israeli–Palestinian negotiations, a history of broken agreements, dead-ended road maps to peace, terror unleashed repeatedly by Islamic Jihad, Hamas, and Hezbollah, the Israel Defense Force's retaliations, and the Israeli government's construction of a controversial wall to prevent terrorist acts all leave the hopes for justice fragile and the chances for lasting peace unsettled.

3. Ethical realism requires one to recognize that retribution is as important as it is unavoidable. Here the assumption is that inflicting harm in return for harm will eliminate a problem, if not by "teaching

people a lesson" then by weakening or destroying others to such an extent that they can do serious harm no more. The dupery in this case is likely to be that winning the war is not the same as winning the peace.

4. The realism, ethical or not, that drives the Israeli–Palestinian struggle reaffirms that a higher ethic is needed. That ethic would be one that stresses the shared humanity of those sustaining and feeling the conflict's impact, one that underscores how people should respect, if not love, each other, one that can help people to transcend differences of nationality and religion. Such an ethic may well be needed, but here, too, deception is not far to find. Its extent depends on how easily and/or thoroughly one thinks the gap between *is* and *ought* can be closed.

Dupery about how easily and/or thoroughly the gap between *is* and *ought* may be closed is illustrated by the arguably well-meaning but misguided actions that were initiated by the Presbyterian Church, U.S.A. (PCUSA) at the meeting of its 216th General Assembly (June 26–July 3, 2004) in Richmond, Virginia. I have written the preceding sentence with regret, for I am a life-long Presbyterian whose father spent his life as a pastor in that denomination. I am also a Holocaust scholar who has tried to improve Jewish–Christian relations, but a PCUSA decision to "initiate a process of phased selective divestment in multinational corporations in Israel" has been taken at a huge price that will not be worth the cost.[3] Presbyterian–Jewish relations deteriorated badly in 2004–05. It will be some time before they can be restored, let alone improved. The Presbyterian initiative, moreover, is unlikely to affect Israeli–Palestinian relations for the better, unless its eventual rejection by the PCUSA turns the church's thought and action in a substantially different direction.

The issue of divestment

To clarify those claims and to eliminate misunderstandings that may surround them, a brief account of the PCUSA's history and structure as well as of the current divestment initiative will be helpful. Tracing its heritage to the Protestant Reformation in sixteenth-century Europe and to the early leadership of the French lawyer John Calvin (1509–64), the PCUSA has about 2.4 million members. They belong to more than 11,000 congregations that are led by some 14,000 clergy. The church's governance, which takes place primarily at the congregational level and in regional jurisdictions called presbyteries, emphasizes the role of elected representatives. Biennially, clergy and laypersons, the latter group consisting of elders who are elected in their home congregations to handle local church affairs, are commissioned from the presbyteries to convene the church's General Assembly, which has responsibility "for matters of common concern for the whole church," including the setting of priorities regarding the church's "witness for truth and justice."[4] The PCUSA has financial assets of approximately $8 billion, including the investment portfolio of its Board of Pensions, which was valued at $6.4 billion at the end of 2004.

In its 1987 document "A Theological Understanding of the Relationship between Christians and Jews," the PCUSA affirmed that its identity is "intimately related" to the ongoing identity of the Jewish people, acknowledged "in repentance" Christian complicity in "anti-Jewish attitudes and actions," and expressed determination to end "the teaching of contempt for Jews."[5] Both before and after that 1987 statement, the PCUSA has affirmed the state of Israel's right to exist within borders that are permanent, recognized, and secure. Such language can be found in the General Assembly's action at Richmond in June 2004, but at the same time a General Assembly Resolution on Israel and Palestine ignited a Presbyterian–Jewish firestorm. Acting on a proposal from the presbytery of St. Augustine, Florida, the General Assembly started a process that could result in the church's divestment in multinational corporations operating in Israel.

As pointed out by Vernon S. Broyles III, a member of the PCUSA Social Justice Ministries staff, various Christian churches have frequently used corporate divestment to protest against environmental abuses and human rights violations.[6] The 1980s apartheid situation in South Africa remains a prominent example. Furthermore, the PCUSA's divestment process requires careful deliberation before any stock is sold. The PCUSA's Mission Responsibility Through Investment Committee (MRTI) is responsible for those evaluations. In the controversial case of possible divestment in certain multinational companies doing business with Israel, the key criteria focus on whether a corporation provides products, technologies, or services (including financial ones) supporting (1) Israel's occupation of Palestinian territory as borders were defined by the Green Line of 1948, and/or (2) violence that targets innocent civilians, and/or (3) the separation barrier or protective wall that the Israeli government erected for security reasons in 2003–04.[7]

Both the General Assembly resolution and the rhetoric used by its defenders make clear that, however nuanced its language, the steps toward divestment tilt decisively in the Palestinians' favor. It does not follow, however, that the tilt actually does favor the Palestinians as much as the advocates of divestment may assume, for the Israeli and Palestinian economies are intertwined and overlapping. Divestment might not affect Palestinians as negatively as it affects Israelis, but those consequences will not fall on Israelis alone. Meanwhile, as the 2004 Resolution on Israel and Palestine sized up the situation, "prospects for a negotiated just peace have so deteriorated that people in the region generally, and particularly the Palestinians, have been driven to the edge of despair and hopelessness."[8] Among other things, that language expressed deep concern for Palestinian Christians, including Palestinian Presbyterians, with whom the PCUSA has close ties. The PCUSA should stand in solidarity with them, just as it should also stand in solidarity with the Jewish people.

Much of the time the Israeli–Palestinian conflict seems to defy resolution, but events in that region are as unpredictable as they are mercurial, as surprising as they are volatile. Less than a year after the General Assembly's bleak prognosis and the very pro-Palestinian resolution that followed from it, circumstances may have changed in ways that make the divestment overture not only lopsided and morally wrong but also embarrassing for its clumsy ill-timing. Although Arafat was not well in June 2004, he was alive and still in enough control that windows of opportunity for a just and peaceful settlement were much harder to discern than they became a year further on. Nothing guarantees that the hopeful notes of 2005 will be amplified, but it is unlikely that the PCUSA divestment initiative will do much to correct the Israeli–Palestinian causes of hopelessness and despair that the Presbyterian proponents of divestment insist they want to relieve. Nevertheless, coupled with Presbyterian proclivities for careful deliberation, which can produce good decisions but not necessarily expeditious responses, the General Assembly's pro-Palestinian tilt is not likely to result in the divestment card's removal any time soon. Sadly, so long as that card remains on the table, Presbyterian–Jewish relations will remain in decline.

The Holocaust should not put the Israeli government above fair criticism by Christians (Presbyterians or otherwise), Jews, Palestinians, or anyone else. But that catastrophe should make post-Holocaust Christians, and now Presbyterians in particular, pause before unfair steps are taken that jar Jewish sensibilities and trust as the Presbyterian divestment initiative has done. Even more specifically, awareness of the Holocaust should warn Christians against using inflaming/defaming language of the kind that Broyles employed when his accusation that the government of Israel is guilty of "gross injustice" was followed by the invidious allegation that "Jewish victimhood makes it impossible for our Jewish sisters and brothers to connect their suffering with that of the Palestinians at the hands of Israelis."[9]

Relationships and obligations

Christianity and Christians have a special relationship and obligation to Judaism and Jews, which is constituted in large part because we Christians owe them a debt that can never be fully repaid. That debt exists especially because the Holocaust would not and could not have happened without many centuries of Christian hostility toward the Jewish people. That judgment does not mean that Christianity caused the Holocaust. Christian hostility toward Jews was not sufficient by itself to produce such horror, but Christianity's animosity toward Jews was a necessary condition for that disaster.

Gas chambers and crematoria did not begin the Holocaust. It started with steps that isolated and separated Jews. Those Nazi policies included economic measures. One can understand that the Presbyterian advocates of divestment feel that they are defending the rights of Palestinians who have been seriously harmed by the Israeli–Palestinian conflict, but that advocacy has been largely tone-deaf and amnesiac with regard to Holocaust history and Jewish memory. In February 2005, when Jay Rock, the PCUSA's coordinator of interfaith relations, tried to explain the church's divestment policy to leaders of the Anti-Defamation League, Rabbi Gary Bretton-Granatoor, the ADL's interfaith director cut to the chase: "When they said 'divestment,' we heard 'boycott.' "[10] Presbyterian disclaimers to the contrary notwithstanding, Bretton-Granatoor did not miss the target, for beyond its symbolic gesture, the PCUSA divestment initiative could not be effective as an economic sanction unless many other institutions took similar decisions.

Presbyterian wealth is considerable, but it is insufficient by itself to influence economic policy substantially, let alone dictate it decisively. Jewish leaders, however, have rightly been concerned that the Presbyterian initiative could encourage what has been called "divestment creep" or even "divestment envy." In fact, some other Christian denominations (e.g., Anglicans and the United Church of Christ) have taken related steps that single out and isolate Israel at the very time when a disturbing upsurge of antisemitism, much of it fueled by anti-Israeli sentiment, has become widespread.

Steps in that direction were already in the making internationally in late February 2005, when the 150-member Central Committee of the World Council of Churches (WCC)—the WCC consists of some 347 Protestant and Orthodox Christian churches—commended the PCUSA's unmistakably pro-Palestinian and anti-Israeli divestment action. Citing Luke 19:42, a New Testament passage that speaks about "the things that make for peace," a WCC document released on February 21, 2005, "reminds churches with investment funds that they have an opportunity to use those funds responsibly in support of peaceful solutions to conflict. Economic pressure, appropriately and openly applied, is one such means of action."[11]

Presbyterians and WCC members who advocate divestment may seek comfort in the hope that they are defending the oppressed and thus occupying high moral ground, but a consequence of their action, unintended though it may be, is to give aid and comfort to antisemitism, thus adding further to the sorry Christian record that has accumulated over the centuries and that climaxed in the Holocaust's near-destruction of the Jewish people. That tragedy is compounded by the fact that the divisive Presbyterian–Jewish confrontation and its unfortunate spin offs could have been avoided without compromising Christian ethics, defense of Palestinian rights, or appropriate and needed post-Holocaust Christian solidarity with the Jewish people.

Much of Christian ethics is shaped by the voices of Hebrew prophets such as Amos and Micah, whose calls for justice and righteousness were echoed by Jesus. Presbyterians are faithful to that tradition when they speak and act against murder and injustice and when they do so fairly. The Presbyterian divestment initiative has been couched in language that not only protests against current Israeli policies but also condemns terrorism and suicide bombings from the Palestinian side. Nevertheless, Jews are right when they say that the Presbyterian initiative emphasizes the former disproportionately and thus gives less than fully justified attention to the latter.

Despite their protests to the contrary, the advocates of divestment are taking the Palestinian side in ways that treat Israel unfairly at the very time—and not for the first time, either—when Israel is making major strides toward a peaceful settlement. In particular, whether the Presbyterian advocates of divestment acknowledge it or not, their actions tend to isolate Israel and drive a deep wedge between Presbyterians and Jews. In this context, it is important to remember that while Israel is a strong country, even one possessing impressive military might, it continues to be surrounded by nations that can scarcely be said to wish her well. A two-state solution to the Israeli–Palestinian conflict is desirable; most Presbyterians, including me, affirm it. One would be duped, however, to assume simply that a two-state solution will bring peace and security to Israel forever. Much depends on the nature of the Palestinian state as well as on the policies of Israeli administrations.

At the February 16, 2005, meeting of the Church Relations Committee of the United States Holocaust Memorial Museum, my colleague David Blumenthal reminded me that when the previously mentioned 1987 document "A Theological Understanding of the Relationship between Christians and Jews" was written, Presbyterians invited Jewish representatives—Blumenthal included—to deliberate with them. Little, if any, consultation of that kind took place before the PCUSA launched its 2004 divestment rocket. One wonders what would have happened if Presbyterians had consulted more widely, bringing to the table not only Palestinian Christian voices but also those of concerned Israelis and American Jews.

The context for such deliberations might have been shaped as follows: To the point of anger, Presbyterians could have said, we are deeply concerned about the suffering of Palestinians during the Israeli–Palestinian conflict. We are equally determined to respect and honor the existence of the state of Israel, whose security has been undermined by Palestinian terrorism. Help us to formulate peace-making policies, including those pertaining to Presbyterian economic resources, so that we can do more to "let justice roll down like waters, and righteousness like an ever flowing stream" (Amos 5:24).

If such consultations had been held, I doubt that the current Presbyterian divestment policy would have been put into play. Perhaps— I am cautious so as not to be duped—a much more creative *investment* policy could have emerged instead. It might—even now; it is not too late—have focused on how Presbyterian financial resources could be better deployed, more wisely used, to support developments, industries, projects of mutual benefit and interest that would bring Palestinians and Israelis together in ways that create the conditions needed for a viable two-state solution. Such an investment policy would give priority to enterprises that bolster and connect both Palestinian and Israeli economic interests, for the chances for peace will be enhanced if economic interests between the two peoples and eventual states are interlocking, interdependent, and structured for mutual well-being. To assist such development, even in the relatively small ways that PCUSA resources could advance them, would provide steps in the right direction that others could emulate. Such planning might mean that some PCUSA economic resources would be reapportioned and reallocated, but instead of divestment that pressures by punishment, the emphasis would be on creative investment planned through consultation and dialogue.

Such a position is one akin to that held by Presbyterians Concerned for Jewish and Christian Relations (PCJCR), a group of PCUSA clergy and laypersons to which I belong. Supporting a two-state solution to the Israeli–Palestinian conflict, PCJCR opposes the General Assembly's divestment posture, calls for postponement of any further action toward divestment, and aims to reverse the 2004 divestment decision at the next General Assembly in 2006. Concurrently, the PCJCR supports "proactive engagement and selective investment of time, talent, and financial resources in companies, not-for-profits, NGOs and diplomatic efforts that are likely to promote a just and lasting peace in the region."[12]

The PCJCR's position may also turn out to be yet another instance of being duped by morality, a phenomenon that has been rife in the Israeli–Palestinian struggle and the world's reaction to it. Be that as it may, the possibility that morality may dupe us does not, must not, mean the demise of ethical reasoning. Where the Israeli–Palestinian conflict is concerned, that possibility entails instead that moral reflection and the policies that emerge from it need to proceed as far as possible with undeceived lucidity about both the threats that Israel continues to face and the needs of Palestinians for an economically and politically viable state of their own. The PCUSA's divestment policy does not pass that test, but a wise investment policy could do so. If the window for peace that opened unexpectedly in 2005 is to be opened further and kept open, such investment policies, which the PCUSA and other Christian churches might help to underwrite, could play important parts, ones that help Palestinians and Israelis alike, ones that heal relations between Jews and Presbyterians, whose sorry state in 2004–05, at least for me, was heartbreaking.

8
The Ethics of Forgiveness

> No, I have not forgiven any of the culprits, nor am I willing to
> forgive a single one of them, unless he has shown (with deeds,
> not words, and not too long afterwards) that he has become
> conscious of the crimes and errors ... and is determined to
> condemn them, uproot them, from his conscience and from
> that of others.
>
> Primo Levi, "A Self-Interview"

To forgive is an act that can have varied but related meanings. To forgive
means to be merciful, to pardon an offense or an offender, to give up a
claim against another individual, to set aside a debt, to relinquish anger
or resentment, however justifiable those feelings may be, to free a person from the burden of guilt. Thus, *forgiveness* is what I call an *after*-word.
It has that status partly because of the Holocaust. Reflection on that fact
is another step that needs to be taken to deepen understanding about
ethics during and after the Holocaust.

Who needs forgiveness?

There could be a world in which the concept of forgiveness is unthinkable.
Such a world would be one devoid of the ideas of right and wrong, justice
and injustice, good and evil, atrocity, genocide, and Holocaust. There
could also be a world in which the concept of forgiveness is thinkable
but in which no one actually needs forgiveness. Such a world would
be one in which nobody ever wronged anyone else. Our world, of course,
is vastly different. Even though we may not agree on their meanings,
concepts of right and wrong, justice and injustice, good and evil profoundly inform human experience. Moreover, in ways large and small,

unintentional as well as intentional, we human beings do harm—often immense harm—to each other. Absent such actions, forgiveness would remain an abstract possibility, but once human-made harm has been done—only then, in fact—forgiveness can become real, specific, concrete, important, needed, and also problematic.

The frequently devastating circumstances that make *forgiveness* an *after*-word can have numbing effects on our moral and spiritual sensibilities, but it remains plausible to say that few people, if any, have never felt the need for forgiveness, asked to receive it, and found relief when it was granted. It is also true that countless people have granted forgiveness to others who have done wrong, often forgiving even when no petition for forgiveness has been made. In many cases, those who grant forgiveness have found relief in doing so.

None of us is perfect. Thus, one credible answer to the question "Who needs forgiveness?" is *all of us do*, at least insofar as the phrase "all of us" refers to men, women, and children who can reasonably be judged responsible for their actions. Religious traditions—the High Holy Days in Judaism, culminating in Yom Kippur, provide a striking example—do much to keep this sensibility alive.

Although they may not include ideas about divinity and sin that are frequently emphasized in religious thought and practice about forgiveness, secular approaches in ethics, psychology, self-help, and politics also stress that human beings fall far short of what is right and good. It is not uncommon to hear public apologies for wrongdoing, sometimes for injustices that took place long ago.[1] Post-Holocaust reparation and restitution efforts and initiatives such as South Africa's Truth and Reconciliation Commission and Rwanda's post-genocide *gacaca* proceedings have also been newsworthy.[2] These efforts often aim at reconciliation. Based on the insight that human beings have to share the earth with one another, and that it is better to do so when mutual understanding and respect prevail, reconciliation refers to resolving disputes so that broken relationships are mended at least enough for life to move beyond hostility, hate, and revenge. Although reconciliation is not equivalent to forgiveness, the two are closely related: Where forgiveness is absent, reconciliation is likely to be incomplete; where forgiveness is present, the chances for reconciliation will be much improved. Wherever steps are advocated and taken to make up for the human deficit between right and wrong, justice and injustice, forgiveness and issues about it will not be far behind.

Note, however, that the question "Who needs forgiveness?" has more bite and greater complexity than these preliminary remarks contain.

Consider, for example, two particular inflections of the question: "*Who* needs forgiveness?" and "Who *needs* forgiveness?" Those versions of the question contain suspicion. The first implies suspicion about the universalizing view that "all of us" need forgiveness. True though that claim may be, the fact of human history is that some people inflict much more harm than others—Heinrich Himmler and his SS men during the Holocaust come to mind—and it is important to measure responsibility accurately and to place accountability where it belongs.

The second inflection—"Who *needs* forgiveness?"— involves suspicion of an even more fundamental kind. It questions the virtue of forgiveness. Far from assuming that forgiveness is simply or purely good, this outlook suspects that forgiveness can become—unwittingly if not expressly—the partner of forgetting, condoning, relativizing, and trivializing. Such dubious partnerships sacrifice justice to indifference, to what the Christian theologian Dietrich Bonhoeffer called "cheap grace," or to self-serving rationalization, which can be a danger lurking especially in some current views of forgiveness—both secular and religious—that stress the importance of *forgiving ourselves* so that we can be liberated from life-repressing guilt and shame. As the Jewish philosopher Emmanuel Levinas put the point, "a world where forgiveness is almighty becomes inhuman."[3]

History and forgiveness

Such ambiguities and problems help to show that *forgiveness* is not only an *after*-word but also a *wounded* word. Its wounded status has a long history, one that requires careful thinking about what forgiveness should and should not mean. But it is also true that the wounded status of forgiveness is an effect of recent events, including the Holocaust in particular. Consider further, then, some aspects of that history, ancient and contemporary, which can be focused by directing attention, first, to the Babylonian Talmud and the biblical book of Isaiah.

At *Berakhot* 7a in the Babylonian Talmud, the rabbis probe a verse from the fifty-sixth chapter of Isaiah: "I will bring them to My sacred mount / And let them rejoice in My house of prayer."[4] Interpreting the text literally to read "And let them rejoice in the house of My prayer," the rabbis indicate that God says prayers. That claim, however, is startling and puzzling: Why and about what would God pray? The unfolding inquiry suggests that God prays for his mercy to prevail so that divine anger stops short of what the Talmud calls "the limit of strict justice."[5] The implication is that God overrides his anger but not completely, for his attributes include anger rightly aroused by disobedience and injustice. Even with God, it seems, tension exists between forgiveness and justice. Otherwise God would not need to pray about the right relationship between them. It should not be surprising, then, that human beings are left to wrestle with versions of that same dilemma.

As the Talmud shows repeatedly, one question leads to another: Even if God suppresses his anger, it remains awesome. Thus, it is important to know the duration of divine anger, especially when the Scripture states that each day includes God's indignation.[6] The Talmud indicates that the duration of God's daily anger is "one moment," but "how long is one moment?" The answer proposed is so minuscule that it scarcely amounts to a split second: "One fifty-eight thousand eight hundred and eighty-eighth part of an hour," *Berakhot* 7a indicates, is the duration of God's daily anger. The point of this response is that God's anger and his inclination to act according to strict justice remain, and their power is *awe-ful*, but they are far less dominant than God's mercy and forgiveness. If that were not the case, the world could not endure the judgment of God's justice.

Embedded in this religious vision are two other factors that merit emphasis. First, no one should presume that God's mercy and forgiveness operate indifferently. Confession of sin and repentance, turning away from injustice and turning toward justice in word and deed, are essential to keep even God's split-second anger at bay. Second, human beings, created in God's image, should do their best to walk in his ways and to emulate God, which strongly implies that men and women should be merciful and forgiving. Arguably, however, that *should* raises as many questions as it answers. Continued exploration of Isaiah 56 helps to explain why.

In addition to its being a text that reiterates God's imperative to "observe what is right and do what is just," Isaiah 56 also contains God's promise to remember those who are faithful to his covenant: "I will give them, in my House / And within My walls, / A monument and a name / Better than sons and daughters. / I will give them an everlasting name / Which shall not perish."[7] That verse is the source of the name Yad Vashem, meaning a monument and a name or, figuratively, a monument and a memorial, which identifies the distinctive Israeli site of Holocaust remembrance and memorialization in Jerusalem.[8]

The Holocaust complicates everything, including forgiveness. Many catastrophes have besieged humankind and the Jewish people in particular, but at least to date none has exceeded the Holocaust. Where contemporary dilemmas about forgiveness are concerned, the Holocaust's complications involve that event's power to call into question the existence of a just God, let alone one who is merciful and forgiving. If the Holocaust affects people in that way, then the issues surrounding forgiveness are altered accordingly: Religiously grounded understandings of or appeals about forgiveness will lack credibility. Advocacy for forgiveness, if it continues to exist, would have to come from other sources—ethical or psychological ones, for example. Even for those who find that the Holocaust does not leave religious perspectives utterly ruined, religiously grounded understandings of or appeals about forgiveness may still be important, but they are not likely to be unwounded. Some Holocaust-related examples can illustrate and deepen these points.

Is forgiveness out of place?

Deported to Majdanek on June 16, 1942, Rudolf Vrba, a Czech Jew born Walter Rosenberg, was transferred to Auschwitz two weeks later on June 30, 1942. He not only survived Auschwitz but also was one of the few to escape. With Alfred Wetzler he did so on April 7, 1944. Their assignments within the camp had positioned Vrba and Wetzler to know how the destruction process worked. Thus, they were able to write what became known as the Vrba–Wetzler Report, a document intended to warn the Hungarian Jews, the last large Jewish group remaining on the European continent, and to provide documentation that would persuade the Allies to intervene more directly against the Third Reich's attempts to destroy the Jewish people.[9]

Vrba published his Holocaust memoir in 1964. He called it *I Cannot Forgive*.[10] That title is significant not because Vrba discussed forgiveness at length. His recollections of Auschwitz are neither religious nor primarily philosophical. He does not dwell on his closing statement that "I cannot forgive the men who made it [Auschwitz] the mightiest murder apparatus ever," except to deny that he was motivated by revenge when he urged West German courts to pronounce death sentences on those they found guilty as Holocaust perpetrators some nineteen years after the World War II ended.[11] Nevertheless, Vrba's title indicates both that forgiveness was on his mind and that he thought it important to reject forgiveness for the Holocaust's perpetrators. Vrba's book does not explain his feelings about forgiveness in much detail, but it seems to me that his outlook, including the tendency not to discuss forgiveness at any length, is widespread not only among Holocaust survivors but among most people who have confronted the Holocaust seriously. There is a sense that forgiveness is out of place where the Holocaust is concerned.

Indeed, the Holocaust is often judged to be unforgivable, and with that judgment the matter ends.

My observations about Vrba do not overlook important departures from his outlook. One of the latter, Simon Wiesenthal's book *The Sunflower*, continues to provoke serious Holocaust-related reflection and discussion about forgiveness, which it has done ever since that Holocaust survivor and famed Nazi hunter first published it in 1969. The dilemma posed in *The Sunflower* traces back to a day in 1944 when Wiesenthal's labor brigade cleared rubbish from a military hospital that the Germans had created in a school that he had attended in Lvov, Poland. By chance, the young Wiesenthal was chosen by the nurse who took him to a 21-year-old, mortally wounded SS man. Karl, as Wiesenthal identifies the German, had participated in the mass murder of Jews. On his deathbed, he wanted a Jew to hear his confession, which apparently was made with the hope that his wish for forgiveness from a Jew would be granted. Wiesenthal scarcely had a choice but to hear the man's confession. Although he found "true repentance" in that testimony, Wiesenthal left the German's hospital room without saying a word.[12] Haunted by this experience, puzzled about whether he had done the right thing, Wiesenthal asked some of his fellow prisoners about it. Their different and conflicting opinions about the matter did not put the matter to rest. Wiesenthal even located Karl's mother after the war, but he left her in war-torn Stuttgart without revealing that her vision of Karl as a "decent young man" who "never did any wrong" was false. Again, Wiesenthal wondered if his silence had been right. Eventually he asked others—Jews and non-Jews, religious and secular thinkers—to consider what they would have done in his circumstances.

Sometimes marked by questioning and tentativeness, other times characterized by conviction and certitude, responses to Wiesenthal's dilemma in *The Sunflower* have been as impassioned as they are varied. For example, identifying himself as "an atheist who is indifferent to and rejecting of any metaphysics of morality," the Auschwitz survivor and philosopher Jean Améry thought that Wiesenthal's anguish was largely irrelevant, except that from a political perspective forgiveness had no place at all. "What you and I went through," he wrote to Wiesenthal, "must *not happen again, never, nowhere*. Therefore—and I have said and written this over and over—I refuse any reconciliation with the criminals and with those who only by accident did not happen to commit atrocities, and finally, all those who helped prepare the unspeakable acts with their words."[13]

In contrast to Améry, Theodore Hesburgh, long-time president of the University of Notre Dame said that his "whole instinct is to forgive.

Perhaps that is because I am a Catholic priest. ... I think of God as the great forgiver of sinful humanity. ... If asked to forgive, by anyone for anything, I would forgive because God would forgive."[14] The Holocaust scholar Lawrence Langer took a very different position. Regarding Wiesenthal's "What would you have done?" to be an illegitimate question because "I have no idea what I might have done in Simon Wiesenthal's place," Langer went on to call the Holocaust "an unforgivable crime." In his view, the SS man in *The Sunflower* had made killing choices, choices to commit atrocities that cannot be encompassed by conventional moral and religious vocabularies that use words such as "misdeed" or even "wrong." The atrocities of the Holocaust have outstripped the categories of conventional ethical and religious discourse. Thus, Langer argued, the SS man's actions "permanently cut himself off from the possibility of forgiveness."[15]

Less certain than Langer, Hubert Locke, a pioneering African-American scholar of the Holocaust and genocide, focused on Wiesenthal's silence. "There is much that silence might teach us," wrote Locke, "if we could but learn to listen to it. Not the least of its lessons is that there may well be questions for which there are no answers and other questions for which answers would remove the moral force of the question."[16] Abraham Joshua Heschel, whose stature keeps growing with the passing of time, identified the moral force of Wiesenthal's question in a way that was more direct than Locke's but not inconsistent with the latter's ethics: No living person, said Heschel, "can extend forgiveness for the suffering of any one of the six million people who perished."[17]

No writer has responded to the Holocaust with greater insight than the Auschwitz survivor Primo Levi. His response to Wiesenthal reflects that fact. Levi thought that Wiesenthal was right to "refuse your pardon to the dying man," but he added that "it is quite easy to see why you were left with doubts: in a case like this it is impossible to decide categorically between the answers yes and no; there always remains something to be said for the other side."[18] Levi's insight is important: Where forgiveness and the issues surrounding it are concerned, a "one size fits all" interpretation may rightly elude or dupe us. Nevertheless, some basic principles still come into view. Levi and others who have been mentioned bring them into focus.

Conditions for forgiveness

Primo Levi once said that "to forgive is not my verb," but he also articulated conditions that might move him to use it. He would be unwilling to forgive any of the Holocaust's perpetrators "unless he has shown (with deeds, not words, and not too long afterwards) that he has become conscious of the crimes and errors ... and is determined to condemn them, uproot them, from his conscience and from that of others. Only in this case am I, a non-Christian, prepared to follow the Jewish and Christian precept of forgiving my enemy, because an enemy who sees the error of his ways ceases to be an enemy."[19]

Levi's statement indicates that forgiveness is voluntary. It is a gift, not a requirement or an obligation. In fact, forgiveness entails that the offended party has a good will that includes a desire to forgive. If such a desire is absent, forgiveness is at an impasse. Furthermore, forgiveness should have conditions that pertain to the one who has caused offense; it ought not to be granted too freely and not unilaterally either.[20] The one who has harmed another must not only want forgiveness sincerely but also be aware of what that desire enjoins, namely, that the one who seeks forgiveness should approach the person who has been harmed both with words that ask for forgiveness and through actions that reveal deep awareness of and regret for the wrong that has been done, plus determination to condemn and uproot attitudes and policies— in oneself and others—that encourage and perpetuate such harm doing. Furthermore, and this condition is of crucial importance, these steps of repentance and atonement must be timely.

Levi suspected that the SS man's repentance in *The Sunflower* had been much too long in coming. Levi pursued no Talmudic inquiry to clarify how long is "too long," but his suspicions about the SS man in *The Sunflower* are instructive. "Everything," said Levi, "would lead one to believe that, had it not been for his fear of impending death, he would have behaved quite otherwise: he would not have repented until much later, with the downfall of Germany or perhaps never."[21] For Levi, the case for forgiveness evaporates with the passage of unrepentant time. Where genuine repentance is concerned, the kind that condemns and roots out the wrong one has done and extends those actions in taking responsibility for others, the rule should be "the sooner the better" as far as any case for forgiveness is concerned. Deathbed confessions remain suspect; they may have their own sincerity, but they may not be much better than no repentance at all. Absent repentance that is as timely as it is heartfelt, Levi indicates, forgiveness is unjustified and even wrong.

In addition, Levi implies, forgiveness would be wrong if it tried to speak for others and particularly for the dead. Levi's reflections about forgiveness are focused on what happened to him and on how he should relate to people who affected him directly during the Holocaust.

His outlook supports the view of Abraham Joshua Heschel, which is widely shared by the respondents to Wiesenthal's dilemma in *The Sunflower*: "It is preposterous," said Heschel, "to assume that anybody alive can extend forgiveness for the suffering of any one of the six million people who perished. According to Jewish tradition, even God Himself can only forgive sins committed against Himself, not against man."[22]

Clarity about forgiveness requires lucidity about who can forgive whom and for what. I can forgive someone for the wrong he or she has done to me. You can do likewise for those who have harmed you. The harm that has been done may have been primarily directed at others and caused me or you to suffer for that reason. Your forgiveness or mine can be for the hurt that is ours, but not for the suffering or loss that another has experienced. They, and they alone, have the prerogative to forgive for that. In no case, moreover, is forgiveness something that can be earned. Nor can it rightly be demanded. The perpetrator can ask; the victim can rightly refuse. As the Belgian-Catholic moral theologian Didier Pollefeyt has wisely said, "Like love, forgiveness must be given freely; otherwise it cannot be real."[23]

How would that view fit, if it does, with the Jewish tradition that a person who sincerely seeks forgiveness three times should be granted it, or with the Christian tradition, which enjoins forgiveness so intently and frequently that a follower of Jesus seems all but duty-bound to grant it?[24] One sound response is that injunctions to grant forgiveness are important because the absence of forgiveness, when conditions for it have been met, is dangerously close to mercilessness, which is, in turn, a condition that makes the world inhuman. Yet even when one should forgive, the forgiveness can only be real when it is neither coerced nor done out of duty alone but instead is freely given.

If the reality of forgiveness depends both on its being freely given and on its being given properly—that is, when conditions for it have been met and in ways that do not exceed the boundaries of authority that the one granting forgiveness needs to observe—what does that perspective imply about whether some actions and events, such as the Holocaust, are unforgivable? My response is as follows: Strictly speaking, as far as human relationships are concerned, many actions and events are unforgivable. If one person, for instance, has murdered another, the murder is unforgivable in the sense that the basic condition for forgiveness has been abolished. The victim is dead. He or she cannot forgive, no matter how repentant the murderer may turn out to be, and no one can speak for the victim. Others may forgive the repentant murderer for what has been done to them, but the offense remains unforgivable in a basic way.

As Primo Levi put the point, "When an act of violence or an offense has been committed it is forever irreparable."[25] It follows that the Holocaust is unforgivable because, as Heschel pointed out, no living person can speak for the millions of Jews who were starved and ravaged by disease in ghettos, worked to exhaustion in concentration camps, shot to death by *Einsatzgruppen*, or gassed at Treblinka, Auschwitz, and the Third Reich's other killing centers. "Forgiveness," as Pollefeyt says, "can only take place between the living."[26]

God and forgiveness

What about God's point of view? Is the Holocaust forgivable by God? It is conceivable that the answer could be *yes*. Heschel, for instance, holds that God cannot forgive sins committed against man but can forgive those "committed against Himself."[27] The Holocaust, of course, was a sin against God or nothing could be. Assuming, and it is a huge but still instructive assumption, that repentant perpetrators stood before God in an afterlife, would God—should God—forgive them for the Holocaust?

Versions of that question were on Elie Wiesel's mind at Auschwitz in late January 1995. When he spoke at a ceremony commemorating the fiftieth anniversary of that camp's liberation, his remarks included prayerful comments as follows:

> Although we know that God is merciful, please God, do not have mercy on those who created this place. God of forgiveness, do not forgive the murderers of Jewish children here. Do not forgive the murderers and their accomplices. ... God, merciful God, do not have mercy on those who had no mercy on Jewish children.[28]

Troubled by Wiesel's statement, the Roman Catholic Holocaust scholar Carol Rittner interviewed him about it in October 1996. Some key points emerged from their exchange. Wiesel affirmed that God can do what he wants where forgiveness is concerned, but Wiesel made equally clear that divine forgiveness for the Holocaust's perpetrators would truly be a cause for protest against God unless two conditions—both unknown to us—have been met. First, it would be obscene for God to show mercy to Holocaust perpetrators if God has not done so for the 1.5 million Jewish children whom they killed during the Holocaust. It is not clear, at least not yet for those of us who still inhabit the earth, that God has been merciful to those girls and boys or to any other Jew murdered by the Germans and their collaborators. Second, Wiesel stressed that forgiveness "presupposes an admission of guilt, contrition, and remorse. I have not seen," he added, "the killers express remorse or contrition, much less guilt."[29]

What if those conditions were met—somehow and somewhere, not in this world but beyond it? Wiesel did not address that issue in his interview with Rittner, but speculative though it is, the question may be instructive. Even if a Holocaust perpetrator admitted guilt and expressed contrition and remorse in an after-life, God might say, "Too late." But given the emphasis that Judaism and Christianity place on God's mercy and love, it seems likely that God would say, "Better late than never," if the admission of guilt and the expression of contrition and remorse were genuine. Arguably, it is this possibility, remote though it might be, that gives Wiesel's petition at Auschwitz—"God of forgiveness, do not forgive"—its most jarring quality. God's ways, however, are not for us to decide, although it is important to underscore two more points that are closely related to Wiesel's prayer at Auschwitz: First, if God forgave even one *repentant* Holocaust perpetrator but did not show mercy to the murdered Jewish children, then there would be additional reasons for protest. Furthermore, if God forgave even one *unrepentant* Holocaust perpetrator, to that extent God would be complicit with that perpetrator, especially if God had not been merciful to the Holocaust's victims. Second, even if all Holocaust perpetrators were genuinely repentant and all Holocaust victims were shown mercy, God still could not rightly grant forgiveness for the entire Holocaust. God could forgive the wrong done to God, but the victims' prerogative to grant or to withhold forgiveness for what happened to them would still be theirs and not God's.

These judgments, focused as they are on circumstances beyond history, also direct attention back to our present world and God's possible relation to it. Who needs forgiveness? If the answer, in part, is *all of us do*, and, in part, *some of us do more than others*, then God may need forgiveness too, for unless God is either nonexistent or lacking in power, God was not merciful during the Holocaust, at least not sufficiently, or God's anger was unleashed in ways that are truly and hideously beyond understanding.

Toward a post-Holocaust ethics of forgiveness

Forgiveness is an *after*-word. It makes no sense until wrong has been done, but how much sense it makes after the Holocaust is a question that shows how dilemmas, deepened and intensified by the Holocaust, have made forgiveness an increasingly wounded word. It is neither a word whose meaning will be shared by everyone nor a quality that everybody will equally regard as virtuous.

Differences about forgiveness, its value and priority, are to be expected, for there is no "one size fits all" approach to forgiveness that is likely to be credible. Nevertheless these reflections may have glimpsed some insights that can be shared by people of diverse experiences and traditions. They point in the direction of a post-Holocaust ethics of forgiveness. In summary, here are six of them:

- Human beings do harm, often immense harm, to one another. Therefore, forgiveness is needed because without it too many wounds will fester unnecessarily.
- Although needed, forgiveness is dangerous because it can minimize accountability, trivialize suffering, and condone injustice, if only inadvertently.
- To avoid the dangers of forgiveness while undergirding the human need for it, basic conditions for granting forgiveness should be met. First and foremost, repentance is required. It includes heartfelt confession that one has done wrong, contrite determination to do all that one can to set matters right, and timeliness in taking those steps. Whenever a person or group wrongs or harms another, such repentance is right, good, and what sound ethics calls for. It is even better, of course, if wrong and harm do not take place at all and in their place are acts of caring and compassion.
- Where forgiveness is concerned, no one alive can speak for anyone else, let alone for everyone and least of all for the dead. Forgiveness is primarily a relationship between specific living persons, one in which a person can seek or grant forgiveness for particular harm that one person has inflicted on another.
- Many deeds and events, including the Holocaust, are unforgivable, at least in large measure, because they involve persons whose lives have been taken from them, and they are in no position to forgive, at least not in any way of which we have knowledge in our current times and places.
- Forgiveness cannot rightly be demanded or coerced. If and when it is granted, forgiveness is a gift. When genuine repentance exists, however, the reasons *for* bestowing and *against* withholding forgiveness grow more compelling.

Reaching the end of these brief reflections on forgiveness, there is no closure. As we struggle with forgiveness as an *after*-word, as a wounded word, the goal is not so much to have the last word but to summon a latent word, to discover anew or for the first time what a post-Holocaust understanding and practice of forgiveness can and should, should not and cannot be.[30] In those explorations, we may also see that time's passage takes us beyond forgiveness in two senses. It may be too late for forgiveness or it may be that, at least in some cases, forgiveness has been achieved, which leaves us to ask what comes after forgiveness. Forgiveness, then, is an *after*-word in more ways than one. In exploring forgiveness we are not only trying to discern what it can mean at a time subsequent to or later than what came *before*. We are also seeking or questing for something we cannot or do not yet have, and thus, again, wrestling with forgiveness leaves us with something we are *after*. In their most fundamental sense, our inquiries about forgiveness are after nothing less than the restoration of a broken human image and the maintenance of any healing we can achieve through forgiveness or in the wake of its impossibility. Reflections about forgiveness are by no means the only path in that direction, but the quest to recover and deepen our humanity will be impeded and impoverished unless we continue to ask and respond thoughtfully to versions of the question "Who needs forgiveness?"

9
The Ethics of Prayer

> If I was God, I would spit at Kuhn's prayer.
>
> Primo Levi, *Survival in Auschwitz*

Absent the possibility of wrong-doing, intentional harm, or evil, there would be no need for ethics, but given the world we inhabit, a place besieged by massive human destructiveness, evil is all too real and the need for ethics is keen. As one considers ethics during and after the Holocaust, it is important to see that the evil experienced by human beings requires at least two intermingling conditions. First, something must *happen*, for evil is scarcely possible without activity. Second, feeling, remembering, and reasoning loom large. No feeling implies no pain or suffering. No remembering entails no continuity of experience. No reasoning means no concepts, no distinctions between right and wrong. Without those ingredients, evil goes missing from human experience.

Richard Rhodes's *Masters of Death: The SS-Einsatzgruppen and the Invention of the Holocaust* recounts how Nazi Germany's mobile killing units murdered more than 1.3 million Jews in eastern Europe during World War II. "Maps in Jewish museums from Riga to Odessa," writes Rhodes, "confirm that almost every village and town in the entire sweep of the Eastern territories has a killing site nearby."[1] Gratuitous and sadistic violence accompanied the slaughter. Rhodes describes one episode as follows: "A woman in a small town near Minsk saw a young German soldier walking down the street with a year-old baby impaled on his bayonet. 'The baby was still crying weakly,' she would remember. 'And the German was singing. He was so engrossed in what he was doing that he did not notice me.' "[2]

If such activity is not evil, nothing could be. But sheer happenings—apart from feeling, memory, and reasoning—are insufficient to produce what we human beings mean by *evil*. Unless activity is experienced in human ways—including reasoning that distinguishes between what is and what ought to be—evil would be neither discernible nor real for us. As Susan Neiman has argued, however, human rationality is characterized by its capacity to differentiate between what is and what ought to be.[3] Far from being tangential, that function is reason's heart. Human beings repeatedly make judgments between right and wrong and about good and evil—to such an extent that we face a tortuous gap between what is and what ought to be. The Holocaust makes that point with a vengeance.[4]

Rhodes contends that "the notorious gas chambers and crematoria of the death camps have come to typify the Holocaust, but in fact they were exceptional. The primary means of mass murder the Nazis deployed during the Second World War was firearms and lethal privation."[5] If Rhodes overstates the case, his claim remains instructive. Privation and shooting dealt death no less than gas, but they were less efficient, and shooting took its toll on the perpetrators' nerves. Gassing made it easier for the killers to kill.[6]

Masters of Death shows that the Holocaust was too vast to be synonymous with any one place alone, but none comes closer than Auschwitz, the most lethal of the Shoah's multiple epicenters. More Jews—about one million—were killed in that camp than at any other Holocaust site. In addition, Auschwitz showed what Nazi Germany's genocidal intentions entailed: the development of factories designed to kill thousands of people a day and to dispose of their remains without a trace, but only after everything of value—labor from those who could work; property, including hair and gold teeth—was taken from them and used to support the Third Reich. Prison, slave labor installation, killing center— Auschwitz, three camps in one, was the most extreme and intensified manifestation of Nazi evil.

At Auschwitz, but not only there, the Third Reich's perpetrators of genocide aspired to be masters of death. At Auschwitz, but not only there, many actions—ordinary, extraordinary, and sometimes both at once—took place as the Holocaust's executioners pursued those aspirations. As one considers not only the consequences of the Holocaust for theology and, in particular, for theodicy—the attempt to vindicate divine justice in the face of evil—but also how evil can most credibly be interpreted and combated in a post-Holocaust world, it is worthwhile to consider an action, both ordinary and extraordinary, that Holocaust history may overlook or too easily dismiss: At Auschwitz, but not only there, people prayed.[7] That fact invites inquiry about the ethics of prayer.

"To write poetry after Auschwitz," the philosopher Theodor Adorno proclaimed, "is barbaric."[8] Tasteless, harsh, crude, brutal, insensitive, inhuman—Adorno's word *barbaric* brings those others to mind. To pray after Auschwitz may also be barbaric in all those senses, but at the very least, it could be argued, to pray after Auschwitz is childish, irrational, and absurd, if not irresponsible and abhorrent. Neither the Holocaust nor Adorno's pronouncement put an end to poetry, although both the Holocaust and Adorno's pronouncement continue to affect what can and cannot, should and should not, be said after Auschwitz.[9] The Holocaust put no end to prayer, either, but that catastrophe also calls prayer profoundly into question.

Should prayer have disappeared in the smoke from Birkenau's chimneys? Should prayer have been buried in the mass graves that the *Einsatzgruppen* filled with Jews? If prayer were to diminish or cease altogether in a post-Holocaust world, what difference would that make? If, as seems more likely, prayer continues after Auschwitz, how should the Holocaust affect it, especially with regard to two of prayer's most common aspects: giving thanks and making petitions for ourselves and others? This chapter invites dialogue about those issues. Such dialogue requires a personal cutting to the chase. It entails sharing honestly one's deepest insights and yearnings about the reality of good and evil, the causes we cherish, and the people we love the most.

Meanings beneath the words

Monowitz, or Buna as it was sometimes called, was one of Auschwitz's many forced labor satellites. In 1944, according to Holocaust survivor Elie Wiesel, the soup distributed to the prisoners on the eve of Rosh Hashanah, the Jewish New Year, went untouched for a time. "We wanted to wait until after prayers," he says in *Night*, noting that ten thousand men joined the solemn service in which the Name of the Eternal was blessed and called upon to inscribe the people of the covenant in the book of life.[10] That Rosh Hashanah service, Wiesel continues, "ended with the Kaddish. Everyone recited the Kaddish over his parents, over his children, over his brothers, and over himself."[11]

Most Jews, then and now, knew and know the Kaddish by heart. Likewise, most Christians memorize the Lord's Prayer. Those facts illustrate that prayer is central to Judaism and Christianity.[12] Neither all Jews nor all Christians pray, but few are those who never have or never will, especially when one recognizes that prayer is not limited to communities gathered for religious observances. William James defined prayer well in his classic *The Varieties of Religious Experience*. Calling it "the very soul and essence of religion," he identified prayer as "every kind of inward communion or conversation with the power recognized as divine."[13] Understood that way, prayer not only persists after the Holocaust, it plays a vital part in Jewish and Christian identity and in human experience generally.

Prayer's forms are numerous. They can be communal and public or personal and private. Spoken, sung, or silent, prayer is not confined to particular times and places; it can take place virtually anywhere and at any time. Prayer's moods are diverse. Its focus may be sharp or diffuse, its intensity high or low, its emotion aroused or restrained. Infused with joy and gratitude, or with fear, grief, and despair, prayer's contents are multiple as well. They can include more concerns and causes, perplexities and persons, than any individual can enumerate. Amidst this variety, however, one aspect of Jewish and Christian prayer is especially striking. Implicitly if not explicitly, prayer acknowledges that the particularities of experience persistently display the characteristics that led Thomas Hobbes to describe human existence as "solitary, poor, nasty, brutish, and short," a view echoed by G. W. F. Hegel when he depicted history as "this slaughter-bench, upon which the happiness of nations, the wisdom of states, and the virtues of individuals [have been] sacrificed."[14]

Both Hobbes and Hegel argued that their dark descriptions were neither complete nor final. Hobbes thought that people could establish civil societies to enhance security and peace. Humanity, contended Hegel, has "an actual capacity for change" and "change for the better."[15] Hobbes's and Hegel's yearnings, like those in the Kaddish and the Lord's Prayer, affirmed that life is good and that it can be better. But, just as dark views were shared by those philosophers, they are not alien to those ancient prayers, either.

On the contrary, even if the Kaddish lacks explicit words about death and the destruction that so often brings it on, that prayer and the contexts in which it finds expression are unthinkable apart from the pain, desolation, and grief that threaten life's goodness and rob its joy. The Lord's Prayer does not mention death explicitly, either. Nevertheless, the "slaughter bench" of history prompts the words that Jesus taught his followers. If evil did not exist, prayers might still be said, but they would be very different from the ones that Jews and Christians typically offer. In our perpetually broken world, prayer testifies that most people, if not all, are in some way discouraged and afraid, needy and suffering, devastated and grieving, to mention only a few of the afflictions that besiege humanity. Thus, when Jews and Christians pray, they often ask God for help to endure and persevere in harsh times, to resist persons who disrespect others, and to overcome powers that destroy dearly loved individuals, communities, traditions, and dreams. In these contexts, prayer petitions God for courage, healing, justice, and peace. Prayer speaks to God on behalf of others and for ourselves. Prayer also voices thanksgiving to God, but such gratitude would be less likely and heartfelt if the world were not such a threatening place. Prayer implies that nothing good should be taken for granted.

Evil prompts prayer; evil destroys prayer's credibility. Wiesel says that as he heard the Rosh Hashanah prayers at Auschwitz in 1944, he rebelled "in every fibre."[16] Amidst the congregation's sighs and tears, Wiesel heard the leader's voice, powerful yet broken: "All the earth and the Universe are God's!" As the words came forth, Wiesel recalls that they seemed to choke in the speaker's throat, "as though he did not have the strength to find the meaning beneath the words."[17]

Night does not explain that meaning, although Wiesel emphasizes that his prayer-provoked rebellion led him to protest against God, a theme that has characterized his religious life and writing ever since. If one thinks with Wiesel about the meaning beneath the words, there are at least three options. In different ways, each is choking. First, an Auschwitz prayer in which it is affirmed that "All the earth and the Universe are God's!" entails the idea that Auschwitz is part of God's domain. That implication, however, only initiates the possible meanings beneath the words. How is Auschwitz part of God's domain? Auschwitz could exist because of God's will; it could exist in spite of God's will. Either way, or in gray zones between those alternatives, the meaning beneath the words can be choking, for the killing did not end speedily and soon. Post-Holocaust prayer, moreover, seems to have done little, if anything, to change that pattern.

Protest against God—calling God to account, insisting that God should be *God*—is one response to the first meaning beneath the words, but a second interpretation of that meaning goes elsewhere. This perspective finds that beneath the words lies God's nonexistence. Auschwitz is part of the earth and the universe, but neither the earth nor the universe is God's because the words *God* and *divinity* refer to nothing real, at least to nothing more real than human ideas. From this perspective, it seems to follow that nothing could be more futile and absurd than to pray during or after the Holocaust, for at the very least that event makes it hard to affirm that prayer was heard and heeded by any divine power. Such a realization gives little cause for celebration. On the contrary, it can be choking because the Holocaust and subsequent genocides show how much the perpetrators of mass killing have become masters of death.

Memory imprints a third way of thinking about meanings beneath the words. Wiesel says that everyone recited the Kaddish, and the praying people remembered persons who were deeply loved and sorely missed. Remembering them involved recollecting times and places far removed from Auschwitz. Before Auschwitz, those times and places were not without suffering and grief, but they contained enough beauty, happiness, and joy to make life irresistibly good and to evoke gratitude for the gift of existence. To say, prayerfully and in Auschwitz, that "All creation bears witness to the Greatness of God!" was choking because Wiesel, his father, and thousands of others like them in that cursed place might still have remembered how good life could be, and they might have yearned for what could have been instead of Auschwitz.[18] Such recollections would have done nothing to reduce their anguish and desolation. On the contrary, memory probably worsened both, as Charlotte Delbo points out when she reflects on what it was like to remember the glory of a Parisian spring amidst the stink of Auschwitz corpses. "Why did I keep my memory?" she wonders. "Why this injustice?"[19]

The contrast between *before* and *after* remained within the injustice that Delbo felt. *Before*, life had been better; it had been good. Even if memory meant that surviving the Holocaust would give rise, as she said, "to such miserable images that tears of despair fill my eyes," the awareness that Auschwitz was contingent, unnecessary, made it possible, perhaps even unavoidable, to think from time to time about a different world, one that might have testified to the greatness of God. Perhaps our world could still do so, at least in part, if genocide ceased and its perpetrators were masters of death no more.

Prayer expresses the heart's cry. That cry is deeply rooted in what once was or could still be but is not now. If that understanding belongs to the meaning beneath the words, then what more might be said about who hears and heeds such cries? Another Auschwitz survivor, Primo Levi, offers important insight into that question.

A journey toward nothingness?

In 1941, Primo Levi took his degree in chemistry from the university at Turin, Italy. Two years later, at the age of 24, and with much of his native Italy occupied by Nazi Germany, he was arrested for resisting fascism. At first, Levi's Jewish identity went undetected, but under his captors' interrogation he acknowledged it and was sent to a detention camp at

Fossoli, near Modena. Deported to Auschwitz in 1944, he ended up in Monowitz. To the best of my knowledge, Levi makes no mention of the autumn Rosh Hashanah services observed there by Wiesel, nor do the two seem to have been aware of each other during their captivity.[20] After his liberation in late January 1945, Levi eventually found his way back to Italy, resumed his career as an industrial chemist, and became an acclaimed author who wrote about the Holocaust with an honesty that few others have matched. In what was probably suicide, a fall down a stairwell in April 1987 cost him his life.[21]

Primo Levi's best-known book about the Holocaust is *Survival in Auschwitz*. It is a classic memoir about his year there, which Levi called "a journey towards nothingness."[22] Although Levi's writings speak about many things, rarely do they say much directly about God. *Survival in Auschwitz*, however, contains a brief but striking exception to that rule. What led to this exception was an Auschwitz "selection" on a Sunday afternoon in October 1944.

All the prisoners in Levi's part of the camp were ordered to their barracks. In each of the barracks (Levi's hut was number 48 out of 60), everyone received "his card with his number, name, profession, age, and nationality" and obeyed orders to "undress completely, except for shoes."[23] Levi and his comrades then waited for the "selection." It would sentence some to the gas chambers. Others would be required to work a while longer.

When the SS inspectors reached hut 48 to process Levi's group, the procedure was as random as it was quick and simple. One by one, the prisoners ran a few steps and then surrendered their identity cards to an SS man who, in turn, passed the cards to a man on his right or left. "This," wrote Levi, "is the life or death of each of us. In three or four minutes a hut of two hundred men is 'done,' as is the whole camp of twelve thousand men in the course of the afternoon."[24] Not quite "done," however, because in Levi's part of the camp it usually took two or three days before those "selected" actually went to the gas. Meanwhile, the prisoners could usually figure out whose cards had gone to the left, whose to the right, and what the difference meant.

Levi's description of this particular October "selection" emphasizes its blending of Nazi logic and capriciousness. October meant that another Auschwitz winter was at hand. In the better weather of spring and summer 1944, the Germans had pitched huge tents to house several thousand prisoners in Levi's part of the camp. As winter approached, the tents came down, and the barracks became increasingly crowded. According to Levi, the Germans disliked such irregularities; they also realized that newly arriving Jewish convoys would make the crowding worse. Thus, the prisoner ranks would have to be thinned. Presumably, the October "selection" would cull the weak and useless prisoners, but Levi believed that the "most important thing" for the Germans was to ensure that "free posts be quickly created, according to a certain percentage previously fixed."[25]

Levi drew that conclusion because he witnessed other "irregularities." A prisoner named Sattler, for example, had been in the camp for only twenty days. Although he was still relatively strong and healthy, the "selection" took him. In the fast-moving inspection, a young and robust man named René went immediately ahead of Levi. Surely, Levi reflects, it was a mistake that René's card went to the left, "the '*schlecte Seite,*' the bad side."[26] And then it occurs to Levi that, yes, a mistake might well have been made, but it was not simply about René's health. More likely, Levi's card, which went to the right, had been mistaken for René's. "The fact that I was not selected," concluded Levi, "depended above all on chance."[27]

Considering the capriciousness that may have spared his life on that Sunday in October, Levi indicates that he felt "no distinct emotion" at the time.[28] Nevertheless, his account does not fully support that judgment, for Levi continues by noting what he observed after the meager portion of soup had been devoured on that post-selection evening and how he felt about what he saw and heard:

> Silence slowly prevails and then, from my bunk on the top row, I see and hear old Kuhn praying aloud, with his beret on his head, swaying backwards and forwards violently. Kuhn is thanking God because he has not been chosen.
>
> Kuhn is out of his senses. Does he not see Beppo the Greek in the bunk next to him, Beppo who is twenty years old and is going to the chamber the day after tomorrow and knows it and lies there looking fixedly at the light without saying anything and without even thinking any more? Can Kuhn fail to realize that next time it will be his turn? Does Kuhn not understand that what has happened today is an abomination, which no propitiatory prayer, no pardon, no expiation by the guilty, which nothing at all in the power of man can ever clean again?
>
> If I was God, I would spit at Kuhn's prayer.[29]

Some forty years after that October night at Auschwitz, and less than a year before his own death, Primo Levi checked the typescript of a series of interviews he had granted to Ferdinando Camon. At the end of one of the interviews, Levi had said, "No, I have never been [a believer]. I'd like to be, but I don't succeed. ... I must say that for me the experience of Auschwitz has been such as to sweep away any remnant of religious education I may have had." Camon sought clarification about those reflections: "Auschwitz," he asked Levi, "is proof of the nonexistence of God?" To that question, Levi gave a reply that is much less simple than it may seem: "There is Auschwitz," he said, "and so there cannot be God."

In those few words, Levi's response seemed done. Not quite done, however, because when Camon received the corrected typescript for the interview, he saw that Levi had penciled a margin note beside his not-quite-final comment: "I don't find a solution to this dilemma," Levi had added; "I keep looking, but I don't find it."[30]

Looking ... not finding ... looking some more: When the question is whether Auschwitz is proof of the nonexistence of God, when the dilemma is whether it could be credible to pray in or after Auschwitz, does that rhythm make sense? By no means would everyone say yes, but Levi's reaction to Kuhn's prayer can intensify reflection about such questions. Levi loathed Kuhn's prayer; perhaps because of Levi's awareness of the capriciousness of the October "selection," Kuhn's prayer seems even to have outraged him. Not only did that prayer affirm divine purpose in a place where Levi found none, it also appeared oblivious to chance, which, as Levi knew from his experience of just hours earlier, could profoundly affect one's life prospects in Auschwitz. If God did exist, Levi thought, God would despise Kuhn's prayer too. To thank God for one's own survival when Nazi Germany's masters of death were annihilating weak and defenseless people by the millions—often doing so through "mistakes" akin to the kind that Levi saw during the October "selection"— such a prayer included an unawareness or indifference as abhorrent as it was blind and self-centered. The same judgment could apply if Kuhn had asked God to protect and spare persons who were especially dear to him and had done so without regard either for chance or for others beyond his family and friends. It would not follow that Kuhn should have been unconcerned about or indifferent to what happened to him or to those he cared about most. If lack of awareness or self-centered indifference diminished Kuhn's integrity, it does not follow that he would have been more fully human if his own fate and that of his loved ones had lost special significance for him.

Levi discredits Kuhn's prayer, but not necessarily all prayer during and after the Holocaust. The atrocities, often compounded by their capriciousness, should always leave the reality and character of divinity in doubt. In that sense, Holocaust-related theodicy, a vindication of God's justice in the face of *Einsatzgruppen* and Auschwitz, seems futile, if not abhorent or dead. Nevertheless, our lives, the histories and contingencies in which they are embedded, the goods we value, and the evils that may engulf us do not account entirely for themselves. Problematic though they may be, the words that Wiesel and perhaps Levi heard on Rosh Hashanah eve in Auschwitz—"All the earth and the Universe are God's!" —still have a meaning as awesome as it is ambiguous. At least for those who take reality to be meaningful, prayer may retain a legitimate place, even if many particular prayers do not.

What Auschwitz indicates is that divinity does not necessarily answer or even hear prayer in the ways people prefer or expect. Reality, largely because of the arbitrary, merciless, and murderous devastation it harbors, does not unfold in ways that conform to our needs and desires, but those needs and desires are part of reality, and prayer can help people to pursue them in their best forms. "Prayers," as Wiesel has written, "do not always coincide with reality, and surely not with truth. But so what? It is up to us to modify reality and make the prayers come true."[31]

At its most profound, prayer involves intense awareness, concentration, and yearning for what deserves to matter most to us as human beings. When prayers are said for justice, peace, and freedom, for relief from hunger, racism, violence, war, and genocide, there can be a quieting and opening of ourselves in recognition that life involves power—at times but not always benign—that transcends our own, and value that extends beyond the boundaries of our finite years. It follows, and this is a kind of answer to our needs and petitions, that we may be encouraged to keep trying and to work toward goals that prayer itself has helped us identify as aims ultimately worthy of the best and the most that we can give. Wiesel's prayer-provoked rebellion and Levi's rejection of Kuhn's prayer at Auschwitz alert one to those possibilities by helping to delineate what post-Holocaust prayer should and should not be. Prayer that is offered well, its meaning dwelling so often beneath the words, resists ignorance, blindness, and self-centeredness. It is an informed expression of and commitment to human solidarity against the masters of death. Prayer is not the only expression of that kind, but humankind would be poorer without it.

Lifetimes of experience: a postscript

The historian and philosopher C. L. R. James, alluding to Hegel as his source, notes that "an old man repeats the same prayers that he did as a boy but now they are pregnant with the experience of a lifetime."[32] For many Jews, that theme applies to the prayers of Rosh Hashanah eve and to the Kaddish. For many Christians, it applies to the Lord's Prayer. These prayers give thanks to God; they also petition God for what is needed to make life good. Many lifetimes of experience, disillusioned by the Holocaust, underscore the fact that God will not deliver us from evil, at least not often or soon enough. To the extent that it occurs, deliverance from evil is like most evil itself—both evil and deliverance come primarily from human hands. Many lifetimes of experience, impassioned by the Holocaust, also emphasize the fact that God will not provide for all our needs or give strength to the weary, at least not sufficiently. To the extent that human needs are met and that our strength is sustained, those results depend on human initiatives. Matured by lifetimes of experience, the meaning beneath the words of prayers that may have been learned in childhood is this: The words focus attention on the things that matter most.

Among the touching children's songs that form the soundtrack for *Into the Arms of Strangers*, the Academy Award winning documentary about the *Kindertransport* program, which rescued several thousand Jewish girls and boys from Nazi Germany in 1938–39, there is a simple prayer sung by a young boy. It is a prayer that loving parents might teach a child to say as darkness falls. It is a song that a loving mother or father might sing to a young son or daughter before sleep overtakes them. "Give us, God, the evening," the words ask, "the evening, the good evening, [and] thus a cheerful morning." For Jewish parents and children during the Holocaust, good evenings and cheerful mornings were few and far between. Memory of that fact makes this prayer worth repeating. The prayer reminds us that we human beings do not create day and night, and that life can be a gift that is incalculably good. Memory of the Holocaust indicates that the quality of day and night, the goodness of life, depends on us. How much it depends on us alone, whether there is life beyond death to ensure that evil is not ultimately overwhelming—these are dilemmas for which lifetimes of earthly experience provide no closure or finality. At least for now, meanings beneath those words remain ours to make.

10
The Holocaust, Genocide, and the "Logic" of Racism

> My mother's Singer sewing machine, too, vanished in the confusion of war like an orphan.
>
> Danilo Kiš, *Garden, Ashes*

When I consider ethics during and after the Holocaust with my students, they often have heard me say that if I had the chance to remove one word, one concept, from human consciousness, my first choice, arguably, would be *race*. Few ideas, if any, have been more pernicious and destructive than that one. *Race* has sometimes been used more-or-less benignly as a synonym for *species* (as in "the human race") or as a word that refers neutrally or in some historical sense to physical, cultural, or ethnic differences among people (as in "the black race"). Overwhelmingly, however, the term *race* has done far more harm than good. Embedded in what can be called the "logic" of *racism*, the reasons are not hard to find, and they shed light on what ethics after the Holocaust needs to do.[1]

Race, racism, and genocide

Uses of the term *race* reflect the interests of human groups. Those interests involve power and control. Racial differentiation, usually traceable ultimately to physical differences such as skin color, has typically entailed distinctions between superiority and inferiority. Attempts to justify such distinctions have often appealed to "nature" or to allegedly empirical corroborations, but deeper inquiry into their origins indicates that such appeals have been rationalizations and legitimations for conceptual frameworks that have been constructed to ensure hegemonies of one kind or another. Far from being neutral, far from being grounded in objective and scientific analysis, racial differentiation has promoted division and advanced the interests of those who want to retain prerogatives and privileges that otherwise might not be theirs. The times when racial distinctions have been benign pale in comparison to those when they have fueled abuse, enslavement, injustice, violence, war, and genocide. Whenever the concept of *race* originated, whatever its forms may have been, seeds of destruction were sown with that concept and schemes evolved from it. The harvest has been as bloody and lethal as it has been long.

The crops of that harvest include *racism* among the most prominent and fecund. The term *racism* can be variously defined, but in common and minimalist usage it refers to prejudice, discrimination, and institutions, including law, based on beliefs about superiority and inferiority that pertain to groups of people who are thought to share lines of descent ("blood"), physical characteristics (such as skin color), and/or cultural features and identities ("civilization" of one kind or another). Separating groups of people into those that are superior and inferior, splitting groups of people into *us* and *them*, and doing so in ways that find the differences to be *essential* and usually *biological*, racism entails that difference among racially defined groups is threatening. Such threats have often been interpreted in ways that are genocidal.

Ruins and absences

These factors noted above remind me that the Serbian novelist Danilo Kiš (1935–89) was the son of a Montenegrin mother and a Jewish father. Subotica, Kiš's Yugoslavian home town, stood near the Hungarian border. When the Germans attacked Yugoslavia in April 1941, Subotica came under Hungary's control. Not until March 1944, when the Germans occupied the territory of their faltering Hungarian allies, did the Jews of Hungary face the Holocaust's full onslaught. When it came, that disaster took Kiš's father to an Auschwitz death.

Narrated from the perspective of a boy named Andi Scham, *Garden, Ashes* is a poignant, semi-autobiographical novel about the Holocaust. In ways unconventional for that genre, Kiš does not take his readers inside a ghetto, a deportation cattle-car, or a death camp. Instead, as the story's title suggests, one is led to consider the Holocaust as an absence, an unredeemed emptiness and unredeemable ruin—ashes—where once there had been life that flowed and flowered like a rich, green garden. The absence is personified by Andi's Jewish father, Eduard, who was taken away and presumably killed at Auschwitz, although his son was never quite sure of that and kept hoping and looking for his father's return, which never came.

Eccentric, difficult, but in his own ways loving and lovable, Eduard Scham was a writer whose masterpiece remained unfinished. The lack of closure, however, was not due entirely to the murder of its author. Scham's project was to be the third edition of his previously published *Bus, Ship, Rail, and Air Travel Guide*. In its revised and enlarged form, this book became a mystical, metaphysical exploration that included not only "all cities, all land areas and all the seas, all the skies, all climates, all meridians" but also spiraling roads and forking paths that carried him "afield in both breadth and depth" so that "abbreviations became subchapters, subchapters became chapters" with no end to their multiplying enigmas.[2]

Like Eduard Scham's travel guide, which led in so many directions without arriving at a certain destination, *Garden, Ashes* lacks closure too. One of the reasons involves the Singer sewing machine that belonged to Andi's mother. The early pages of the novel describe it; a sketch of the machine in one of the novel's pages adds to the specificity that Kiš conveys. Andi's mother created beauty with that machine, and thus the sewing machine itself was beautiful, for it signified home and a world in which one could be at home. It is even possible that the destination sought by Eduard Scham's travel guide might have been the place where that sewing machine belonged and where it could be found. The sewing machine, however, was not to be found. Apparently it belonged nowhere, for it "vanished in the confusion of war," writes Kiš.[3] The garden it had helped to create was turned to ashes by the Holocaust.

Consistency and inconsistency

For three reasons, I have referred to Kiš's *Garden, Ashes* in these reflections on "Genocide and the 'Logic' of Racism." First, the detail of this narrative is a reminder of the particularity that is often hidden by terms such as *genocide* or *racism*, which are concepts in ways that fathers, gardens, and sewing machines are not. Second, the destruction of such particularities—and many more—is what racism implies, and that implication also means that, at its core, racism tends to be genocidal. Third, whether there will be, even can be, any closure with regard to this connection, particularly in the sense of dissolving the connection and destablizing the ideas that comprise it, is something that remains to be seen. At least in part the outcomes depend on what philosophy and philosophers turn out to be.

What happened to Eduard Kiš helps to make these points clear. He was deported to Auschwitz because he was a Jew. Antisemitism was at the heart of Nazi ideology. Within that ideology, Nazi antisemitism meant that race—specifically the "purity" of German blood and culture—counted for everything. Nothing could be tolerated that might pollute the racial strength on which the Third Reich depended. According to Nazi theory—practice, too, as events unfolded—Jewish life posed this threat to a degree that surpassed all others. Germans, the Nazis argued persuasively, could not afford to let Jews remain in their midst.

As the history of Nazi Germany so emphatically shows, racism's "logic" leads tellingly, if not inevitably, to genocide. For if you take seriously the idea that one race endangers the well-being of another, the only way to remove that menace completely is to do away, once and for all, with everyone and everything that embodies it. Thus, the Holocaust took the lives of approximately 1.5 million Jewish children who were under fifteen. If most forms of racism shy away from such extreme measures, Nazi Germany's antisemitism was more consistent. It followed the path that racism's "logic" mapped out.

Genocides are never identical, but all of them share features in common. The goals of genocide can be diverse, including acquiring wealth or territory, or advancing a belief or ideology, but all cases of genocide entail one or more targeted groups—national, ethnic, racial, or religious—that the perpetrators seek to eliminate in one way or another. Although not the same in each case, steps to isolate and separate people take place. The means and duration of murder are not uniform, but most genocides, if not all, involve mass killing. The perpetrators are always particular people; so are the victims. Nevertheless, whatever their ethnicity or group identity may be, there are perpetrators and victims in all genocides. There are also bystanders. Without them, neither the causes nor the mechanisms of genocide would have their way so easily.

How does racism fit with this pattern of similarity and difference among genocides? In response, two main points loom the largest. First, *the "logic" that operates in and between racism and genocide indicates that racism can exist without genocide, and yet racism tends to be genocidal nonetheless.* Racism can exist at lower or higher levels of intensity. It may express itself in various policies and institutions. Racial discrimination need not be as overt or visible as segregation, *de jure* or *de facto*, makes it; racial prejudice need not be as extreme or violent as lynchings or pogroms. Nevertheless, insofar as racism is not self-contradictory but true to its fundamental impulses, it has to take seriously the idea that racial difference is fundamentally at odds with what one deeply values.

Much racial thinking and racism in particular are self-contradictory. One's racial group is thought to be better than another, but the idea is not taken seriously enough to produce sustained or systematic action based on racial discrimination, perhaps because cultural values make it politically incorrect to do so. Racism's impulses can be muted, but such pressures do not eliminate the "logic" of racism, which entails that a perceived racial threat to one's own racial group cannot be ignored with impunity. Furthermore, a savvy racism will include the understanding that in the case of racial threats to one's own racial group, there are many ways—sexual, cultural, political, religious—in which there can be incursions that pollute what is valued and weaken what allegedly should be authoritative. It follows for the "logic" of racism that racial threats to the purity and hegemony of a privileged racial group must be dealt with in a thoroughgoing manner.

Insofar as one harbors racism, whether in full consciousness or only dimly, a person or even a group can be dishonest and inauthentic in failing to acknowledge (1) that a consistent racism will want to rid itself of the threat that racial difference poses, and (2) that this goal can be achieved fully, once and for all, only through genocide. The "logic" of racism calls for an "honest" racist to be genocidal—not necessarily to agitate for genocide *now* but to be prepared to incite and implement genocide if and when the times for it are opportune. Ironically, such a realization might produce a fortunate step that could reduce racism, for it may be that those who practice racial discrimination (however inadvertently), and are racists to that extent, do not want to be murderous and would even resist pressures in that direction. Nevertheless, it would be unwise to take much comfort from the fact that racism may often be of a lukewarm and inconsistent variety. An inconsistent racism may not be overtly genocidal, but inconsistency does not defang racism, at least not completely. One can be inconsistent today and consistent tomorrow. The history of genocide bears witness to that.

Continuing the exploration about how racism fits within patterns of similarity and difference among genocides, the second point that looms largest goes as follows: *Although genocide can be incited and committed, at least in principle, without explicit appeals to racial difference, superiority and inferiority, few genocides, if any, are devoid of racism in one form or another* To justify this claim, note, first, that racism involves more than dislike of behavior, disagreement with political or religious views held by others, or even disputes about national identities. Behavior can shift so that the provocation for dislike is removed. A person's or a group's political perspectives or religious beliefs can be altered so that the grounds for disagreement are taken away. Even citizenship is negotiable and change-able; the irritations that activate disputes about differences in those areas can also be dissolved.

With racism, however, more is at stake than behavior, belief, and even citizenship. To have the dubious distinction of being worthy of the name, racism is typically about *essential* and usually *biological* differences. Racism trades in the allegedly unchangeable. What is taken to be unchangeable may be masked by what is changeable and changing, but claims about what is *essential* remain at the heart of racism nonetheless. The "logic" of these considerations works in two related ways.

First, racism's "logic" encourages one to think that when a racial threat is perceived, there is something that must be preserved and pro-tected against that threat. What is valued, racism's "logic" understands, could be harmed, compromised, polluted, ruined—the unfortunate verbs multiply their invidious distinctions. Racist feeling is often aroused because it is sensed that such polluting actions have taken place and that they have weakened the privileged racial identity that deserves hegemony. The remedy is to restore health to the privileged race and to purge the forces that are contaminating threats. Within this "logic" is the idea that the privileged race is essentially what it is. Even if compro-mised and contaminated, it remains and requires vindication lest it be lost, which could happen if vigilance diminishes. Such vigilance, if it is thoroughly and consistently focused on the perceived threats, will tend to have genocidal inclinations.

Second, where either genocidal inclinations or actual implementations of genocide are concerned, racism is likely to be an accompanying and energizing factor. At first glance, that claim might seem at odds with the formal definition of genocide, which in the United Nations' formulation speaks of potentially targeted groups as "national, ethnical, racial or reli-gious" and identifies a variety of acts that can be carried out with intent to destroy such groups "in whole or in part."[4] At second glance, however, far from eliminating racism, those identifying marks clarify how racism works in genocide and how it is even required for some genocides to take place.

Where the intent is genocidal, the "logic" of that intention means that destruction "in part" is always second-best. The optimal realization of genocidal intent is to destroy a targeted group "in whole." There are practical and philosophical reasons that back such "logic." The Nazi SS leader Heinrich Himmler captured both dimensions of this "logic" in a speech about the destruction of Jewry that he delivered to his men in October 1943. "We had to answer the question: What about the women and children?" Himmler observed. "Here, too, I had made up my mind. ... I did not feel that I had the right to exterminate the men and then allow their children to grow into avengers, threatening our sons and grandchildren. A fateful decision had to be made: This people had to vanish from the earth."[5]

Destruction of a group "in part" rightly qualifies as an instance of the crime of genocide, but Himmler's reasoning cogently underscores that the "logic" involved here would find it imprudent not to finish the job once the tasks of genocide have begun and the opportunity to continue to the end is available. Most genocides do not go "all the way," but that outcome takes place either because pressure or force from the outside intervenes, which happens mostly too late and too little, or because exhaustion of one kind or another sets in, or because of some combination of the two. But the "logic" of genocide says that the destruction, once started, should continue to the end. Not to achieve that outcome is to come up short.

The UN Convention indicates that there can be an intention to commit genocide halfway—"intent to destroy ... in part," as the wording might be read. One need not deny that such intent could be and even has been real, but in those cases a kind of inconsistency has entered into the intentionality. In the case of the Nazis, for instance, it was not understood that 50 percent of the European Jews were a threat or even that only the destruction of the European Jews was the optimal goal to be achieved. Better still and even necessary, as Himmler put it, was action that would make the Jewish people disappear from the earth. Nor, according to the Hutu leadership in Rwanda, was it merely 100,000 Tutsi who had to be destroyed. Better still and even necessary, the "logic" of genocide in Rwanda meant that it would be desirable, if possible, for all the Tutsi in Rwanda and, arguably, elsewhere to disappear from the face of the earth as well.

An objection to this line of reasoning might invoke the possibility that genocide can simply be instrumental and thus its perpetrators might not want or intend to go "all the way" because doing so would be contrary to their interests. The latter, for example, might involve decimating a population but also sparing some portion of it for enslavement or other forms of exploitation. Such theory and practice can certainly be genocidal, but in such cases one would still have to ask: Why must so many, if not all, of these people be decimated?

That question brings back into view the fact that genocide does more than envision instrumental opportunities. Its deepest impulse is to remove a threat. The threat, in turn, will scarcely be describable as such unless the targeted population is portrayed as endangering the prerogatives, the hegemony, and superiority of the perpetrator group. From the perspective of the "logic" of genocide, these threats, moreover, are rooted in what are taken to be, at least by implication, characteristics or qualities that cannot be assimilated into the perpetrator group. If one's group thinks with a genocidal "logic," then that group cannot embrace the national, ethnic, or religious other, even though in principle and over time, all of those identities could change. It cannot embrace them because at the bottom line an essentialist mind set is typically embedded in genocidal "logic," and in the context of genocidal mentalities that essentialist mind set is closely related to racism, if not virtually synonymous with it.

Not all essentialist ways of thinking are racist, but racism is a form of essentialism, and genocidal mentalities typically reflect forms of essentialism that are racist. At the end of the day, racism and genocide inflame each other. The "logic" of the one often entails the "logic" of the other. If there are exceptions, they prove the rule: Usually genocide includes racism of one kind or another, and racism tends to be genocidal.

Paradigmatic genocide that it was, the Holocaust emerged from a deeply racist Nazi ideology. The Rwandan genocide, the clearest case of post-Holocaust genocide, was also rooted in racism. Linda Melvern, a discerning scholar of the Rwandan genocide has documented the following points:

> The Hutu extremists believed that the Tutsi were a different race and that they had come from elsewhere to invade Rwanda. Hutu Power taught that the Tutsi were different, that they were lazy; that they did not want to work the land, that they were outside human existence— vermin and subhuman. The effect of the Hutu Power radio, with its catchy nationalistic theme tunes and its racist jingles must never be underestimated. The broadcasts of *Radio–Télévision Libre des Milles Collines* (RTLM) were an integral part of the genocide plot and it was thanks to the propaganda that spewed over the airways that by April 1994 a large number of people in Rwanda had come to believe that the elimination of the Tutsi, or "cockroaches" as they were called, was a civic duty and that it was necessary work to rid the country of them.[6]

Raising voices in abysses of horror

In late June 1994, as the killing incited by the RTLM was still going on, Pope John Paul II sent Cardinal Roger Etchegaray as his envoy to Rwanda.

Addressing the Rwandan people after his arrival, Etchegaray spoke of "the abyss of horror" created by the mass murder that sundered them. Lest that phrase be taken merely as a rhetorical flourish, consider it in more detail.

The word *abyss* has at least three meanings. It denotes, first, a gulf or pit that is bottomless. This meaning suggests that anything or anyone entering an abyss is utterly lost. Second, *abyss* means chaos or even hell; it refers to disorder in which secure existence for anything or anyone would be impossible until order is created or restored. Third, *abyss* has not only spatial, geographical, or cosmological connotations. The term also refers to the ways in which the human mind and spirit as well as its physical condition can be overwhelmed and left bereft by events that apparently elude rational comprehension. In such cases, the human condition itself becomes abysmal.

Events that elude rational comprehension are often riddled with *horror*, another term that should not be spoken or taken lightly. *Horror* refers to intense feelings of a particular kind and to the actions or conditions that cause them. The feelings, which run deep because they are intense and primal, are those of fear, terror, shock, abhorrence, and loathing. Genocide is a primary instance of *horror* or nothing could be. An *abyss of horror*, then, would be a reality so grim, so devastating, so full of useless pain, suffering, death, and despair that it fractures the world—perhaps forever. Genocide is an *abyss of horror* or, again, nothing could be. Racism is not the only force that opens that abyss, but if racism were absent, it would be possible to have at least a cautious optimism about responses to the question "Will genocide ever end?"

A genocidal abyss of horror cannot be closed, at least not completely. Nor can the questions that it raises be answered with confidence and finality. What can be done is to recognize that abysses of horror remain and that the questions they raise deserve to be confronted as we human beings assess and take up our responsibility for both—the abysses and our responses to the questions they leave before us. As one pursues those points, it is well to remember that every form of power includes, even depends upon, raising voices. Leaders have to raise their voices to state their principles, express their visions, and rally their supporters. Governments have to raise their voices to define policies, defend interests, and justify decisions. Supporters of leaders and governments have to raise their voices to back visions and policies; otherwise the power of principles and interests declines and even disappears.

To be effective, the "logic" of racism and genocide also depends on raising voices. That "logic" can have little force unless divisions between people are constructed by speech, fears are expressed in ideology and propaganda, and killing is unleashed by voices that proclaim it to be necessary. The "logic" of racism and genocide also depends on "unraising" voices; it counts on the silencing of dissent and on the acquiescence of bystanders. Every voice unraised against that "logic" gives aid and comfort to those who call for and support genocide, that crime of crimes. Genocide can be prevented before it happens, and it can be stopped after it is under way. Neither prevention nor successful intervention, however, can happen without power. Rwanda's genocidal tragedy resulted from the fact that raising voices against it came too late and too little.

Here an objection may be raised: Raising voices may not count for much, because actions speak louder than words, and attention should be directed much more on what people do than on what they say. That point has validity, but it underestimates the relationship between raising voices and taking action. Racism and genocide do not appear out of the blue. Intentions, plans, and many people are necessary to make them operational. Absent raising voices, the coordination of thought and action required by racism and genocide will not and cannot be in place. The same can be said of resistance to the "logic" of racism and genocide.

Philosophy and philosophers have important contributions to make when it comes to raising voices. Where genocide prevention is concerned, one of those contributions can and should be the continuing deconstruction of racial thinking. For if such thinking is curtailed, especially in contexts where philosophers equally emphasize the idea and ideals of universal human rights, then racism may be neutralized. With that outcome, one of the most potent causes of genocide would be kept in check. Philosophy is by no means the only discipline that emphasizes logical analysis. Nor are philosophers by any means the sole experts in the critical analysis of reasoning. But philosophy and philosophers are in the vanguard of those who value and practice thinking that questions assumptions, asks for evidence, and tracks the connections and implications of ideas. They can do much to criticize, expose, and demystify the ways of thinking that lead to genocide, including the powerful inducement that racism has provided for it. Philosophy and philosophers ignore this task at the risk of leaving humankind in further abysses of horror.

In closing, my thoughts move from Rwanda and back to the Europe of Danilo Kiš and the Holocaust. His novel *Garden, Ashes* ends on somber notes.[7] "We are witnesses to a great breakdown in values," Kiš writes, and Andi Scham observes that his vanished world has left him in a house with a kitchen stove that cannot "generate a real flame: we lacked a real blaze, there was no glow." The novel's last words belong to Andi's mother, who has no husband and no Singer sewing machine: "Lord," she says, "how quickly it gets dark here." The "logic" of racism remains, and with it the specter of genocide shadows our twenty-first-century world. None of us alone can remove that shadow, but each of us can do something. For philosophers, that responsibility includes raising voices to unmask and deconstruct the "logic" of racism, raising voices to reveal and undermine that logic's murderous, genocidal impulses. High on philosophy's—indeed on humanity's—priorities should be the task of diminishing, if not eliminating, the destructively influential parts that the concept of *race* has played in human history and the work of advancing views of universal human rights that can be as persuasive and credible as possible in a world that remains profoundly wounded by and vulnerable to the threats of genocide.

11
Will Genocide Ever End?

> I promise you that after.
> Elie Wiesel, *One Generation After*

On October 2, 1938, less than a year before Nazi Germany's invasion of Poland began World War II, the British philosopher R. G. Collingwood put the finishing touches on his autobiography. Its observations underscored his belief that "the chief business of twentieth-century philosophy is to reckon with twentieth-century history."[1] Collingwood's primary intention was to urge philosophers to pay more attention to the discipline of history—its methods, consciousness of context, and attention to detail—so that philosophy might be less abstract, more aware of its own historical heritage, and directed more fully to inquiry about problems raised by historical thinking (e.g., how is historical knowledge possible?). At least by implication, this call for an up to-date philosophy of history meant that philosophy's responsibilities included paying close attention to twentieth-century events as well.

Unfortunately, twentieth-century philosophy did relatively little to meet Collingwood's expectations. Whether philosophy will do better in the twenty-first century remains to be seen. Illustrative evidence for those latter judgments can be found by noting that the late December 1985 meeting of the American Philosophical Association's Eastern Division featured a symposium on the Holocaust. An article in the prestigious *Journal of Philosophy* provided a prelude for that event. Authored by Emil Fackenheim (1916–2003)—with a brief commentary by Berel Lang—the essay was entitled "The Holocaust and Philosophy." As if echoing Collingwood in a minor key, it began with a lament: "Philosophers," wrote Fackenheim, "have all but ignored the Holocaust."[2] Twenty years on, Fackenheim's indictment is less devastating than it was in 1985.

Philosophical attention to the Holocaust has grown and continues to do so.[3] To that degree, philosophers have not ignored genocide entirely, for the Holocaust is a paradigmatic instance of that crime, but when one thinks of philosophy and genocide before and after the Holocaust, a version of Fackenheim's judgment remains valid. To a large extent, philosophers have ignored and still overlook genocide. Correction of that unfortunate situation is important if genocide is to end.

Philosophy and genocide

While the Holocaust raged in the 1940s, Raphael Lemkin, a Jewish lawyer who fled from Poland, coined the term *genocide*. Initially defining it to mean "the destruction of a nation or of an ethnic group," he observed that the term denoted "an old practice in its modern development," for the plight of the Jews under Hitler was not a simple repetition of past historical patterns.[4] From the slaughter of Hereros in the German colony of South West Africa in 1904, the Turkish destruction of Armenians in 1915–16, and the Holocaust to the Rwandan genocide in 1994 and, arguably, what happened a decade later in the Darfur region of Sudan, genocide's modern development has taken an immense toll on human life and civilization in the twentieth century and now in the twenty-first as well. It is no exaggeration to say that we live and philosophy exists in an age of genocide.

Writing in the December 2002 issue of the *International Social Science Journal*, the Holocaust historian Omer Bartov argued persuasively that the modern development of genocidal catastrophes can neither be understood nor prevented in the future unless one grasps that "scholars have played a prominent role in preparing the mindset, providing the rationale, and supplying the know-how and personnel for the implementation of state-directed mass violence."[5] Philosophers and philosophy are not exempt from Bartov's indictment.

Even though the history of philosophy shows that philosophers have done much to advance human rights and to defend human equality, the same history shows that genocide has been aided and abetted by philosophies that have advanced racism and antisemitism and by philosophers who have encouraged—inadvertently if not explicitly— political regimes and cultural agendas that turned genocidal. When the topic is philosophy, genocide, and human rights, the problem is not simply that philosophy has ignored genocide and that philosophers need to pay more attention to that crime. The problem is also that philosophy and philosophers bear more responsibility for genocide than they have usually admitted. In our post-Holocaust world, nations, businesses, churches, and professions such as medicine and law have been called to account for their complicity or for bystanding while Nazi Germany committed genocide against the European Jews.[6] To some extent philosophers have been held accountable too, but when the history of genocide is taken into account, philosophy and philosophers have not been sufficiently self-critical about their bystanding and complicity.

Generally speaking, philosophy and philosophers have high estimates of themselves. Philosophy depicts itself as occupying high moral ground. Philosophers tend to see themselves—I include myself in these judgments—as extending a tradition that serves free inquiry, truth, goodness, beauty, and justice. But philosophy and philosophers have darker sides, and they have been less than forthcoming about them, especially with regard to genocide. As the history of the Holocaust shows, and other genocides follow similar patterns in this regard, the expertise and cooperation, or at least the passivity, of virtually every professional group within a state and a society—teachers, professors, scholars, and philosophers among them—are needed for genocide to take place. Philosophy and genocide exist in the same world. Unfortunately, their relationship has not always been one of opposition. Philosophy's association with genocide does not leave philosophy unscathed and untarnished. For the sake of humanity's well-being and philosophy's integrity, philosophers should come to grips with that reality.

Although philosophy often highlights characteristics shared by all persons, its history contains theories that have negatively emphasized differences—religious, cultural, national, and racial.[7] Such theories have encouraged senses of hierarchy, superiority, and "us versus them" thinking in which genocidal policies may assert themselves, especially in times of economic and political stress. If philosophy is divided between views upholding that all people are equal members of humanity and others stressing differences between groups as fundamental, how can philosophy contribute to stopping or mitigating genocide?

Philosophy is critical inquiry about reality, knowledge, and ethics. It explores what is, what can be known, and what ought to be. Typically, philosophers have not given genocide priority as a field of study. However, there are some twenty-first-century signs that a welcome change may be taking place. A small but growing number of philosophers are focusing on evil.[8] More than that, they recognize that the paradigmatic cases of evil are not only produced by human beings but also are to be found in the Holocaust and other genocides. This emphasis also drives home the importance of human rights, but with a difference that Bartov captures when he argues that it cannot be credible to philosophize "by applying, as if nothing had happened, the same old humanistic and rational concepts that were so profoundly undermined" by genocidal catastrophes.[9] Genocide puts profound challenges before philosophers and before all critically thinking people. Much depends on how those challenges are met.

Sudan and the "G word"

When American voters went to the polls on Tuesday, November 2, 2004, a brief article in the *New York Times* reported that the Sudanese army had not only surrounded the camps of internally displaced people in Sudan's western region of Darfur but also was likely to relocate them forcibly, which it subsequently proceeded to do. At that time, the number of the homeless in Darfur numbered more than 1.5 million. Another 200,000 refugees had fled to Chad, where they were in dire straits. Less than six months later, reliable estimates put the figure for forced displacements at 2.4 million. The United Nations indicated that 70,000 people had died from disease and malnutrition in the seven months preceding the American election.[10] That count rapidly rose to 300,000 by the time of this writing in April 2005.[11]

In late September 2004 but very briefly—for no more than four minutes, to be precise—the situation in Sudan was addressed by John Kerry and George W. Bush in the first of their three debates in the 2004 American presidential campaign. Jim Lehrer, the debate's moderator, initially asked Kerry whether American troops should be sent to Sudan. Following the lead taken on July 22, 2004, when both houses of the US Congress overwhelmingly denounced the atrocities in Darfur as genocide, and on September 9, 2004, when Colin Powell, then the US Secretary of State, also called the situation in Sudan a genocide, Kerry too applied the "G word" to Darfur.[12] In the two minutes he was given to address Lehrer's question, the Democrat's nominee urged "logistical" as well as humanitarian support. "If it took American forces to some degree to coalesce the African Union," he added, "I'd be prepared to do it because we could never allow another Rwanda. It's a moral responsibility for us in the world."

Lehrer gave Bush, the Republican incumbent, ninety seconds to respond and to express his position on Darfur. The American president, too, called the Darfur situation genocide. He mentioned that $200 million in aid had been committed by the United States. He noted US support for the UN in Darfur. He also stated that the United States "shouldn't be committing troops," and he expressed the hope that "the African Union moves rapidly to save lives."[13]

Those four minutes represented the sum total of attention that genocide received during the 2004 presidential campaign in the United States.[14] There and elsewhere, the record of philosophers has been considerably better, but not so much better as to be a cause for congratulation because the situation in Darfur has deteriorated further. For example, an early December 2004 report by UN Secretary-General Kofi Annan stated that "in Darfur, chaos is looming as order is collapsing."[15] Annan indicated that 2.3 million people, more than a third of Darfur's population of about six million, were in desperate conditions as the Sudanese government and its proxies, the Arab militias known as Janjaweed, continued their decimating assaults against the Aranga, Fur, Jebel, Masalit, and Zaghawa, the key black African tribes in western Sudan. The methods employed in the onslaught included lethal dehydration as wells and water supplies in the arid environment were ruined, rape, starvation (partly produced by hijacking relief goods or preventing relief agencies from gaining access to those in need), forced relocation, and outright killing by shootings and bombings. Despite these genocidal signs, a UN commission of inquiry found on January 31, 2005, that the evidence did not lead to the conclusion that the Sudanese government has committed genocide. Evidence of genocidal intent was lacking. According to the UN report, "generally speaking, the policy of attacking, killing and forcibly displacing members of some tribes does not evince a specific intent to annihilate, in whole or in part, a group distinguished on racial, ethnic, national or religious grounds."[16] The US Department of State saw the situation differently. Released on February 28, 2005, its 2004 report on human rights abuses contained a lengthy analysis of the situation in Sudan, which confirmed that "genocide had been committed in Darfur, and the Government and the Jinjaweed bore responsibility."[17]

The most important matter, however, is not to settle an argument about whether use of the "G word" is appropriate for the disaster in Sudan. People in Darfur kept dying while those wrangles continued. Whether one agrees with the US Department of State or the UN with regard to Sudan and the "G word," the most important concern is that the killing and dying should stop. One contribution of philosophy and philosophers—indeed of caring people everywhere—is to say so, but what else might they contribute to diminish mass death and its suffering?

"After? Meaning what?"

The writings of Elie Wiesel, a survivor of Nazi Germany's genocide against the Jews, sometimes include Holocaust-related dialogues.[18] Spare and lean, they often consist of just a few hundred words or less. These dialogues are distinctive not only for their minimalist qualities but also because their apparent simplicity, their unidentified settings, unnamed characters, abrupt and open endings, raise fundamental questions in moving ways.

In Wiesel's *One Generation After*, for example, one partner in a dialogue tries to rescue the other from a downward-spiraling sadness. "Look around you," says the upbeat voice. "The trees in bloom. The shop windows. The pretty girls. What the hell, let yourself go. I promise you that after ..."

After—but not allusions to spring's new life—that's the word, the problem, that gets the other's attention. "After?" asks the downcast voice. "Did you say: after? Meaning what?"[19] The dialogue ends with that question, but far from being over, it has only begun.

After—that word is ordinary because human life is thick with time. Encountering what is present, anticipating what lies ahead, our living is always *after*, whose meanings denote a subsequent or later time and a seeking or questing for something one does not have. In those senses, philosophy is an after-word. When Plato contended that philosophy begins in wonder, he understood that philosophy does not come first but comes to life in the aftermath of preceding experience. Once it comes to life, philosophy takes on life of its own, which can be life-giving or life-threatening or many other things in between. As history has unfolded, philosophy now lives after genocide, a fact that makes, or should make, philosophers wonder about what philosophy's promise is to be.

Sadly, there is a sense in which those who perpetrate genocide tend to have a crucial advantage. Those who intervene or prosecute or philosophize after the fact usually arrive too late. The horror unleashed by human hands makes it unclear that justice can be achieved. The repetition of genocide since the Holocaust makes it hard to glimpse how prevention can happen. My friend, Hank Knight, a Holocaust scholar at the University of Tulsa in Oklahoma, is a fine song writer, and his lyrics in a song called "Hardly Ever Again" capture moods and concerns that should make people, including philosophers, think long and hard:

In '45, remember when
The world said, "Never, never again!

Never again: six million lost;
Never again: the Holocaust."
"Never," we said, "Never again,"
But this is now and that was then.

"Hardly ever again."
Is that what we meant to say?
"Hardly ever again."
Will we turn and walk away?
This is now and that was then;
And we meant "hardly ever again." ...

But this is now and that was then.
When will we ever mean "never again"?[20]

The historian and legal scholar Michael Bazyler argues persuasively that the model of reparations and restitution in Holocaust-related cases helps to put on notice individuals and institutions that pursue human rights abuses, including genocide. That notice, he contends, indicates that those who commit genocide or violate human rights in other ways will be held responsible for their misdeeds.[21] With the Nuremberg Trials of 1945–46 as one of their precedents, post-genocide trials, such as the one in the International Criminal Court at the Hague, where Slobodan Milosevic is the first head of state to be put on trial for genocidal atrocities—specifically the ones that took place during the 1992–95 Bosnian War—reparation and restitution come *after*. Legal proceedings and acts of reparation and restitution that come *after* may help to forestall genocide by putting people on notice, as Bazyler contends, but trials and acts of reparation and restitution are only two arrows in the hoped-for quiver of genocide prevention. What about others that are needed as well and how might philosophy, philosophers, and all caring persons contribute to them?

Confronting the beast of genocide

"The beast of genocide," says Gregory H. Stanton, director of the International Campaign to End Genocide, "lurks in the dark." Roméo Dallaire, the Canadian general who headed the United Nations Assistance Mission in Rwanda, makes a related point when he urges that "the need is to stop the disconnect between the experiential and the intellectual."[22] To the extent that Stanton's warning is heeded in ways that advance Dallaire's imperative, the answer to the fundamental question, "Will genocide ever end?" can at least be *perhaps*. That realistic conclusion is ever-so-tentative. Yet it is not without hope and substance because international awareness about what it will take to move beyond genocide is becoming clearer. More effectively than they have done so previously, philosophers and all caring persons can raise their voices in this cause.

Consider five overarching themes on these topics. First, genocide prevention is a goal that exceeds any single person's expertise, any discipline's methodology, or any government's reach. Genocide prevention requires working together at every point. Second, no automatic link exists between intellectual analysis of genocide and the action that is needed to prevent it. That connection can be made only through political will. How to muster and sustain that political will is among the most important questions raised by the continuing threat of genocide in our world. Third, governments, even if they are alert and activated, will not—indeed, cannot—do everything that is necessary to prevent, stop, or heal the wounds that genocide inflicts. That fact requires the mobilization of other agencies that may be able to lend a hand in this crucial work. Fourth, at times there is no substitute for military intervention, which is essential to maintain stability and security. Military intervention, however, is not enough to meet the needs that genocidal threats present. Crucial needs include political, economic, and educational aid—somewhat along the lines of a post-World War II Marshall Plan—to defuse potentially genocidal situations. Fifth, prevention of and intervention in genocide are long-term commitments, otherwise genocide prevention will remain ineffective. The long-term commitments must involve all sorts of institutions, and not least of all the media, which have the power to alert, inform, and urge the need for action. In all of these areas, philosophy and philosophers have much needed contributions to make. They can ask crucial questions, provide conceptual clarity, identify and undermine ideologies that are genocidal, persistently call attention to differences between right and wrong, advance and assess arguments that pertain to those differences, bolster support for human rights, and encourage creative responses to educational needs. Importantly, philosophy and philosophers can do these things not abstractly but with attention focused on the particularities of existing situations, genocide—actual and threatened—among them.

Good news/bad news

These five overarching themes have a series of good news/bad news implications, which identify key areas in which vigilance and hard work, including vigilance and hard work for philosophy and philosophers, remain if the temptations of genocide are to be curbed in the twenty-first century. Although my account calls specific attention to the responsibilities of philosophy and philosophers, I have also been suggesting that these responsibilities, and others related to them, also belong to all ethically concerned persons. What I am saying calls philosophy and philosophers to account, but the calls beckon much more widely as well. Here, very compactly, are several of the implication clusters that most deserve attention if the chances for ending genocide are to be improved.

1. We have the concept of genocide. It is defined, for example, by the United Nations Convention on Genocide. The concept helps us to identify genocide when it happens and, importantly, when it may be coming. But the bad news is that education about genocide is lacking, and, in addition, the scope and meaning of the concept remain debatable. As a result, even though genocide has a place in international law, there are loopholes in the legal frameworks about genocide. The concept's definition, moreover, is not likely to be universally agreed upon. Even if it were agreed upon, the sense of obligation to prevent genocide may remain ambiguous. Deeper study and better education about genocide are needed if genocide is to end. If they are moved to do so, not only philosophy and philosophers but every ethically concerned person can provide help in these areas and in all the others that I shall continue to identify.

2. Prevention and proof of genocide depend on determining perpetrator intent, which is not easily done, especially in pre-genocidal situations. Nevertheless, there is good news about demonstrating intent, because we know that ideologies can show it. Some ideologies are genocidal; philosophy can help to identify them and thus contribute to early warnings against genocide. Yet, even if we can sense genocide's coming by study of ideologies, the control of hate-inflaming communication, education, and media—crucial though it is—remains both problematic and lacking. If genocide is to end, there must be media usage and control in that direction. Here the signal for philosophy, philosophers, and all caring persons is that they will need to become more engaged in public life and discourse than their often abstract theorizing and highly specialized academic projects have inclined them to be.

3. The good news includes the fact that we have worthwhile analyses of risk assessment and credible approaches to early warning where genocide is concerned. Nevertheless, too often no one gives the perpetrators—potential or actual—reason to pause. Early warning is an important piece, but still a small one, in a very large and complicated genocide

puzzle. If genocide is to end, early warning systems must produce policies and actions that give its agents reason to pause. Philosophy and philosophers have encouraged thinking that is creative, imaginative, and original. Often genocide confronts us with what is unimaginable, or so it seems, but its extremity requires us to stretch our minds and to energize our wills to find ways that can check the advantages that genocide's perpetrators often enjoy. At the very least, philosophy can offer encouragement that helps to keep genocide's perpetrators—potential or actual—at bay.

4. Military intervention can be effective in preventing and stopping genocide. Such intervention is crucial for establishing security in which genocide cannot erupt or prevail. Yet, military power is state-focused; what it can do depends on state authority, and states jealously guard their sovereignty. Where genocidal situations are involved, how states will allow their military power to be used, if at all, for prevention and intervention remains at issue. Genocide's threats are unlikely to disappear until more effective international military cooperation against genocide becomes operational. Philosophers can do more than they have done before to advance these aims.

5. We know too much for it to be a surprise when genocide happens. Nevertheless, genocide indicators are difficult to operationalize for genocide prevention. Accountability is among the most crucial aspects of this problem. Who, for example, does one call to get preventive action going when genocide is threatened or under way? If genocide is to end, calls of that kind must be placed and answered. Accountability for genocide prevention must be put in place. Philosophers know how to think well about responsibility and accountability. Many other people do as well. If they put their minds to it, they can lend assistance in these areas too.

6. The good news is that we know a great deal about what to do to check genocide or to keep it from re-erupting after it has happened. Those steps include: establishing security, neutralizing genocidal leaders, engaging in regional planning, ensuring that political moderates have a voice, avoiding ethnic-based governments. In spite of such knowledge, however, genocides continue. They reveal either the failure or the inadequacy of basic institutions—political, religious, humanitarian. Genocide's threat will not end until those institutions perform better than they have thus far done. Philosophers have a part to play in getting those institutions to make the improvements that are needed. That work may properly emphasize the importance of philosophy's self-criticism, which may be needed to move philosophers to give concerns about genocide a higher priority than has typically been the case.

7. National interest is not always a barrier to genocide intervention. The case can be made that prevention and intervention are parts of a nation's values and thus of its interests. On the other hand, decisions are often made on the basis of political considerations that override appeals to "higher values." When that happens, value-based appeals for prevention and intervention are muted and unheeded. Genocide is unlikely to end unless the tendency to override ethical considerations is reversed. If philosophy, philosophers, and caring people everywhere fail to rise to this challenge, then the quality of human life will be jeopardized far more than necessary.

8. It is good news to know that religion can be a powerful and persuasive force in genocide prevention. The negative example of Rwanda bears witness to this claim, for virtually all analysts of that genocide are convinced that it could have been prevented or stopped if strong religious protests against the genocide had been raised. But that same negative example also shows that religion is a key part of the problem where genocide is concerned. Religion can separate people; it can legitimate violence that is genocidal. If the quality of religious life improves by becoming less exclusive and more inclusive, so will the odds in favor of genocide prevention. Philosophy and philosophers have often worked successfully to help make religion less dogmatic and sectarian, more thoughtful and inclusive. Focused with genocide more consciously in mind, this work needs to continue.

9. Reports, testimonies, films, books, courses, acts of memory and memorialization, legal proceedings, reparation and restitution settlements—these responses keep attention focused on what happens in genocide. They make it more difficult to perpetuate genocide and to ignore the brutality, the killing, and its aftermath. Unfortunately, reports can be buried. Films, books, and courses may be forgotten. Apologies may ring hollow. The past recedes. Life goes on. Reparation and restitution cannot bring back the dead. Justice may not take place. Legal proceedings drag on. Long-term rebuilding falters. Denial gets a hearing. Perpetrators go back to business as usual. Nevertheless, the antidotes for genocide include resistance against the disappearance of what has been seen and felt in genocide's killing fields. Even though they cannot set everything right, reparation, restitution, and courts of law play crucial parts in the process of preventive memory and policy. Philosophical reflection on genocide has its part to play in these activities, and if it does not take place, memory will be less deep and ethical than it ought to be.

10. Not only are there many non-governmental organizations (NGOs) that do have deep commitments to humanitarian causes, but those

organizations, along with many governmental ones, are staffed by individuals who often display immense courage, persistence, and resilience in battling against genocidal threats. Yet the bad news includes the fact that NGOs may unwittingly aid and abet potentially genocidal regimes by creating or intensifying one set of problems as they respond to another. When to disengage as well as when to engage remain issues that can often be riddled with ambiguity and unintended negative consequences. Such difficulties are among those that never make it possible for us to say with complete assurance that genocide will end, but greater confidence that it can and will end can be legitimately found if philosophy and philosophers bring their critical judgment to bear on these issues of engagement and disengagement.

11. The media possess immense power and sophistication to report accurately, to keep us informed of events in real time, and to cover the globe. Where genocide is concerned, the excuse that "I did not know" or "we were unaware" can no longer have much credibility. But the bad news is that too often the media spin, simplify, and scoop. The spins are multiple, contested, incomplete, more-or-less true, and they reflect "interests"—political, economic, philosophical—that contribute to the ideologies and mistrust in which genocidal dispositions thrive. In no small part, then, the prevention of genocide depends on media committed to that goal. Philosophers and all ethically motivated people also have a part to play in holding the media accountable in this way. The ethical analyses and moral questions of philosophy suggest steps that can be taken in these directions.

Establishing accountability

Giving testimony about his experiences in Bosnia in the 1990s, Kemal Pervanic, a survivor of genocidal ethnic cleansing in the Balkans, said that his story, unfortunately, was "nothing new." Then, as if echoing what Elie Wiesel might have said, he added: "I heard the concept of genocide first *after* it happened."[23]

Along with all ethically concerned persons, philosophy and philosophers can engage in the work of genocide prevention, which hinges first and foremost on establishing institutional accountability—governmental and non-governmental—aimed in that direction. As a result, the questions that most need answering include the following: How do we best establish, support, and encourage institutions to take responsibility to prevent or check genocide and to keep that goal among the highest priorities? Few, if any, questions are more important than that one. After genocide has taken place in the age of genocide that is ours, the credibility of the world's future and philosophy's as well requires philosophers and all caring people to put that question high on their list of priorities.

The beast of genocide does lurk in the dark, as Gregory Stanton said, but the dark is not only the darkness of murderous ignorance, lethal discrimination, and bloodthirsty arrogance. Instead, genocide lurks largely in the darkness of irresponsibility and non-accountability, which prevents too little and intervenes too late. General Dallaire got it right: the disconnection between the experiential and the intellectual must be stopped. He might have substituted *philosophical* for *intellectual*. If that disconnection is stopped, then perhaps genocide can be stopped as well. Caring persons, especially the philosophers among them, have no right to regard those objectives as hopeless.

12
The Holocaust and the Common Good

> I promised to show you a map you say but this is a mural
> then yes let it be   these are small distinctions
> where do we see it from is the question
>   Adrienne Rich, *An Atlas of the Difficult World*

As I worked on this book at the Center for Advanced Holocaust in the United States Holocaust Memorial Museum, the route to my office took me past the Washington Monument and then through an entry and corridors whose walls are inscribed with the words of an American idealism that stands in the sharpest contrast to the aims of Nazi Germany and the "Final Solution" of the so-called Jewish question, which marked so indelibly the aspirations of that genocidal regime. Those inscriptions include Thomas Jefferson's July 4, 1776, affirmations in the Declaration of Independence: All men are created equal. There are inalienable human rights, including "life, liberty, and the pursuit of happiness." They also include a September 27, 1979, statement by Jimmy Carter, the American president who appointed the Commission on the Holocaust that led to the building of the Holocaust Memorial Museum. "Out of our memory ... of the Holocaust," said Carter, "we must forge an unshakable oath with all civilized people that never again will the world ... fail to act in time to prevent this terrible crime of genocide ... We must harness the outrage of our memories to stamp out oppression wherever it exists. We must understand that human rights and human dignity are indivisible."

Carter's statement raises many questions. For example, to what extent does his phrase "never again" ring true, and what should be done with the word *must*, which is repeated three times. In this chapter, however, there are two other points that are especially worth highlighting.

First, there is Carter's emphasis on memory. That emphasis is important because memories (and I use the plural form intentionally so as to include our remembering of particular things) are so crucial to our humanity. Memories are not entirely in our control, but without them we would not be human. More particularly, absent memories we could not be moral creatures, for history would dissolve, and we would be able neither to identify one another as persons nor to make the connections on which ethical decisions depend. Ethics, in short, cannot exist without memory, but given that we human beings have memories, responsibility and specifically moral responsibility are thrust upon us.

Second, Carter's statement about memory is memorable because it has an "edge." He noted, for example, that memories can be *outraged*. Indeed, he suggested that we would not be fully human or ethical if some events, the Holocaust in particular, failed to make our memories outraged. Memories, of course, are a key ingredient in happiness. Without memories, celebration of good things would not make much sense; it could scarcely contain and express much joy. It is also true, however, that memories can be outrageous and outraging because history is so lethal and murderous. The German philosopher G. W. F. Hegel described history aptly when he called it a slaughter-bench. History charges memories with feelings. Outrage is high on that list. Absent such ingredients, ethics would lack passion, intensity, and urgency, although it might be less prone to melancholy and despair.

When Carter spoke about memories being outraged, he used two powerful verbs in that context. Outraged memories have to be *harnessed*, he emphasized. *Harnessed* does not mean hamstrung or paralyzed. As Carter used the term, I think he meant that outraged memory has to be focused, directed, and governed so that attention is paid and work is done in the service of what is good and right. The purpose of harnessing outraged memories, Carter went on to assert, is to *stamp out* oppression wherever it exists. What such a phrase means, how it might be put into practice, what policies it would energize—these are crucial issues to consider. Carter's statement and the questions it raises are part of what can be called the ethics of memory. Such ethics involves deciding what we ought to do with what we have experienced and with what we know. With specific reference to the Holocaust, the ethics of memory would entail that questions otherwise unasked will be raised, that silence otherwise unbroken will be lifted, that indifference otherwise unchallenged will be disputed, that protest, resistance, and compassion otherwise unexpressed will find expression. Put another way, a Holocaust-related ethics of memory should orient people to care for the common good.

What is the common good?

The Holocaust and the common good—those ideas are antithetical or none could be. But as we ponder that relationship and do our best to uphold it, we also need to drive our reflection deep by observing that Nazi Germany did not lack a vision of the common good. To the contrary, its conception of the common good did much to unleash the Holocaust, for Nazi ideology held with a vengeance that the common good, at least for Nazi Germany, entailed a world in which Jews and other allegedly inferior people would not exist. Where the common good is concerned, the Holocaust provides a dual warning: First, that concept's meanings are neither simple nor should they be taken for granted. Second, memory of the Holocaust is crucial for clarifying and defending what the idea of the common good ought to mean. Impressionistically and mural-style, as this chapter's epigraph suggests, consider those propositions further.

Much more than is the case today, discourse used to employ the term *commonwealth*, which American states such as Massachusetts and Kentucky still use in referring to themselves. As that old word implies, people have shared interests and concerns, hopes and aspirations, or they can scarcely be a community at all. Some of those public interests involve respect for the fulfillment of private needs, but many of those interests show that our selves are public. They are constituted by communal ties.

There is no society without individual men and women, but as people live together, a social reality that is more than them, individually or collectively, manifests itself and exerts its influence. Individualistic outlooks tend to lose sight of the fact that living together binds people together by social ties that elude reduction to individual choices and decisions, likings and dislikings. Nevertheless, even individualistic outlooks can recognize the importance of traditions that emphasize how the good of the whole is crucial. That emphasis contends that there is a public interest or, better still, a *common good*. This good refers to the basic features of life that every person needs to thrive, including a home that is safe and secure, sound education, worthwhile work to do, and respect for one's life and liberty.

Such goodness is social. More than the sum of individual efforts and parts, this goodness cannot be entrusted conveniently to "invisible hands" that will secure it—somehow or in the long run, the optimistic assurance always says—as individuals pursue self-interest. The tuning of human loyalties toward what deserves fundamental respect is essential for that outcome. Properly understood, and this point is crucial for our deliberations, such loyalties emphasize realities not only that all Americans or all Germans need but also that all people need—individually and collectively. This qualification is basic, for to the extent that one group's "common good" jeopardizes, intentionally or even inadvertently, the well-being of other groups, then critical scrutiny and correction must loom large.

Among the elements that all people need are justice, truth, and compassion. Such qualities are not abstractions. We feel their presence or absence in the particularities of our lives, even as those qualities transcend such particularities by giving us the perspectives we need to understand, judge, and improve the specific times and places in which we live. Here it is important to underscore that the common good is not separated from self-interest, especially when self-interest is "rightly understood," an important qualification that properly makes a distinction between self-interest and selfishness. To be "rightly understood," self-interest must reveal that we are public selves. We have our private needs, but our selves are public nonetheless because our private needs always have public dimensions. Unless our self-interest is so rightly understood that the common good is cared for in its own right and attended to for its own sake, the significance of life, for each and all, will be less than it can and ought to be.

Mapping a difficult world

One of my favorite American writers is the poet Adrienne Rich. Some of her best work appears in *An Atlas of the Difficult World*. In ancient Greek religion, Atlas was a Titan. He challenged Zeus and paid a price. His punishment was to hold up the sky, although he is sometimes pictured as the one who must hold up the earth. Atlas can make us think of strength. Most often, however, the word "atlas" makes us think of something else. It suggests a book of maps. In this sense, an atlas does not hold up the earth, much less the sky, and yet it does suggest strength of another kind. A good atlas helps us to know where in the world we are, where the earth has been, and what has been happening in it. These days, of course, atlases keep going out of date. The map-drawing and map-revising businesses thrive with the many political, economic, geographical, and religious upheavals that the world has witnessed in the last decades of the twentieth century and the early years of the twenty-first. Good maps, carefully drawn, are needed to help us see where we are going and where we need to be headed.

As the title for a book of poetry, *An Atlas of the Difficult World* suggests a variety of themes: poems as maps, for example, or the poet as Atlas. Rich's poems are about a difficult world, one that she tries to map and perhaps to hold in ways that keep the skies from falling or the earth from going completely out of orbit.

Rich does not view the earth from the sky, however. Whether she writes "From an Old House in America" in Vermont or, in this case, from out West along California's Pacific shore, she stands firmly on American ground. "Here is a map of our country," she begins one entry from her *Atlas*. And then this poetic cartographer lines out words about haunted rivers and seas of indifference, battlefields and shrines, capitals of money and suburbs of acquiescence, blind alleys, crumbling bridges, air inversions, and cemeteries of the poor.[1] Hers is not a map of America the Beautiful. It's about a wasted land, a country that blights nature and corrupts young and old alike, a place that betrays its best ideals and squanders hope. Yet Rich's lamentation is no conventional litany of woe. To the contrary, her yearning for a deeper and higher goodness, her loyalty to truth, justice, and love, makes her map point the way toward the "never-to-be-finished, still unbegun work of repair."[2]

Rich charts poisoned environments. She explores issues of race, class, and gender. Her atlas exposes illusion and disillusionment. But Rich plots all of this decay to protest against the waste that forgets, ignores, or marginalizes "those who could bind, join, reweave, cohere, replenish / ... those needed to teach, advise, persuade, weigh arguments / those urgently needed for the work of perception."[3] The themes that Rich explores in her *Atlas of the Difficult World*, the dilemmas she probes, the memories and hopes she echoes—all of these elements make contact with deep human yearnings.

I can explain what I mean by focusing on some additional examples from Rich's *Atlas*. One of them is a poem about suicides. Drawing on her Jewish tradition, Rich offers a "Tattered Kaddish," a raveled prayer for the dead. This poem praises life even "though it crumbled in like a tunnel / on ones we knew and loved."[4] Rich's praise is inseparable from grief and even rage. It savors the gift, the goodness of life. "How they loved it, when they could," Rich says in honoring those who lived but could not stand to do so anymore. Yet her "Tattered Kaddish" also questions the gift and, implicitly, the Giver of lives that can be so good and yet so broken, so wonderful and yet so full of despair, so filled with love and yet so lonely and bereft.

In 1942, Rich turned 13. Looking back in a 1989–1990 series of poems called "Eastern Wartime," she asks, "What's an American girl in wartime / her permed friz of hair / her glasses for school and the movies / between school and home and ignorantly Jewish / trying to grasp the world through books"?[5] And then this poem jars the reader by quoting a telegram.

Containing information conveyed by German industrialist Eduard Schulte to Dr. Gerhart Riegner, the World Jewish Congress representative in Geneva, the telegram is dated August 11, 1942. Its message, sent through the American legation in Bern, Switzerland, to the US State Department in Washington, DC, reported the existence of a plan for the systematic annihilation of Europe's Jews. Those who received the telegram dismissed its message as unbelievable.

I do not know what, if anything, Adrienne Rich knew about the Holocaust while it was actually happening. Clearly, however, that catastrophe decisively marked her identity. For instance, in a 1990 poem called "1948: Jews," she apparently ponders her college experience at Radcliffe when she observes, "It was a burden for anyone / to be fascinating, brilliant / after the six million / Never mind just coming home / and trying to get some sleep / like an ordinary person."[6] Rich is intent on remembering, on taking the responsibility to be moved by memory. In profound ways the Holocaust is one of her answers to the question "Where do I see it from?"

Where do we see it from, and what do we see? Just as a young American dreamer named Stingo experiences a "voyage of discovery" in *Sophie's Choice*, William Styron's controversial novel about the Holocaust raises other versions of that question.[7] Initiated by Sophie Zawistowska, a fictional Polish Catholic, who, like thousands of her actual Polish sisters and brothers, experienced Auschwitz, Stingo learns in 1947 about a world very different from his own. As Sophie's story unfolds, Stingo undergoes shocks of recognition, including, as he relates the incident, "the absurd fact that on that afternoon, as Sophie first set foot on the railroad platform in Auschwitz, it was a lovely spring morning in Raleigh, North Carolina, where I was gorging myself on bananas."[8] On that day—Styron says it was April Fool's Day, 1943— Stingo was seventeen. He was desperately trying to make the weight requirement for enlistment into the US Marines. He squeaked by. He had not heard of Auschwitz.

American dreams and Holocaust questions—in some ways these dimensions of life are as different as the experiences of Sophie and Stingo in April 1943. And yet those realities intersect and challenge each other. Sometimes they produce shocks of recognition in ways that make one wonder about the interdependence of all human actions, about what is—and is not—sacred and ultimately deserving of loyalty. Additional lines in Styron's narrative about Stingo and Sophie show how and why.

In Styron's novel, Stingo meets Sophie Zawistowska in "a place as strange as Brooklyn," but their shared experience climaxes in Washington, DC. "We walked through the evening in total silence," Stingo recalls. "It was plain that Sophie and I could appreciate neither the symmetry of the city nor its air of wholesome and benevolent peace. Washington suddenly appeared paradigmatically American, sterile, geometrical, unreal." The reason, Stingo adds, was that Auschwitz "stalked my soul."[9]

Stingo's experience in Washington, DC, would have taken place almost sixty years ago. Although the city is still paradigmatically American and its symmetry remains, much about our nation's capital has also changed. On one hand, now there is probably less an "air of wholesome and benevolent peace" than there was then. On the other, perhaps there are today more people walking through the evening in total silence. For now Americans not so different from Stingo are visiting the United States Holocaust Memorial Museum in huge numbers—millions since the Museum was formally dedicated on April 22, 1993—and thus, like Stingo, they may be finding that Auschwitz stalks their souls too. If so, what would that presence do to American dreams? Should it make them "paradigmatically American, sterile, geometrical, unreal" or should Holocaust questions make something else of those dreams?

As we Americans consider those questions, it bears remembering that David S. Wyman, the leading authority on the subject, hits the target when he writes about "the abandonment of the Jews" by the United States during the Hitler era.[10] In the late 1930s, restrictive immigration possibilities meant that the American Dream of Emma Lazarus—the Jewish poet whose words "Give me your tired, your poor, / Your huddled masses yearning to breathe free" are inscribed on the Statue of Liberty— would be a dream tragically deferred for many of her own people who might have escaped the Holocaust. "Negative attitudes toward Jews," Wyman shows, "penetrated all sectors of wartime America."[11] Even after public governmental acknowledgment in December 1942 that the Jews were being slaughtered en masse, the American government was not moved to take action specifically directed at alleviating Jewish plight. Not least of the reasons for that inaction was American antisemitism, some of it deeply imbedded in American Christianity. According to Wyman, polls taken from August 1940 until the war's end showed that 15–24 percent of the respondents "looked upon Jews as 'a menace to America.' "[12] Such ingredients conspired to yield a record less noble than the American Dream might like to envision.

Nor does the Holocaust's shadow on American ground stop there. Formerly the director of the Office of Special Investigations, a division of the US Department of Justice established in 1979 to identify and prosecute Nazi criminals in America, Allan S. Ryan, Jr., hoped the nation's "record in dealing with Nazi war criminals is not entirely beyond salvage," but he also estimated that hundreds, if not thousands, of German and Eastern European war criminals found a haven here after World War II. "The record is clear," asserts Ryan. "Preventing the entry of Nazi criminals to the United States was not a high priority, and was not taken seriously."[13]

Such a report would have saddened but not surprised Ralph Ellison. In 1945 he was working on a different narrative when what he identified as the "blues-toned laughter" of his great novel *Invisible Man* began to dominate his imagination. Eventually the laughter compelled him to give full expression to its voice, which belonged to the invisible man "who had been forged," the author noted, "in the underground of American experience and yet managed to emerge less angry than ironic."[14]

Ellison's postponed story was to be about an American pilot. Downed by the *Luftwaffe* and interned in a Nazi POW camp, he was the highest ranking officer there and thus, owing to war's conventions, the spokesman for his fellow prisoners. Like Ellison himself, the American pilot was black. Prisoner of racists and also the "leader" of prisoners who in normal American circumstances would not see him as their equal, let alone as their superior, Ellison's pilot would have to navigate his way between the democratic ideals he affirmed and "the prevailing mystique of race and color." This dilemma, Ellison adds, was to be "given a further twist of the screw by [the black pilot's] awareness that once the peace was signed, the German camp commander could immigrate to the United States and immediately take advantage of freedoms that were denied the most heroic of Negro servicemen."[15]

If Ralph Ellison never finished that story, his pilot's voice, like that of *Invisible Man* would seem to echo Langston Hughes's 1938 poem, "Let America Be America Again": "Oh yes, / I say it plain, / America never was America to me, / And yet I swear this oath—/ America will be! / Its dream lies deep in the heart of me."[16]

Auschwitz shadows the American Dream. In William Styron's story about Sophie Zawistowska, an SS doctor gave her a choiceless choice. She could pick which of her two children, Jan or Eva, should go to the gas. "Ich kann nicht wählen!"—I cannot choose—she screamed.[17] Sophie could not choose. And yet, so as not to lose them both, she let

Eva go. Limited though it was, Sophie's choice was real. So was her sense of guilt. Set free in 1945, she found her way to the United States. "But," as the lyric from *Les Misérables* so aptly states, "there are dreams that cannot be, / And there are storms we cannot weather." Liberation left Sophie in the shadow of Birkenau. She found inescapable the conclusion that her own life, even in America where she hoped for a new beginning, was not worth living. In 1947 Sophie let it go—also by choice.

Dreams die hard in America. In *Sophie's Choice*, Stingo, the white Presbyterian Southerner, cannot prevent Sophie's suicide. But Stingo endures, having learned much about himself, about American racial guilt, about his own American Dream. Three fragments from a journal he kept in 1947 form the novel's conclusion. "*Someday I will understand Auschwitz*"—like many American dreams, that vow, Stingo reflects years later, is "innocently absurd." "*Let your love flow out on all living things*"— that one is worth saving "as a reminder of some fragile yet perdurable hope." Finally, some poetry: "*Neath cold sand I dreamed of death / but woke at dawn to see / in glory, the bright, the morning star.*"[18] Facing despair, Stingo finds ways to revive determination to choose life and hope again. If freedom to choose destroyed Sophie, apparently Stingo tries to resist that fate by using choice against itself in a struggle to make life more worth living and not less so.

Styron does not tell us whether Stingo succeeded, but the question "Where do we see it from?" remains. The responses we make to it, including what we see in that process, will either inform the atlas of our difficult world or we shall lack a map of our country to guide us well in pursuing the common good that all of us need to honor and respect.

Responsibility during and after the Holocaust

It is a long trip from Washington, DC, to a village called Le Chambon, for that place is situated in southeastern France. Le Chambon is not exactly a household name. Still, that place has become much better known than its residents could have imagined sixty years ago. The story that surrounds the attention it has received merits consideration in the context of our reflections about the Holocaust and the common good.[19]

For decades, centuries even, Le Chambon and the farms in its vicinity had little that was noteworthy about them. Located well off the beaten track on a plateau in a rather mountainous region of France, Le Chambon had a population that was poor and Protestant. For the most part, the families of Le Chambon were descendants of a Huguenot religious minority that had been violently persecuted in earlier French history. In 1934, a couple named André and Magda Trocmé had come to live among them. During World War I, André Trocmé had lived in a part of France occupied by Germany, a fate that would repeat itself during World War II. As Trocmé saw the devastation of World War I, he became friends with a German medic who believed that Christians should not kill. Influenced by the medic's example, Trocmé gradually forged a religious outlook that stressed nonviolent resistance to evil, which he defined as doing harm to human life. In Trocmé's view, the injunction not to kill, however, was insufficient; it had to be supplemented by positive action to relieve suffering and to block harm's way.

Trocmé's views, which he came to hold as a Protestant pastor, were not widely popular, and so it was that he had been shunted to the backwater community of Le Chambon, where he was serving as the minister of the main church in the area when Nazi Germany invaded France in May 1940. France fell to the Nazis in a few weeks. Geography placed Le Chambon in Vichy, the unoccupied region south of the Loire River where the Germans permitted a puppet government, under France's World War I hero, Henri Philippe Pétain. Within a few months of the fall of France, the Vichy regime enacted its own harsh anti-Jewish legislation and authorized the internment of foreign Jews. Measures in the occupied zone were even more punitive and swiftly applied. Deportations of Jews from France to Auschwitz began in March 1942. By late 1942, as the Allies rolled back German gains in North Africa, the Germans occupied the Vichy zone of France, leaving few havens of any kind for Jews on French soil. Le Chambon, however, would remain one of them.

Earlier, during the winter of 1940–41, Magda Trocmé had answered an evening knock at her door. A frightened woman identified herself as a German Jew. She had heard that there might be help in Le Chambon. Could she come in? Magda Trocmé's answer was "naturally." That single word says a great deal. From then on, Jewish refugees arrived in Le Chambon almost daily. None was turned away. They were fed, hidden, and whenever possible spirited across the Swiss border by cooperating Christians, some devout and some not, who were convinced that it was simply wrong to leave anyone in harm's way.

Why these acts did not bring full German retribution to Le Chambon has not been fully explained, for the activities were never completely secret. One crucial reason, however, has been identified, namely, a Major Julius Schmäling, the German officer who had governmental responsibilities for two years when the Germans occupied this region of France. He knew what the people of Le Chambon were doing and let it happen. Likewise, André and Magda Trocmé and their followers knew that they had some protection, and they did not let their opportunity slip away.

Some 75,000 Jews in France lost their lives in the Holocaust. The lifeguards of Le Chambon rescued about 5,000 Jews. In the Holocaust's immense destruction, that number is relatively small. Nevertheless it also stands as large because it shows not only what did happen when those people were determined to save lives that were in harm's way but also what might have happened if others had followed their example.

At this point, depart from the narrative to consider two other significant aspects of our knowledge about Le Chambon. First, and this point is one that I will revisit later, it is important to see that the people of Le Chambon did not do "everything" but instead did what they could for the common good. For instance, they saved lives, several thousand of them, and in the process they prevented the Germans from harming those people too, but the people of Le Chambon did not and could not prevent World War II or stop the Holocaust. Nevertheless, they did what they could. Indeed, without expecting recognition or reward, they arguably did *all* that they could to help the most needy among them.

When asked why they did these things, the rescuers in Le Chambon were extremely modest. Needy people such as those who knocked on Magda Trocmé's door should be helped, they said. It was the natural and right thing to do. Wouldn't anyone do the same? To me, and perhaps to you, such reasoning creates huge challenges. The people of Le Chambon were moral heroes or no persons could be, but the reason that they were notable was not because they "saved the world" or did "everything." It was because they did what they could in the particular times and places where they lived and worked. That challenge is the one that the example of Le Chambon puts before anyone who is concerned about ethics and the common good after the Holocaust. It should make us see and remember that limited though our power may be, we still have time and energy that can be used to prevent harm, save lives, and improve the chances for people to care for one another. Such work is not ours to complete, but it is ours to do, lest it goes undone and too little blocks and reverses harm's way.

Second, it is worth noting that two people, in particular, have played leading parts in making Le Chambon well known. As we think about the Holocaust and the common good, a word about each of them can be helpful. About twenty-five years ago, I met a film maker in Los Angeles, who happened to be taking an evening course that I was teaching about the Holocaust and the writings of Elie Wiesel. As I got to know Pierre Sauvage, I learned not only that he was making a film about Le Chambon but also that he had been born there in 1944, for his parents were among the Jewish refugees who had found refuge in that village. Sauvage has established a foundation that has built a memorial and a museum at Le Chambon, but his film about the village has probably done more than anything to call attention to that place and to the moral example it embodies.

Weapons of the Spirit is the title of Sauvage's film. That title comes from the New Testament passage on which André Trocmé preached soon after France fell to Nazi Germany. The text of that sermon still exists, and in it Trocmé referred to the importance of what St. Paul calls the weapons of the spirit or the weapons of righteousness, which are to be used to resist evil. Those weapons, as Trocmé and Sauvage have understood them, are acts that seek to remove people from harms's way, which entails trying to remove the conditions in which harm-doing flourishes.

Meanwhile, Sauvage's research for the film turned up many other fascinating details. One of them is that a member of the French Resistance, Albert Camus, the French novelist and philosopher, lived in the vicinity of Le Chambon when that community rescued Jews. It is likely that Camus knew of the activities there while he was writing his important metaphorical novel, *The Plague*. Set in the Algerian city of Oran in the 1940s, Camus's story chronicles the battle that Dr. Bernard Rieux fights against a lethal outbreak of bubonic plague. In the novel, the plague eventually leaves Oran, but Dr. Rieux, who did all that he could to fight it, finds nothing final about the victory. "The plague bacillus never dies or disappears for good," he says at the novel's end. The fight against it, he concludes, must be "never ending."[20]

A few years before Pierre Sauvage completed his film, a philosopher named Philip Hallie (1922–94) published a book about Le Chambon, which is called *Lest Innocent Blood Be Shed*. He is the second person who contributed greatly to our early knowledge about the French village and the rescuers who lived there. An American Jew and a World War II veteran, Hallie spent his life teaching and writing about ethics, about what he called "the preciousness of human life." But he was also haunted by his military experience in Europe, which involved unleashing artillery barrages that had killed many people. With intended irony, he spoke of himself as a "decent killer." Hallie admired Le Chambon greatly. He was also intently interested in Major Schmäling, the German officer who had made a contribution to the rescue efforts there. However, Hallie also said that something in him "resented the village," because, as he put it, the people in Le Chambon had done little to stop Hitler. It had taken "decent killers" like himself, said Hallie, to crush Nazi Germany's cruel march.[21]

"No ideas but in facts," Hallie liked to say, "no ideas but in things."[22] He called himself a skeptic. His skepticism, I believe, helps to support the common good, for it had two parts: (1) a suspicion of abstraction, closure, and finality and (2) a conviction that details, particularities, and facts contain moral insights and have lessons to teach if we pay attention. "Lucidity and passion," he urged, "that's my motto." Hallie knew much about ancient philosophy. He reminded people that the early skeptics were doctors. Lucidity meant getting as clear as possible about what was happening, especially if disease was the focal point. Knowing what was going on was not enough, however, especially if disease was the focal point. Passion sharpened the focus. Hallie's skepticism entailed that one must be moved to act and, in particular, stirred to get people out of harm's way and to give them help.

Hallie's skepticism resisted moral indifference and ethical relativism. His blend of lucidity and passion, forged in the continuing collision between his wartime killing and his moral philosophy's emphasis on the preciousness of individual human life, stressed that right and wrong are matters of fact, not opinion. To say that it is wrong to be tortured or starved, or to say that the people of Le Chambon did the right thing when they welcomed Jewish refugees, should not succumb to the relativist's subverting and often bullying question, "Who's to say?" When challenged to prove that more than opinion is involved in those judgments, Hallie understood that "I cannot prove this belief in the way I can prove that I am alive," but, he argued, there is an expert, qualified judgment in such cases, and it belongs especially to "the drowned ones and the saved ones. ... They know."[23]

For Hallie, knowledge could never be purely "objective," for there is no such thing as pure objectivity. Knowledge roots itself in experience; human experience, in turn, depends on our embodied selves and the times and places of the communities in which we live and on which we depend. The fact that knowledge exists in a historical context, however, does not mean that it is reduced to opinions on the grounds that human judgments are merely "subjective." Instead, Hallie's skepticism understood that the quality of experience determines the qualifications of the knowledge claims that are made. It is not, for instance, the judgment of the perpetrators or the bystanders that counts the most, if at all, when the claim in question is that the Holocaust was wrong. As Hallie put the point, "cruelty has authority and that authority is its *victims*. The victim of cruelty has an empirical authority like the authority of a doctor who's observing a patient, or better yet, like the authority of a patient about his or her own feelings."[24]

Hallie was an eloquent storyteller. Wrestling with the dilemmas he felt from his own life and its contrast with Le Chambon, he sometimes referred to a hurricane. One year, he recalled, a hurricane had reached his Connecticut home, where he observed its havoc. But havoc was not all that Hallie saw. Even while the storm raged all around, there was space for calm and quiet within the hurricane's eye. Hallie's eye, moreover, was drawn to the pale blue sky overhead. From an ethical point of view, I believe, blue was his favorite color.

Hallie's hurricane experience contained vision that provided him with moral insight. Hallie embraced much of Albert Camus's thought, and thus in ways akin to Dr Rieux's struggle with the plague, Hallie liked to say that we are in the hurricane, and we must not forget how menacing that place will always be. Within the storm, however, there can be space like the haven provided by Le Chambon. More than that, Hallie's passion, as he put it, was to "expand the blue." Some persons, he added, "make a larger space for blue, for peace, for love." Such work, he insisted, "takes power as well as love. It takes force of will. It takes assertion and commitment."[25] Without those qualities, he could have gone on to say, the common good is weakened and imperiled.

Along with Dr Rieux, Camus himself served the common good by battling the plague. Philip Hallie said "it's the hurricane we're in. Don't forget it." Like Camus, he did not see that condition as one that should bring on resignation, indifference, and hopelessness. To the contrary, he saw that our condition also contained the possibility of resistance and creative change. In such possibility, ethical resources to keep the plague from paralyzing us and the hurricane from overwhelming us can be found. Even in the shadow of Birkenau such resources are all around and within us, waiting to be discovered and rediscovered for the common good, if only we do not overlook the fact that even small deeds and modest actions can be lifesaving and if we remember to take nothing good for granted.

Epilogue: Standing Here

> How you stand here is important.
> William Stafford

About as far from Birkenau as one can get, the town where my granddaughter lives is called Winthrop. It sits small in the Methow Valley, a place of spectacular beauty on the eastern slope of the majestic Cascade Range, far north in the state of Washington. Native Americans knew that valley and its glistening rivers long before it became one of the last places in the American West to be settled by white men and women. While I was working on this book during a December 2004 visit with my granddaughter, Keeley Brooks, I was also reading the words of a writer who was new to me, just as Elie Wiesel had been some thirty-five years ago. I discovered that the poet William Stafford (1914–93) is one of America's national treasures.

Stafford's poems focus on the natural world, often on our abuse of it. Also drenched in history, his verse laments the carnage we human beings inflict and encourages resistance against it. Although the Holocaust was not Stafford's theme, he knew plenty about war and genocide—his Indian heritage saw to that—and in works such as *Traveling Through the Dark* and *The Darkness Around Us Is Deep*, he wondered, as Wiesel did in *Night*, whether, ultimately, only the darkness was there. In a poem called "Meditation," for example, he writes as follows: "Animals full of light / walk through the forest / toward someone aiming a gun / loaded with darkness. / That's the world: God / holding still / letting it happen again, / and again and again."[1] Such words are not ones of resignation and despair. They voice protest and the possibility of creative change instead.

In Washington, DC, the United States Holocaust Memorial Museum stands next to the headquarters of the US National Forest Service. So it is worth observing that two forest rangers contacted William Stafford one day. They had an unusual request: Would he help them create "poetry road signs" for the North Cascades highway? Winter snow buries that breathtaking road, and the threat of avalanches closes it down for five or six months each year. But several of William Stafford's specially written poems are there to reappear and offer guidance when the road reopens and travelers are on their way through the mountains again.

One of those poems is called "Being a Person." It invites a reader/viewer to contemplate the Methow River as its clear, cold water rushes to the Columbia and then to the Pacific. Its reflections make a good ending and beginning for any stock-taking, but especially one that asks how we should respond to what happened to ethics during the Holocaust and what we should make of ethics in the shadow of Birkenau. "Be a person here," writes Stafford. "How you stand here is important. How you / listen for the next things to happen. How you breathe."[2] Whatever else it may be, ethics after the Holocaust is about those things: what we hear as we listen for what is happening, how we breathe, how we stand. Nothing could be more important.

Notes

Prologue: Only the Darkness?

1. Elie Wiesel, *Night*, trans. Stella Rodway (New York: Bantam Books, 1982), p. 22.
2. Ibid., p. 24.
3. Ibid., p. 22.
4. Ibid., p. 23.
5. Ibid., p. 22.
6. Ibid., p. 24.
7. Ibid., p. 24.
8. Ibid., p. 25. David Olère (1902–85), the exceptional Jewish artist who drew "Krematorium III, Auschwitz 2 Birkenau," which appears on this book's cover, saw the flames and shadows of Birkenau close up. Born in Warsaw, Poland, he was in France when a roundup trapped him on February 20, 1943. Soon deported to Auschwitz, where he was interned from March 2, 1943, to January 19, 1945, Olère was conscripted into the *Sonderkommando*, special squads of inmates whom the Nazis required to facilitate the gassing and burning of Europe's Jews. He was one of the few who survived that hideous work. After his May 1945 liberation from the Nazi camp at Ebensee, a subcamp of Mauthausen in Austria, he used his artistic ability to portray and document what he had seen. His art raises the question, "What happened to ethics during and after the Holocaust?" For more information about Olère and his Holocaust art, see David Olère and Alexandre Olèr, *Witness: Images of Auschwitz* (N. Richland Hills, TX: West Wind Press, 1998). The cover art comes from *Witness*, p. 19, and is used by permission.
9. Wiesel, *Night*, p. 31.
10. Ibid., p. 32.
11. This statement is from Elie Wiesel's foreword to Harry James Cargas, *Shadows of Auschwitz: A Christian Response to the Holocaust* (New York: Crossroad, 1990), p. ix.
12. Elie Wiesel, *All Rivers Run to the Sea: Memoirs* (New York: Alfred A. Knopf, 1995), p. 76. The change in the spelling of Madame Schächter's name is Wiesel's.
13. Ibid., p. 79.
14. See Hilberg's comments in Claude Lanzmann, *Shoah: An Oral History of the Holocaust* (New York: Pantheon Books, 1985), p. 70.
15. I shall use the terms *antisemitism and antisemitic* instead of *anti-Semitism* and *anti-Semitic*. Particularly in the later decades of nineteenth-century German politics, and then with a vengeance during the Nazi years, the term *Semite* was exploited to set Jews apart from non-Jews, including even from other so-called Semitic peoples—Arabs, for example—and particularly to reinforce a negative, race-based perception of Jews and Judaism. The hyphenated and capitalized form *anti-Semitism* and its variations honor, however inadvertently, distinctions that are erroneous and misleading. Jews are not a race,

nor is the category "Semite" a clear one. The forms *antisemitism* and *antise-mitic* retain the prejudicial, anti-Jewish meaning, but they also protest the harmful confusions that attend the hyphenated and capitalized forms of those terms. Spelling can be a consequential matter. In this case, it is an important part of ethics during and after the Holocaust.

1   The Philosopher's Project

1. Jostein Gaarder, *Sophie's World: A Novel about the History of Philosophy*, trans. Paulette Møller (New York: Berkeley Books, 1996), p. 30.
2. See Immanuel Kant, *Critique of Pure Reason*, trans. Norman Kemp Smith (New York: Macmillan, 1963), p. 635.
3. See Henri Bergson, *Mind-Energy: Lectures and Essays*, trans. H. Wildon Carr (London: Macmillan, 1920), pp. 57–8. Although born Jewish, Bergson, who won the Nobel Prize for literature in 1927, was not a practicing Jew. During World War II, after France capitulated to Nazi Germany in June 1940, the puppet Vichy regime installed by the Germans offered to excuse the famous philosopher from its anti-Jewish laws. Bergson refused to accept this exemption and identified with the Jewish community by registering as a Jew. His long wait in the winter cold to do so probably contributed to the illness that took his life in early January 1941 at the age of 81.
4. Gaarder, *Sophie's World*, p. 513.
5. José Ortega y Gasset, *What Is Philosophy?*, trans. Mildred Adams (New York: W.W. Norton, 1964), p. 224. The subsequent quotations from Ortega are also found in *What Is Philosophy?* See pp. 61, 62, 66, 74, 84, 220, and 223.

2   Why Study the Holocaust?

1. Charlotte Delbo, *Auschwitz and After*, trans. Rosette C. Lamont (New Haven, CT: Yale University Press, 1995), p. 258. Portions of this chapter draw on my *Holocaust Politics* (Louisville, KY: Westminster John Knox Press, 2001).
2. After the Holocaust, Delbo gathered as much information as she could about every woman who was on her Auschwitz transport. Their stories are told in Charlotte Delbo, *Convoy to Auschwitz: Women of the French Resistance*, trans. Carol Cosman (Boston, MA: Northeastern University Press, 1997). The book was originally published in France in 1965.
3. Charlotte Delbo, *Days and Memory*, trans. Rosette C. Lamont (Marlboro, VT: Marlboro Press, 1990), p. 2.
4. The quotation is from Littell's concluding plenary speech at Remembering for the Future 2000, a major international conference on the Holocaust held in Oxford, England, July 16–23, 2000. See John K. Roth and Elisabeth Maxwell, eds., *Remembering for the Future: The Holocaust in an Age of Genocide*, 3 vols. (New York: Palgrave, 2001), 3:8–9.
5. On these points see Zygmunt Bauman, *Modernity and the Holocaust* (Ithaca, NY: Cornell University Press, 1991) and Jonathan Glover, *Humanity: A Moral History of the Twentieth Century* (New Haven, CT: Yale University Press, 2000).
6. Calel Perechodnik, *Am I a Murderer? Testament of a Jewish Ghetto Policeman*, ed. and trans. Frank Fox (Boulder, CO: Westview Press, 1996).
7. Ibid., p. 9.

8. Richard L. Rubenstein, *The Cunning of History: The Holocaust and the American Future* (New York: Harper Torchbooks, 1987), p. 91. The italics are Rubenstein's.

9. For an important study of bystanders during the Holocaust, see Victoria J. Barnett, *Bystanders: Conscience and Complicity during the Holocaust* (Westport, CT: Praeger, 2000), which eloquently makes the case that the inaction and indifference of the bystander—a category containing vastly more human beings than those of perpetrator, victim, or rescuer—is extremely important when the questions are "Why did the Holocaust happen?" and "Will genocide ever end?" Omer Bartov complements Barnett's account when he writes: "The majority of the estimated 300 million people under German rule during the Holocaust were neither victims of the camps nor perpetrators. They were bystanders of various degrees and types. Some belonged to Greater Germany, and their kin were either fighting for Hitler or running his camps. Others belonged to Germany's allies, and more likely than not were more supportive of the partnership with the Third Reich in the early phases of the war than toward the end. Others still belonged to the occupied nations, and stood a good chance of becoming victims themselves, especially if they resisted Nazi policies or tried to protect those slated for extermination. But by and large, those who did not carry out genocide and related atrocities, and those who were not subjected to these policies, namely, the vast majority of German-occupied Europe's population, mostly watched in silence or did their best not to see at all. ... Genocide cannot take place without a majority of passive bystanders." See Omer Bartov, ed., *The Holocaust: Origins, Implementation, Aftermath* (New York: Routledge, 2000), p. 204. Points akin to those emphasized by Barnett and Bartov are effectively amplified in Gordon J. Horowitz, "Places Far Away, Places Very Near: Mauthausen, the Camps of the Shoah, and the Bystanders," in Michael Berenbaum and Abraham Peck, eds., *The Holocaust and History: The Known, the Unknown, the Disputed, and the Reexamined* (Bloomington: Indiana University Press, 1998), pp. 409–20. See also Gordon J. Horowitz, *In the Shadow of Death: Living Outside the Gates of Mauthausen* (New York: The Free Press, 1990).

10. Michael Berenbaum, *The World Must Know: The History of the Holocaust as Told in the United States Holocaust Memorial Museum* (Boston, MA: Little, Brown and Company 1993), p. 220.

11. An insightful study of rescue during the Holocaust is David P. Gushee, *The Righteous Gentiles of the Holocaust: A Christian Interpretation*, rev. edn. (St. Paul, MN: Paragon House, 2003).

12. For an important discussion of these themes, see Peter J. Haas, *Morality after Auschwitz: The Radical Challenge of the Nazi Ethic* (Philadelphia, PA: Fortress Press, 1988). Related topics are discussed in Claudia Koonz, *The Nazi Conscience* (Cambridge, MA: Harvard University Press, 2003) and John K. Roth, ed., *Ethics after the Holocaust: Perspectives, Critiques, and Responses* (St. Paul, MN: Paragon House, 1999).

13. Even with respect to Berenbaum's appealing idea that the Holocaust is a negative absolute, this judgment remains valid. There is no guarantee that universal moral reason or intuition exists or that, if they do, they will automatically conclude without disagreement that the Holocaust is a negative absolute. In ethics, the human will is decisive in determining how good and evil, right and wrong are understood. Reason and intuition inform our willing and choosing, but without the latter, our senses of good and evil, right

and wrong, lack the force that gives them full reality and makes them effective. Willing and choosing alone do not determine what is ethical, but in the fullest sense no determination of right and wrong takes place without them. For a careful and important ethical study that emphasizes rationality in a more universalistic way, see David H. Jones, *Moral Responsibility in the Holocaust: A Study in the Ethics of Character* (Lanham, MD: Rowman & Littlefield, 1999).

14. Rubenstein, *Cunning of History*, p. 90.
15. Ibid., p. 89.
16. Jean Améry, *At the Mind's Limits: Contemplations by a Survivor on Auschwitz and Its Realities*, trans. Sidney Rosenfeld and Stella P. Rosenfeld (New York: Schocken Books, 1986), p. 86. The book was originally published in 1966.
17. Ibid., p. 28.
18. Ibid., pp. 94–5.
19. Ibid., p. 89.
20. Perechodnik, *Am I a Murderer?*, p. 211.
21. Ibid., p. 209.
22. Ibid., p. 211.
23. Lawrence L. Langer, *Preempting the Holocaust* (New Haven, CT: Yale University Press, 1998), p. 10.
24. Delbo, *Auschwitz and After*, p. 5.
25. The quotation is from a speech that Himmler gave to SS leaders in October 1943. See Paul Mendes-Flohr and Yehuda Reinharz, eds., *The Jew in the Modern World: A Documentary History*, 2nd edn. (New York: Oxford University Press, 1995), p. 685.

3 Handle with Care

1. Peretz's testimony is quoted in Dan Cohn-Sherbok, ed., *Holocaust Theology: A Reader* (New York: New York University Press, 2002), p. 35. The complete text of Bond's poem "How We See" can be found in John K. Roth, *Holocaust Politics* (Louisville, KY: Westminster John Knox Press, 2001), p. 282.
2. See Christopher R. Browning, *Collected Memories: Holocaust History and Postwar Testimony* (Madison: University of Wisconsin Press, 2003), p. x. Browning quotes the late George Mosse, who once said, "Those of us who survey the broad landscape still love the twigs and bushes."
3. See Gideon Greif, *We Wept Without Tears: Testimonies of the Jewish Sonderkommando from Auschwitz* (New Haven, CT: Yale University Press, 2005).
4. Raul Hilberg, *Sources of Holocaust Research: An Analysis* (Chicago: Ivan R. Dee, 2001), p. 204.
5. See, for example, Bauer's letter to the editor in *Holocaust and Genocide Studies* 18 (Spring 2004): 182–3 and also his book *Rethinking the Holocaust* (New Haven, CT: Yale University Press, 2001).
6. I quote from Bauer's letter to the editor, *Holocaust and Genocide Studies*, p. 183.
7. Isaiah Trunk, *Jewish Responses to Nazi Persecution: Collective and Individual Behavior in Extremis*, trans. Joachim Neugroschel and Gabriel Trunk (New York: Stein & Day, 1979), pp. 70–1.
8. Primo Levi, *Survival in Auschwitz: The Nazi Assault on Humanity*, trans. Stuart Woolf (New York: Simon & Schuster, 1996), p. 17.
9. Ibid., p. 123.

10. For the phrase quoted from Levi, see ibid., p. 123.
11. Theodor W. Adorno, *Negative Dialectics*, trans. E. B. Ashton (New York: Seabury Press, 1973), p. 362.
12. Isaiah 43:10. The following paragraphs in this essay are derived from my contributions to Carol Rittner, Stephen D. Smith, and Irena Steinfeldt, eds., *The Holocaust and the Christian World* (London: Continuum Books, 2000), John K. Roth, *Holocaust Politics* (Louisville, KY: Westminster John Knox Press, 2001), and Richard L. Rubenstein and John K. Roth, *Approaches to Auschwitz: The Holocaust and Its Legacy*, rev. edn. (Louisville, KY: Westminster John Knox Press, 2003).
13. Genesis 4:10.
14. A related theme is stressed in *Dabru Emet*, an important contemporary Jewish statement on Christians and Christianity, which was released on September 10, 2000, and endorsed by many leading Jewish rabbis and scholars. In the words of that text, "Without the long history of Christian anti-Judaism and Christian violence against Jews, Nazi ideology could not have taken hold nor could it have been carried out. ... But Nazism itself was not an inevitable outcome of Christianity." The full text of *Dabru Emet* is available on the Internet at: http://www.jcrelations.net/en/?id = 1014.
15. Deuteronomy 6:6–7.
16. See, for example, the April 2, 2004, survey issued by the Pew Research Center for the People and the Press, "Belief That Jews Were Responsible for Christ's Death Increases," which is available on the Internet at: http://people-press.org.
17. Deuteronomy 6:4–5.
18. See Matthew 22:34–40.
19. Luke 10:25–37.
20. The apostle Paul reflects a version of this idea in Romans 11.
21. See Clark M. Williamson, *A Guest in the House of Israel: Post-Holocaust Church Theology* (Louisville, KY: Westminster John Knox Press, 1993).
22. Deuteronomy 30:19.
23. See Gilbert Levine, dir. *The Papal Concert to Commemorate the Holocaust*, The Royal Philharmonic Orchestra (Houston: Justice Records, 1994). The quoted statements are taken from the narrative text that accompanies the recording.
24. Primo Levi, *Collected Poems*, trans. Ruth Feldman and Brian Swann (London: Faber and Faber, 1988), p. 56.

4   Raul Hilberg's Ethics

1. Raul Hilberg, *The Politics of Memory: The Journey of a Holocaust Historian* (Chicago, IL: Ivan R. Dee, 1996), p. 39.
2. Ibid., pp. 39–40.
3. Ibid., p. 40.
4. See Claude Lanzmann, *Shoah: An Oral History of the Holocaust* (New York: Pantheon Books, 1985), p. 70. This book contains the complete text of the film.
5. Raul Hilberg, *The Destruction of the European Jews*, 3 vols. (New Haven, CT: Yale University Press, 2003), p. xii. The quoted words are from Hilberg's preface to the second edition (1985) of *The Destruction of the European Jews*. The third edition (2003) contains Hilberg's prefaces to all of the editions, the first of which appeared in 1961. In this chapter, citations from this book refer to the third edition.

6. I owe the metaphor to Christopher R. Browning, *Collected Memories: Holocaust History and Postwar Testimony* (Madison: University of Wisconsin Press, 2003), p. x. Browning quotes the late George Mosse, who once said, "Those of us who survey the broad landscape still love the twigs and bushes."
7. For the quoted passages, see Lanzmann, *Shoah*, pp. 141–2.
8. Hilberg, *The Politics of Memory*, p. 18.
9. Raul Hilberg, *Sources of Holocaust Research: An Analysis* (Chicago, IL: Ivan R. Dee, 2001), pp. 71, 204.
10. Adler is quoted in Hilberg, *The Politics of Memory*, pp. 202–3.
11. Ibid., p. 202.
12. Raul Hilberg and Stanislaw Staron, "Introduction," in Raul Hilberg, Stanislaw Staron, and Josef Kermisz, eds., *The Warsaw Diary of Adam Czerniakow: Prelude to Doom*, trans. Stanislaw Staron and the Staff of Yad Vashem (Chicago, IL: Ivan R. Dee, 1999), p. 64.
13. Hilberg, *The Politics of Memory*, p. 187.
14. See Lanzmann, *Shoah*, p. 190.
15. Hilberg, *The Politics of Memory*, 188.
16. See Lanzmann, *Shoah*, p. 71.
17. Hilberg tells this story in an article called "The Holocaust," which appears in Paul Woodruff and Harry A. Wilmer, eds., *Facing Evil: Confronting the Dreadful Power behind Genocide, Terrorism, and Cruelty* (Chicago, IL: Open Court, 1988), pp. 99–100.
18. Hilberg, *The Destruction of the European Jews*, p. 1173.
19. See Raul Hilberg, ed., *Documents of Destruction: Germany and Jewry 1933–1945* (Chicago, IL: Quadrangle Books, 1971), p. vi.
20. Hilberg, *The Destruction of the European Jews*, 1090.
21. Ibid., p. 1173.
22. Raul Hilberg, "Incompleteness in Holocaust Historiography," in Jonathan Petropoulos and John K. Roth, eds., *Gray Zones: Ambiguity and Compromise in the Holocaust and Its Aftermath* (New York: Berghahn Books, 2005), p. 75.
23. John K. Dickinson, *German & Jew: The Life and Death of Sigmund Stein* (Chicago, IL: Ivan R. Dee, 2001), p. viii.
24. See Hilberg's introduction in ibid., p. xvii.
25. Ibid., pp. xvii–xviii.
26. I was unaware of this book until an essay by Hilberg called it to my attention in 2004. I purchased a copy "on sale" from a table of remaindered books at the United States Holocaust Memorial Museum.
27. Hilberg, "Incompleteness in Holocaust Historiography," pp. 84–5.
28. Hilberg, *Sources of Holocaust Research*, p. 202.
29. Raul Hilberg, *Perpetrators Victims Bystanders* (New York: HarperCollins, 1992), p. 268.
30. Here my commentary is based on my copy of the videotape of Hilberg's lecture at the University of Oregon. To the best of my knowledge, the lecture has not been published, but some of its historical content, especially comparisons that Hilberg draws between the situations of Jews in Warsaw, Poland, and in Copenhagen, Denmark, can be found in *The Destruction of the European Jews*, pp. 1123–24.

Among the moving moments in Hilberg's lecture at the University of Oregon is a story he tells about a young soldier whose name Hilberg does not mention. It is also important for detecting his ethics. In the summer of 1945, as Hilberg recounts the episode, a unit of American soldiers was in Europe after the Germans had surrendered in May of that year. Some of the veterans were headed home. The younger and less combat-experienced soldiers awaited orders that would send them to the Pacific theater, where many would lose their lives in the final campaigns against the Japanese. Then on August 6, 1945, a major announced that an atomic bomb had been dropped on Hiroshima. "Are there any reactions?" the officer asked. Dead silence prevailed until a 19-year-old GI rose and said, "An atomic bombing that destroys a city is an immoral act." He sat down. No one else said a word.

Having reviewed the Hilberg lecture as I was writing this chapter, I wondered—not for the first time—how Hilberg knew this story. Perhaps, it occurred to me, that young soldier was Hilberg himself. On February 16–17, 2005, I spoke with Hilberg at the United States Holocaust Memorial Museum. In those conversations, he confirmed my hunch. He also talked about the killing of SS men at Dachau by American soldiers. He did not witness those events first-hand but saw photos of the killing and talked with people who knew about it. Those Americans, Hilberg believed, did not kill sadistically but out of anger after seeing train cars filled with corpses. The victims had simply been left to die after being transported from Buchenwald to Dachau, which did not want to receive them. Hilberg further stated that he had changed his mind about the death penalty after the trial and execution of Adolf Eichmann in 1961. When I asked why, Hilberg gave two reasons. First, on utilitarian grounds, he would have wanted to interview Eichmann and his ilk. Second, as an atheist, he felt that the line that had to be held to prevent nihilism was the right to life, which he takes to be absolute.

31. Hilberg, *The Destruction of the European Jews*, p. 1085.
32. For an instructive source on this point, see Leon Goldensohn, *The Nuremberg Interviews: An American Psychiatrist's Conversations with Defendants and Witnesses*, ed. Robert Gellately (New York: Alfred A. Knopf, 2004). Goldensohn monitored the mental health of the Nazi defendants who stood trial before the International Military Tribunal at Nuremberg in 1945–46. He also interviewed Nazis who were witnesses in those trials, including Rudolf Höss, the former SS commandant of Auschwitz, and Otto Ohlendorf, the SS general who commanded *Einsatzgruppe* D on the eastern front, a shooting squadron responsible for some 90,000 Jewish deaths. Goldensohn's interviews show these men to be largely devoid of anything resembling guilt, remorse, or repentance for their actions.
33. Hilberg, *The Destruction of the European Jews*, pp. 1059, 1084.
34. See ibid., pp. 1085–1104.
35. Hilberg, *Sources of Holocaust Research*, p. 134.
36. Hilberg, *The Destruction of the European Jews*, p. 1296.
37. I am indebted to the historian Gregory Weekes, who video-recorded Hilberg's response at Brown University and kindly shared that document with me.

5 Gray Zones and Double-Binds:
Holocaust Challenges to Ethics

1. See "The Essential and the Superfluous," Levi's 1987 interview with Robert Di Caro, in Primo Levi, *The Voice of Memory: Interviews, 1961–1987*, ed.

Marco Belpoliti and Robert Gordon, trans. Robert Gordon (New York: The New Press, 2001), p. 175.

2. Primo Levi, *The Drowned and the Saved*, trans. Raymond Rosenthal (New York: Summit Books, 1988), p. 38.
3. Ibid., p. 48.
4. Ibid., p. 53.
5. Ibid., p. 41. In an important book called *Jewish Resistance during the Holocaust: Moral Uses of Violence and Will* (New York: Palgrave Macmillan, 2004), James M. Glass shows how the Holocaust produced a disintegration of ethics akin to the outcomes that Levi witnessed in Auschwitz. He describes two types of Jewish resistance to that disintegration. One form, spiritual resistance, did not eliminate useless suffering and death, but it allowed the dying a modicum of dignity and perhaps helped to keep ethical hopes alive. The other form, violent resistance, developed an ethic of its own, one that gave priority to survival and legitimated what was necessary to improve the odds for it. Glass's lucid and realistic account helps to show how the status and content of understandings of right and wrong are influenced by power configurations.
6. Levi, *The Drowned and the Saved*, p. 202.
7. Ibid., p. 69.
8. See Peter J. Haas, *Morality after Auschwitz, The Radical Challenge of the Nazi Ethic* (Philadelphia, PA: Fortress Press, 1988). For further discussion on this important theme, see also John K. Roth, ed., *Ethics after the Holocaust* (St. Paul, MN: Paragon House, 1999).
9. Claudia Koonz, *The Nazi Conscience* (Cambridge, MA: Harvard University Press, 2003), p. 1.
10. Quoted in ibid., p. 2. Both Roman Catholic and antisemitic, Schmitt (1888–1985) was a leading German jurist and professor whose expertise included constitutional and international law. He joined the Nazi Party in 1933. His philosophy of law became immensely influential within the Nazi regime. His career in jurisprudence and political philosophy continued long after the defeat of the Third Reich.
11. William T. Stooksbury, ed., *Ethics for the Marine Lieutenant* (Annapolis, MD: Center for the Study of Professional Military Ethics, US Naval Academy, 2002), p. ii.
12. My biographical sketch of Böhm draws on Robert N. Proctor, *Racial Hygiene: Medicine under the Nazis* (Cambridge, MA: Harvard University Press, 1988), pp. 83–5. For this reference and other information about the ten commandments regarding marriage in Nazi Germany, I am indebted to Susan Bachrach at the United States Holocaust Memorial Museum. She served as the project director for the Museum's "Deadly Medicine" exhibit.
13. For more detail on the history covered in the "Deadly Medicine" exhibit, see Dieter Kuntz, ed., *Deadly Medicine: Creating the Master Race* (Washington, DC and Chapel Hill, NC: United States Holocaust Memorial Museum and University of North Carolina Press, 2004). The text cited from Hermann Böhm's book appears on p. 72.
14. Haas, *Morality after Auschwitz*, p. 3.
15. Koonz, *The Nazi Ethic*, p. 1.
16. Hermann Böhm, *Darf ich meine Base heiraten?* (Berlin: Reichsausschuss für Volksgesundheitsdienst, 1935), p. 67.

17. See Koonz, *The Nazi Conscience*, pp. 4–8.
18. Quoted in ibid., p. 7.
19. Ibid., p. 3.
20. Ibid., p. 252.
21. Sarah Kofman, *Smothered Words*, trans. Madeleine Dobie (Evanston, IL: Northwestern University Press, 1998), p. 39.
22. Jean-Luc Nancy, "Foreword: Run, Sarah!" in Penelope Deutscher and Kelly Oliver, eds., *Enigmas: Essays on Sarah Kofman* (Ithaca, NY: Cornell University Press, 1999), p. ix. Deutscher and Oliver provide helpful background—biographical and philosophical—about Kofman in "Sarah Kofman's Skirts," their introduction to *Enigmas*, which also contains a detailed bibliography of Kofman's publications. See pp. 1–22 and 264–75.
23. See especially Charlotte Delbo, *Auschwitz and After*, trans. Rosette C. Lamont (New Haven, CT: Yale University Press, 1995). Delbo was not Jewish, but her activity in the French Resistance led to her arrest and deportation to Auschwitz, which took place on January 24, 1943. She survived Auschwitz and Ravensbrück, a Nazi camp established especially for women.
24. For the English translations of these books, see Kofman, *Smothered Words* and Sarah Kofman, *Rue Ordener, Rue Labat*, trans. Ann Smock (Lincoln: University of Nebraska Press, 1996). Kofman's memory of her father plays an important part in both. *Smothered Words* is dedicated to him and also to the philosophers Maurice Blanchot (1907–2003) and Robert Antelme (1917–90). Blanchot's controversial career included the prewar articles that he wrote for right-wing, antisemitic publications, but also assistance to French Jews during the German occupation and post-war reflections on the Holocaust, particularly *L'Ecriture du désastre* (1980), which influenced Kofman considerably. Antelme was arrested by the Germans because of his work in the French Resistance. His survival of Buchenwald and Dachau led to *L'Espèce humaine* (1957), a philosophical memoir that made an especially strong impression upon Kofman. "To have to speak without being able to speak or be understood, to have to choke," wrote Kofman in *Smothered Words* (p. 39), "such is the ethical exigency that Robert Antelme obeys in *The Human Race*." For the English translations of the books by Blanchot and Antelme, see Maurice Blanchot, *The Writing of the Disaster*, trans. Ann Smock (Lincoln: University of Nebraska Press, 1986) and Robert Antelme, *The Human Race*, trans. Jeffrey Haight and Annie Mahler (Evanston, IL: The Marlboro Press/Northwestern University Press, 1998). All citations from Antelme and Blanchot as well as from *Rue Ordener, Rue Labat* and *Smothered Words* are from the English editions I have noted.
25. Kofman, *Rue Ordener, Rue Labat*, p. 31.
26. Kofman adds the following information about her father:

On 16 July 1942, my father knew he was going to be picked up. It had been rumored that a big roundup was planned for that day. He was rabbi of a small synagogue on the Rue Duc in the 18th arrondissement. He had left home very early that day to warn as many Jews as he could to go into hiding immediately.

Then he came home and waited; he was afraid that if he too were to hide his wife and six young children would be taken in his place. He had three girls and three boys between two and twelve years old.

He waited and prayed to God that they would come for him, as long as his wife and children could be saved (*Rue Ordener, Rue Labat*, p. 5).

About eighty thousand Jews from France were killed in Nazi Germany's extermination camps, mostly at Auschwitz. Approximately one-third of them were French citizens; the majority were immigrants and refugees. Foreign Jews were first deported from France to Auschwitz on March 27, 1942. Facilitated by French police, the roundups and deportations intensified during the summer of 1942. For more background and detail, see David Weinberg, "France," in Walter Laqueur, ed., *The Holocaust Encyclopedia* (New Haven, CT: Yale University Press, 2001), pp. 213–22.

27. Among the multiple double binds that the Holocaust created were the complex dilemmas of identity encountered by hidden children. Kofman illustrates an aspect of that bind when she briefly describes the journey that took her from Rue Ordener, her home street, to a place of hiding and relative safety on Rue Labat. Her reaction seems to run as deep as it was physical. Short in distance and time though it was, that journey "seemed endless to me, and I vomited the whole way" (*Rue Ordener, Rue Labat*, p. 31). Kofman indicates that Mémé, her rescuer, was "not without anti-Semitic prejudices." She also detached Kofman from her mother and Judaism. Yet, Kofman says that she came to love Mémé "more than my own mother." Ending *Rue Ordener, Rue Labat* with Mémé on her mind, Kofman writes, "I was unable to attend her funeral. But I know that at her grave the priest recalled how she had saved a little Jewish girl during the war" (*Rue Ordener, Rue Labat*, pp. 47, 58, 85).

28. Kofman, *Smothered Words*, p. 10.

29. Ibid., pp. 10–11. In this passage Kofman includes two quotations from Blanchot, whose words, along with Antelme's, are frequently quoted in *Smothered Words*. The first quotation is from "After the Fact," Blanchot's afterword to his *Vicious Circles*, trans. Paul Auster (Barrytown, NY: Station Hill Press, 1985), p. 68. The second passage is from *The Step Not Beyond*, trans. Lycette Nelson (Albany: State University of New York Press, 1992), p. 61. Elsewhere Blanchot amplifies and complicates the point made in the first passage quoted by Kofman. "The disaster ruins everything," he writes, "all the while leaving everything intact." That relationship epitomizes another of the Holocaust's double binds, which are so vividly illustrated in Kofman's life and authorship. See Blanchot, *The Writing of the Disaster*, p. 1.

In "A Note on Translation," which helps to introduce *Smothered Words*, Madeleine Dobie observes that Kofman's frequent use of quotations, a style often found in her later writings, "may be seen to attenuate the mastery of the narrative voice through the interposition of the voices of others, and thereby of the Other, the style that Kofman, following Blanchot, calls 'writing without power'. ... *Paroles suffoquées*," continues Dobie, "is at once a scholarly piece that develops arguments supported by quotations and footnotes, and a meditation in the style of Blanchot, in which the conventional privileging of the signified—arguments or ideas—over the signifier—form or the very process of writing itself—is called into question" (p. xxiv). My discussion of Kofman, replete with quotation of her words, modestly tries to emulate her style in that regard.

30. Kofman, *Smothered Words*, p. 9.

31. Kofman, *Smothered Words*, p. 34.
32. Ibid., p. 9.
33. Ibid., p. 9. Kofman cites Theodor Adorno's *Negative Dialectics* as an influence on her thinking about this point.
34. See Richard Rorty, "Human Rights, Rationality, and Sentimentality," in Patrick Hayden, ed., *The Philosophy of Human Rights* (St. Paul, MN: Paragon House, 2001), p. 251.
35. Kofman, *Smothered Words*, p. 39.
36. Kofman, *Rue Ordener, Rue Labat*, p. 3.
37. Ibid., p. 3.
38. Antelme, *The Human Spirit*, p. 3.
39. See Kofman, *Smothered Words*, p. 58, and Antelme, *The Human Race*, p. 220.
40. Kofman, *Smothered Words*, p. 66.
41. Ibid., p. 70.
42. Ibid.
43. Ibid.
44. Ibid.
45. Kofman ends *Smothered Words* with this quotation from Blanchot (see p. 73). The quoted passage comes from *The Infinite Conversation*, trans. Susan Hanson (Minneapolis: University of Minnesota Press, 1993), p. 135.
46. Kofman, *Smothered Words*, p. 73.
47. Ibid., pp. 89–90. Here one thinks of the Nietzschean theme of the revaluation of values.
48. Ibid., p. 73. Kofman mistakenly attributes the quoted phrase to Antelme, but as her translator points out, Theodor Adorno's *Negative Dialectics* is the correct source. "After Auschwitz," he said, "there is no word tinged from on high, not even a theological one, that has any right unless it underwent a transformation." See Theodor Adorno, *Negative Dialectics*, trans. E. B. Ashton (New York: Seabury Press, 1973), p. 367.

6   Post-Holocaust Restitution of a Different Kind

1. See Craig S. Smith, "Leaders Gather to Mark Liberation of Auschwitz," *New York Times*, January 27, 2005.
2. US Department of State, "Report on Global Anti-Semitism, 1 July 2003–15 December 2004," submitted by the Department of State to the Committee on Foreign Relations and the Committee on International Relations in accordance with Section 4 of PL 108–322, December 30, 2004, and released by the Bureau of Democracy, Human Rights, and Labor, January 5, 2005. See p. 1. Available online at: http://www.state.gov/g/drl/rls/40258.htm. All references are to the online version, which is designated hereafter as Report on Global Anti-Semitism.
3. See the Web site for the PBS series: www.pbs.org/Auschwitz. For the Bukiet citation in particular, see: www.pbs.org/auschwitz.understanding/lessons.html.
4. Jacques Chirac, "Discours a l'occasion de l'inauguration du memorial de la Shoah," Paris, January 25, 2005. "L'antisemitisme n'a pas sa place en France," said Chirac. "L'antisemitisme n'est pas une opinion. C'est une perversion. Une perversion qui tue. C'est une haine qui plonge ses racines dan les profondeurs

du mal et dont nulle resurgence ne peut être tolérée." I owe this reference to Paul Shapiro, director of the Center for Advanced Holocaust Studies, United States Holocaust Memorial Museum.

5. *Report on Global Anti-Semitism*, pp. 1–2.
6. Ibid., p. 4.
7. Ibid., pp. 1, 2.
8. Stuart Eizenstat, *Imperfect Justice: Looted Assets, Slave Labor, and the Unfinished Business of World War II* (New York: Public Affairs, 2003), pp. 130, 137–8, 353. Eizenstat's book is an important study of the post-Holocaust reparation and restitution process. The quotation that serves as the epigraph for this chapter is from pp. 344–5. Also indispensable in this field of study is Michael J. Bazyler, *Holocaust Justice: The Battle for Restitution in America's Courts* (New York: New York University Press, 2003).

Perspective on the immense economic damage that the Holocaust inflicted has been provided in April 2005 by an Israeli government report, which took seven years to complete. It puts the material losses inflicted on the Jewish people during the Holocaust—not only looted property but also lost income and wages between US$240 and US$330 billion at current monetary values. The report breaks down those totals as follows: US$125 billion for looted property; US$104 to US$155 billion in lost income; US$11 to US$52 billion in unpaid wages for forced labor. Although various reparation and restitution processes date back to 1948, only a small fraction of the material loss has been recovered. At most, these processes can only approximate justice. They do more to produce political than personal reconciliation. See "Report: Holocaust Damages Cost Up to $330B," *New York Times*, April 20, 2005. In the analysis that follows, I shall emphasize *restitution*. Typically that concept refers to property and possessions (personal or communal) that have been stolen and that ought to be returned to their rightful owners or heirs. Reparations usually involve monetary payment to compensate people or their heirs for abuses of multiple kinds. As the following discussion intends to show, Christians need to make restitution to Jews by doing all that Christians properly can to restore the vitality of Jewish life, which was so much stolen from the Jewish people by Christian hostility toward Jews.

9. Jean Améry, *At the Mind's Limits: Contemplations by a Survivor on Auschwitz and Its Realities*, trans. Sidney Rosenfeld and Stella P. Rosenfeld (New York: Schocken Books, 1986), pp. 30–1. The following commentary about Améry and Jonathan Glover as well as the discussion of useless experience are adapted from my article, "Useless Experience: Its Significance for Reconcilation after Auschwitz," in David Patterson and John K. Roth, eds., *After-Words: Post-Holocaust Struggles with Forgiveness, Reconciliation, Justice* (Seattle: University of Washington Press, 2004).

10. The quotations in this paragraph are from Jonathan Glover, *Humanity: A Moral History of the Twentieth Century* (New Haven, CT: Yale University Press, 1999), pp. 327 and 396.

11. Eventually Nazi "logic" would have put Christianity at risk, too, but unquestionably the racially antisemitic core of National Socialism made the elimination of every trace of Jewish life a "logical," if not political, priority that no other exceeded.

12. Améry, *At the Mind's Limits*, p. 31.
13. This recognition grips me as a Christian who has taught and written about the Holocaust for more than thirty years. Non-Jews can and should do such work, but our consciousness in doing it is fundamentally different from the Jew's because we are not part of the Jewish people, the ones who were targeted for destruction and death. Especially in post-Holocaust circumstances, this crucial difference between Jew and non-Jew remains, no matter how much we non-Jews may express solidarity with the Jewish people, and that difference deserves respect. We non-Jews carry our own Holocaust legacies— usually related to bystanders or perpetrators—and those responsibilities can be awesome enough, but they are not the same as the trauma that stalks Jews whose families were decimated and who themselves would not be alive today if National Socialism's "logic" had prevailed.
14. The quotations in this paragraph are from Primo Levi, *The Drowned and the Saved*, trans. Raymond Rosenthal (New York: Summit Books, 1988), pp. 106, 109, 111, and 119.
15. Améry, *At the Mind's Limits*, p. 24; Glover, *Humanity*, p. 326.
16. Levi, *The Drowned and the Saved*, p. 126.
17. The quotations in this paragraph are from Emmanuel Levinas, "Useless Suffering," in *Entre Nous: On Thinking-of-the-Other*, trans. Michael B. Smith and Barbara Harshav (New York: Columbia University Press, 1998), pp. 94, 97, and 99.
18. Charlotte Delbo, *Auschwitz and After*, trans. Rosette C. Lamont (New Haven, CT: Yale University Press, 1995), pp. 58–9.
19. Levi, *The Drowned and the Saved*, p. 200.
20. Delbo, *Auschwitz and After*, p. 230.
21. Daniel Jonah Goldhagen, *A Moral Reckoning: The Role of the Catholic Church in the Holocaust and Its Unfulfilled Duty of Repair* (New York: Alfred A. Knopf, 2002), pp. 241, 261.
22. Ibid., p. 193.
23. For the most part in this chapter, the capitalized word *Church* refers specifically to the Roman Catholic Church. But much of the discussion focused on that institution is also applicable to other churches and to Christians generally.
24. Goldhagen, *A Moral Reckoning*, p. 21.
25. Ibid., p. 23.
26. Ibid., p. 267.
27. Ibid., p. 167.
28. Ibid., p. 15.
29. See "We Remember: A Reflection on the Shoah," in Carol Rittner, Stephen D. Smith, and Irena Steinfeldt, eds., *The Holocaust and the Christian World: Reflections on the Past, Challenges for the Future* (New York: Continuum, 2000), p. 260.
30. Goldhagen, *A Moral Reckoning*, p. 80.
31. Ibid., p. 165.
32. Ibid., p. 219.
33. Ibid., p. 246.
34. Ibid., p. 259.
35. Ibid., p. 7.
36. Ibid., p. 3.

37. Ibid., pp. 262, 266.
38. On these points, see Andy Newman, "Jewish Groups Mostly Praise the New Pope As a Partner," *New York Times*, April 20, 2005, p. A8.
39. See "The New Pope, In His Own Words," *Washington Post*, April 20, 2005, p. A14.
40. For Goldhagen's reaction to Ratzinger's elevation to the papacy, see "A German Lesson: The Fallacy of One True Path," *Los Angeles Times*, April 22, 2005.
41. Quoted in Daniel Williams, "Benedict XVI Assumes 'This Enormous Task,' " *Washington Post*, April 25, 2005, p. A12.
42. Quoted in Newman, "Jewish Groups Mostly Praise the New Pope As a Partner," p. A14.
43. My account of Pope Benedict XVI's trip to Cologne, Germany, is drawn from Ian Fisher, "At Synagogue, Pope Warns of Rising Anti-Semitism," *New York Times*, August 19, 2005, and Craig Whitlock, "Pope Notes 'Insane' Ideology of Nazis During Synagogue Visit," *Washington Post*, August 19, 2005. Approximately 11,000 Jews from Cologne perished in the Holocaust.

7 Duped by Morality?

1. Emmanuel Levinas, *Totality and Infinity: An Essay on Exteriority*, trans. Alphonso Lingis (Pittsburgh, PA: Duquesne University Press, 1969), p. 21.
2. See Peter J. Haas, *Morality after Auschwitz: The Radical Challenge of the Nazi Ethic* (Philadelphia, PA: Fortress Press, 1988) and Claudia Koonz, *The Nazi Conscience* (Cambridge, MA: Harvard University Press, 2003).
3. The quotation is from the Resolution on Israel and Palestine (2004) that was approved by a vote of 431 to 62 at the 216th General Assembly of the PCUSA. The complete text of the Resolution, plus discussion pertaining to it, is available through the Internet at www.pcusa.org.
4. For the source of the quoted passages and for more information about the General Assembly, go to the PCUSA Web site, www.pcusa.org/generalassembly, and use the link for the General Assembly.
5. This document is available through the Internet at www.pcusa.org.
6. See Vernon S. Broyles III, "Money, Morals & Israel: The Presbyterian Case for Divesting from Israel," *The Christian Century*, February 8, 2005. Broyles's article is part of an important symposium in *The Christian Century*, a leading Protestant weekly. Responses from Barbara Wheeler, president of Auburn Theological Seminary, and Ira Youdovin, executive vice president of the Chicago Board of Rabbis and president of the Council of Religious Leaders of Metropolitan Chicago, disagree with Broyles, whose rebuttal is also part of the exchange. The symposium is available through the Internet at www.christiancentury.org/article.php?articleid=139.
7. See the MRTI's "Guidelines for the Implementation of Divestment Related to Israel and Palestine" (adopted November 6, 2004), which can be found through the Internet at www.pcusa.org. Meeting in Seattle, Washington, on August 5, 2005, the MRTI announced that it would focus attention on four corporations that allegedly contribute to Israeli violence against Palestinians: Caterpillar, ITT Industries, Motorola, and United Technologies. In an attempt at evenhandedness, a fifth company, Citigroup, was also singled out for

allegedly moving "substantial funds from charities later seen to be fronts funneling money to terrorist organizations. Some of these funds ended up as payments to the families of Palestinian suicide bombers." In the MRTI's process of "progressive engagement," the initial strategy is to persuade the corporations to change policies that are judged to enable or support violence between Palestinians and Israelis. If persuasion fails, divestment could follow. It is estimated that the PCUSA's holdings in the five companies total approximately US$60 million. For more detail, see "Mission Responsibility Through Investment" on the PCUSA Web site at: http://pcusa.org/mrti/ actions.htm. See also Laurie Goodstein, "Threat to Divest Is Church Tool in Israeli Fight," *New York Times*, August 6, 2005.

8. The text of the resolution is available through the Internet. See note 3 above.
9. Vernon S. Broyles III, "Occupation Is the Issue: A Rebuttal," *The Christian Century*, February 8, 2005.
10. Bretton-Granatoor was quoted in James D. Davis, "Church Plans Roil Jewish Leaders," *South Florida Sun-Sentinel*, February 13, 2005. From the time that the PCUSA divestment initiative was first announced, Jewish reaction has been sharply critical, as illustrated by the following examples. One Jewish critic is US Congressman Howard L. Berman (D-CA). His letter of protest (dated September 14, 2004) to Clifton Kirkpatrick, Stated Clerk of the General Assembly, charged that "the Presbyterian Church has knowingly gone on record calling for jeopardizing the existence of the State of Israel." His letter contained signatures from thirteen other members of Congress, four of them Jewish, three of them Presbyterian. The letter is available through the Internet at www.house.gov/apps/list/press/ca28_berman/presbyletter.html. Rabbi Eric H. Yoffe, president of the Union for Reform Judaism stated that the PCUSA's action "has caused utter dismay in the Jewish community." See Alan Cooperman, "Israel Divestiture Spurs Clash," *Washington Post*, September 29, 2004, p. A8. Dennis Prager, a respected Los Angeles commentator on religious affairs was even more direct. "Incredibly," he wrote on July 20, 2004, "the General Assembly of the Presbyterian Church (USA) joins the list of religious groups committing evil." Calling the PCUSA action "immoral, sinful and bigoted denigration of the Jewish state," Alan Dershowitz's essay in the *Los Angeles Times* (August 8, 2004) went on to find the divestment initiative "so one-sided, so anti-Zionist in its rhetoric and so ignorant of the realities on the ground that it can only be explained by the kind of bigotry that the Presbyterian Church itself condemned in 1987 when it promised 'never again to participate in, to contribute to, or (insofar as we are able) to allow the persecution or denigration of Jews.' " These examples of criticism, and others like them, did not always grasp correctly all of the details of the Presbyterian divestment initiative, but they made clear how deeply the church's position wounded Presbyterian–Jewish relations. Those relations were harmed further when two PCUSA officials, Kathy Lueckert and Peter Sulyok, members of an October 2004 fact-finding trip to the Middle East, met with officials from Hezbollah, a recognized terrorist organization. They left their PCUSA jobs but not before more needless damage had been done. Jewish unhappiness with Presbyterians was also deepened by the church's support of Congregation Avodat Yisrael, a church for Messianic Jews in the Philadelphia area. Steps have been taken, effective July 1, 2005, to dissolve that relationship.

11. See the WCC Central Committee's news release (February 21, 2005), "WCC Central Committee Encourages Consideration of Economic Measures for Peace in Israel/Palestine," which is available through the Internet at www.2.wcc-coe.org/pressrelease.nsf/index/pr-cc-05-08.html. Noting that "the desire for a just and equitable peace is growing," the WCC document reiterates its 1992 position that "criticism of the policies of the Israeli government is not in itself anti-Jewish," which is a viable distinction but also one that may contain dupery. The WCC approaches that line because its statement is couched in ways that accuse Israel of decades of illegal occupation and "illegal activities in occupied territory [that] continue as if a viable peace for both peoples is not a possibility." The WCC places the fault for the Israeli–Palestinian conflict primarily and emphatically on the doorstep of every Israeli administration since 1967, if not before. Therefore, Christians as well as Jews should think carefully about the most credible responses to the following question: At what point does the distinction between criticism of Israeli policy and anti-Jewish sentiment collapse and/or legitimate, however unintentionally, postures and policies contrary to the interests of the Jewish people precisely because those stances are anti-Israeli? Probably most Jews will answer that question very differently from the WCC. They will be right to do so because their realistic sensibilities about the importance of the state of Israel, its significance for the vitality of the Jewish people, and its precarious situation in the Middle East, which pronouncements from Christian groups can do little to improve but much to worsen, will run deeper and stronger than any Christian's are likely to do. Meanwhile, as this book went to press in the summer of 2005, other Christian denominations in the United States had joined the PCUSA and the WCC in considering divestment or other economic pressures against Israel. They included the Episcopal Church U.S.A., the United Church of Christ, and two regions of the United Methodist Church. Resolutions calling on Israel to dismantle barriers that separate Israeli and Palestinian territory, such as one passed by the Disciples of Christ, were also under consideration. Rabbi Abraham Cooper of the Simon Wiesenthal Center in Los Angeles aptly summarized the reaction of many Jews when he was quoted as calling the churches' actions "functionally anti-Semitic." See Goodstein, "Threat to Divest Is Church Tool in Israeli Fight."

12. The quotation is from the PCJCR media release, "Presbyterians Challenge PCUSA Divestment Decision," December 8, 2004.

8 The Ethics of Forgiveness

1. What is the relationship and the difference between *apology* and *forgiveness*? An apology is a confession of harm doing, an open acknowledgment of responsibility and even of guilt, that is offered by a person or group that has inflicted harm on another person or group. Typically, an apology is made with the hope, if not the expectation, that it will be accepted by those to whom it is properly directed. In many cases, the acceptance of an apology is taken to be equivalent to forgiveness, but there can be significant differences as well.

First, making an apology and asking for forgiveness are not necessarily the same. The latter includes confession of harm doing but often contains a depth of feeling and awareness that the making of an apology does not convey. Contrition, remorse, the sense both that the wrong done cannot be set right and yet that one must try as best one can to do so—these are qualities that often distinguish petitions for forgiveness from statements of apology. The line between them may not always be easily discernible, but it does exist. Likewise, the acceptance of an apology and the granting of forgiveness may have different qualities of depth that should be recognized. Acceptance of an apology does not necessarily grant forgiveness, nor should it. The reason is that while an apology may deserve acceptance it may not have the degree of repentance that warrants forgiveness. To accept an apology is to acknowledge that another person is admitting responsibility for harm or wrongdoing and to recognize that this person regrets what he or she has done; it is also to indicate that a broken relationship has been restored but not necessarily to the point of forgiveness, unless the apology that is accepted is actually, explicitly, a petition for forgiveness, which commits a person or a group much more profoundly to acts of repentance than words of apology typically require. One of the reasons why apologies can seem hollow, even when they are accepted, is that they neither reflect nor require the commitment to transformation and repair that make a petition for forgiveness authentic and the granting of forgiveness responsible.

2. Among the most helpful studies about these topics are Elazar Barkan, *The Guilt of Nations: Restitution and Negotiating Historical Injustices* (New York: W. W. Norton, 2000) and Priscilla B. Hayner, *Unspeakable Truths: Confronting State Terror and Atrocities* (New York: Taylor & Francis, 2002).

3. Emmanuel Levinas, *Difficile liberté: Essais sur le judaïsme* (Paris: Albin Michel, 1963), p. 37. The translation is Didier Pollefeyt's.

4. The quotation is from Isaiah 56:7 as found in *Tanakh: The Holy Scriptures* (Philadelphia, PA: Jewish Publication Society, 1988). Citations from the Hebrew Bible refer to this translation and edition.

5. For this discussion see *Berakhot* 7a, trans. Maurice Simon, in I. Epstein, ed., *Hebrew-English Edition of the Babylonian Talmud* (London: Soncino Press, 1990).

6. See Psalms 7:12.

7. Isaiah 56:5.

8. See James E. Young, *The Texture of Memory: Holocaust Memorial and Meaning* (New Haven, CT: Yale University Press, 1993), pp. 243–60, esp. p. 244.

9. Vrba and Wetzler's escape route took them to Slovakia, where they gave their information and warning to the *Judenrat* (Jewish Council). By early May 1944, if not late April, their report was also in the hands of Hungarian Jewish leaders, but its contents were not widely shared with the Hungarian Jews, who were deported to Auschwitz—approximately 437,000 of them—in a matter of weeks during the late spring and summer of 1944. A perceptive discussion of this history is available in Ruth Linn, *Escaping Auschwitz: The Culture of Forgetting* (Ithaca, NY: Cornell University Press, 2004). An Israeli scholar, Linn raises crucial questions about the Vrba–Wetzler report not only in its wartime context but also with regard to the relative silence about it in post-Holocaust Israel. Linn facilitated the first Hebrew publication of Vrba's Holocaust memoirs, which took place in 1998. She believes that the Vrba–Wetzler report and Vrba's memoirs were long obscured in Israeli scholarship and education about the Holocaust because both raise uncomfortable questions about the complicity of some Hungarian Jewish leaders in the Holocaust and the roles that they went on to play in Israeli society.

10. Vrba's book appeared in British, American, and German editions in 1964. A French edition followed in 1988. In some subsequent and expanded editions, the title was changed to *44070—The Conspiracy of the Twentieth Century* or to *I Escaped from Auschwitz*.

11. Rudolf Vrba with Alan Bestic, *I Cannot Forgive*, expanded edn. (Vancouver: Regent College Publishing, 1997), p. 268. Vrba's reasoning about the death penalty was that the German people, who had achieved what he called "the twin peaks of barbarity and humanity," needed to carry it out against Holocaust perpetrators to convince the world and themselves that "the people of music, of poetry, of philosophy, of science, and even of genius have triumphed and that the dark elements which swamped them have been obliterated forever" (p. 269).

12. Simon Wiesenthal, *The Sunflower: On the Possibilities and Limits of Forgiveness*, rev. and expanded edn. (New York: Schocken Books, 1997). All citations are to this edition, which includes an updated symposium edited by Harry James Cargas and Bonny V. Fetterman. Born in 1908, Wiesenthal died in 2005.

13. Ibid., p. 108.

14. Ibid., pp. 163–4.

15. Ibid., pp. 177–8.

16. Ibid., p. 192.

17. Ibid., pp. 165–6.

18. Ibid., p. 182.

19. See Giorgio Calcagno's interview with Levi, regarding the latter's 1986 book *The Drowned and the Saved*, in Primo Levi, *The Voice of Memory: Interviews 1961–1987*, ed. Marco Belpoliti and Robert Gordon and trans. Robert Gordon (New York: The New Press, 2001), p. 111. See also "A Self-Interview: Afterword to *If This Is a Man* (1976)," in ibid., p. 186. In the quoted passage, Levi's specification that he is not a Christian is a significant one. As Levi himself would have understood, his Jewish identity is well known. Ordinarily there would have been no need for him to state that he is not a Christian. He did so, I believe, because he was speaking about forgiveness, even suggesting that there might be Holocaust perpetrators who could once have been worthy of it. Conventional wisdom sometimes holds that forgiveness is more a "Christian" quality than a "Jewish" one. Levi may have wanted to clarify that his outlook was not buying into a Christian ethic of one kind or another. On the issue of whether the Christian tradition emphasizes forgiveness more or at least differently than Judaism does, a one-size-fits-all resolution is not to be found. It can be said, however, that a position such as the one articulated by Theodore Hesburgh in *The Sunflower*, and noted above, would be consistent neither with Jewish teaching nor even with all forms of Christian theology and ethics.

20. An important objection requires a response at this point, for it could be argued that the purest and most virtuous form of forgiveness is the kind that is freely given without a petition for forgiveness being offered by the offender or any other condition being met on that person's part. Expecting or requiring nothing, such forgiveness would seem to flow from the most generous of spirits. There is no doubt that such unilateral forgiveness can be real. It may bring a kind of release and liberation from resentment, bitterness, or hatred on the part of the person who forgives. Nevertheless, such unilateral forgiveness

truncates, even removes, the relational qualities that give true forgiveness depth and authenticity. To be fully what it can be, forgiveness entails a relationship, one where people are engaged with one another and respond to one another in transforming ways. Forgiveness that involves one party—the one who gives it—but not the activity of a repentant harm- or wrongdoer can have value, but it does not represent forgiveness at its fullest and best, and it may even excuse offenders only to find that injustice and indifference to it increase.

Related problems attend another form of unilateral forgiveness—namely, what can be called forgiving oneself. At least in some cases, such forgiveness can have value. In catastrophic situations one's survival may bring about feelings of guilt, as has often been the case with Holocaust survivors who understand that their survival was largely a matter of luck and that others who were better or more deserving than they were—at least in the judgment of the survivors— did not come out alive. Or there are instances where Holocaust survivors made decisions—sometimes they were what Lawrence Langer calls "choiceless choices"—that doomed others. Their plight in extreme situations indicates that the survivors' fate was scarcely in their own hands and their ranges of freedom were severely curtailed. In these cases, forgiving oneself can be an important way of removing unreasonable senses of guilt and providing a release that allows people to have less tortured lives, even though their lives remain deeply impacted by trauma. Nevertheless, the idea of self-forgiveness becomes problematic as soon as it is extended beyond relatively confined boundaries. Without careful understanding of when and where it is legitimate, self-forgiveness overlooks and excuses too much, and thus it increases the likelihood that injustice will have its way. Self-forgiveness is legitimate and should be encouraged only in those instances where a reasonable analysis—one that could withstand critical, unbiased inquiry by others who are capable of evaluating the circumstances in question—finds that one's feelings of guilt are undeserved.

21. Wiesenthal, *The Sunflower*, pp. 182–3.
22. Ibid., pp. 165–6.
23. Didier Pollefeyt, "Forgiveness after the Holocaust," in David Patterson and John K. Roth, eds., *After-Words: Post-Holocaust Struggles with Forgiveness, Reconciliation, Justice* (Seattle: University of Washington Press, 2004), p. 61.
24. The Gospels of the Christian New Testament make clear that Jesus expects his followers to be forgiving people. A classic text is Matthew 18:21–22. Peter asks how often one should forgive a person who sins against him. "As many as seven times?" he wonders. "Not seven times," Jesus replies, "but, I tell you, seventy-times seven."

The context surrounding this passage is important because it illustrates that Jesus typically insists not that forgiveness should be given no matter what, but that the imperative to forgive is especially strong where the person who has harmed another is repentant toward that individual. It is even important for a community to hold its members accountable, to point out the error of their ways, so that repentance is encouraged. Then, if and whenever repentance is genuine, forgiveness should follow, for that is God's way, and Jesus urges his followers to walk in that path. Indeed, only if Jesus' followers forgive those who have repented after trespassing against them, can they expect God's forgiveness for their own sins.

Jesus also makes clear that timeliness is important. Repentance and forgiveness should come the quicker the better, for God's judgment is at hand. In this context, Matthew 5:23–26 has important light to shed. In that passage, Jesus teaches that repentance before a brother or sister who has "something against you" takes precedence over making an altar gift to God, the implication being that the gift to God could be neither authentic nor well regarded by God if a person is unrepentant about wrong or harm he or she has done to another. Likewise, Jesus urges his followers to "come to terms quickly with your accuser." Here the implication is that the accusation is just, and that one needs to come to terms about it and in a timely manner. If not, says Jesus, "your accuser may hand you over to the judge, and the judge to the guard, and you will be thrown in prison. Truly I tell you, you will never get out until you have paid the last penny." Jesus did not dispense "cheap grace," nor should his followers.

When the Christian emphasis on repentance and judgment gets muted, that tradition is open to the charge that it does dispense "cheap grace." Thus, Christians need to be careful about some New Testament texts that seem to make forgiveness imperative even where repentance is not evident. Mark 11:25, for example, might appear to be an unqualified imperative that does not make repentance a condition for forgiveness: "Whenever you stand praying," says Jesus, "forgive, if you have anything against anyone; so that your Father in heaven may also forgive you your trespasses." This passage should not be regarded as trumping the far more pronounced emphasis that Jesus places on repentance as a condition for forgiveness, but it can and should be read to stress that followers of Jesus are to be predisposed to granting forgiveness. When the right conditions for forgiveness are present, a follower of Jesus will not hold back forgiveness any more than God himself would do so. It is important for Christians to be clear that Christianity is not a religion of "cheap grace." It is also important for Christians to be forgiving when repentance is forthcoming.

25. Wiesenthal, *The Sunflower*, p. 181.
26. Pollefeyt, "Forgiveness after the Holocaust," p. 64.
27. Wiesenthal, *The Sunflower*, p. 166.
28. The quotation from Wiesel is taken from Carol Rittner's important chapter, "What Can a Christian Say about Forgiveness?" in Carol Rittner and John K. Roth, eds., *"Good News" after Auschwitz? Christian Faith within a Post-Holocaust World* (Macon, GA: Mercer University Press, 2001), p. 121. Rittner's careful research about Wiesel's statement is significant. "Although Wiesel includes a version of this prayer in his memoir, *And the Sea Is Never Full*," says Rittner, "I have taken the version I am using from the *New York Times*, January 27, 1995. This version is corroborated by what was reported in the *Washington Post*, January 27, 1995, and also by the excerpt of his speech reprinted in *McLean's* (February 22, 1995). The version in Wiesel's memoirs appears to be slightly edited from what appeared in the news media almost immediately following his presentation" (pp. 121–2, n.17).
29. See Rittner's interview with Wiesel, "What Can a Christian Say about Forgiveness?" p. 125.
30. In this context, Bernhard Schlink, the German novelist and philosopher of law, makes an important contribution. He asks what comes *after* forgiveness,

both in the sense of our being in situations where the passage of time renders forgiveness increasingly impossible because the parties who can be in the relationship of forgiveness are no longer alive, and in the sense that forgiveness may have been achieved but life goes on after forgiveness.

In the former case, there are still relationships that may exist between those in the succeeding generations of those who were harmed and those who inflicted harm. One thinks, for example, of the succeeding generations of Holocaust perpetrators and victims. In the latter case, where forgiveness between those who were harmed and those who harmed them may actually have been achieved, the relationship is not necessarily at an end because life goes on. What should these various relationships include? Schlink's suggestion is that at least three ingredients are important: remembrance, recognition, and tact. Here is how I interpret his suggestions.

As time passes, forgetting is unavoidable, but where forgiveness has taken place, the importance of remembrance remains lest we lose sight of the need for vigilance against injustice. And where it has become too late for forgiveness, remembrance remains as an occasion for very different generations to take responsibility for themselves and for each other in ways that may help to keep injustice at bay. As time passes, identities change, but where forgiveness has taken place, recognition of who the people were and who they have become can provide models for future healing that the world needs. And where it has become too late for forgiveness, recognition of the relationships that still exist between the succeeding generations of those who inflicted harm and those who received it can also be an impetus for healing that the world needs. Last but not least, what Schlink calls tact, which I take to mean a heightened awareness of the other's vulnerability and a concern not to exacerbate it, plays a part in his suggestions about what to do after forgiveness has happened or after it is too late for forgiveness. As time passes, insensitivity may remain, but where forgiveness has taken place it enjoins both the imperative not to repeat the wrong that was done and the reminder that the healing of forgiveness includes routine, everyday actions that show respect and courtesy among people and that keep people alert to guard against the small ways as well as the large ones in which suffering can be inflicted. And where it has become too late for forgiveness, tact has its place too, for it signals sensitivity about the unrelieved burdens that succeeding generations carry because of what their ancestors have done or suffered. (My interpretation of Schlink's position is based on his presentation at a symposium on "Forgiveness after the Holocaust" in which I also participated. The symposium took place on September 19, 2004, at the Museum of Jewish Heritage in New York City.)

9   The Ethics of Prayer

1. Richard Rhodes, *Masters of Death: The SS-Einsatzgruppen and the Invention of the Holocaust* (New York: Alfred A. Knopf, 2002), p. 121. This chapter draws on my contributions to David Patterson and John K. Roth, eds., *Fire in the Ashes: God, Evil, and the Holocaust* (Seattle: University of Washington Press, 2005).
2. Ibid., p. 140.

3. See Susan Neiman, *Evil in Modern Thought: An Alternative History of Philosophy* (Princeton, NJ: Princeton University Press, 2002), especially pp. 1–13 and 314–28. Neiman is one of a small but growing number of philosophers who are concentrating on issues about evil with specific reference to the Holocaust. "*Auschwitz*," she writes, "stands for all that is meant when we use the word *evil* today" (p. 3). By focusing on evil, she seeks to reorient philosophy to "the real roots of philosophical questioning" (p. 13). For a related inquiry, see Richard J. Bernstein, *Radical Evil: A Philosophical Interrogation* (Cambridge: Polity Press, 2002). Acknowledging that many twentieth-century philosophers have been reluctant to speak about evil—to do so would seem too theological or too close to a "vulgar Manichaeism"—Bernstein notes that "the problems concerning evil come back to haunt us" (p. 3). Contending that "there is a prevailing sense of the irrelevance of theodicy"—if that concept is understood as "the attempt to find some 'justification' for the evil and useless suffering that we encounter"—he also underscores that "Auschwitz signifies a rupture and break with tradition and that 'after Auschwitz' we must rethink both the meaning of evil and human responsibility" (pp. 2–4).
4. In addition to acknowledging that people may identify evil differently, Neiman emphasizes two further points echoed below. First, human beings not only discern evil but also are its primary sources. Second, human-made evil is contingent. Evil is humanity's responsibility twice over. We produce it; we must deal with it.
5. Rhodes, *Masters of Death*, p. 156.
6. Rhodes makes the problematic statement that "shooting was not less efficient than gassing." He argues that "shooting began earlier, continued throughout the war and produced far more victims if Slavs are counted, as they must be, as well as Jews." The factors that Rhodes emphasizes, however, are insufficient to make his case about efficiency. When one considers the continental sweep of the "Final Solution" and the assembly-line intensity of the killing at Belzec, Treblinka, and Birkenau, then the efficiency of those killing centers looms large enough to make Rhodes's claim less than convincing. See ibid., p. 156.
7. At Auschwitz and other Holocaust sites, prayers were said by perpetrators and bystanders as well as by victims. Owing to space constraints, this chapter concentrates on the latter. A full discussion about prayer and the Holocaust would also need to consider the two former groups.
8. Theodor R. Adorno, "Cultural Criticism and Society," in *Prisms*, trans. Samuel and Shierry Weber (London: Neville Spearman, 1967), p. 34. This essay was originally published in 1951.
9. Adorno's dialectical form of philosophizing meant that he often brought criticism to bear on his own judgments, and in his own way he opened the door for the right kind of prayer to be not only permissible but also of decisive importance in the shadow of Birkenau. "Perennial suffering has as much right to expression as a tortured man has to scream," Adorno said, "hence it may have been wrong to say that after Auschwitz you could no longer write poems." Poetry, however, would still be barbaric to the extent that it failed to remember, respond, and return to the Holocaust. All of this could be said of prayer as well. See Theodor W. Adorno, *Negative Dialectics*, trans. E. B. Ashton (New York: Seabury Press, 1973), p. 362.

10. Elie Wiesel, *Night*, trans. Stella Rodway (1958; New York: Bantam Books, 1989), p. 63.
11. Ibid., p. 65.
12. In the Hebrew Bible, God is identified as One who answers prayer (see, for example, Psalms 65:2 and I Kings 9:3). In addition to the Psalms, most of which are prayers, the Hebrew Bible contains "over ninety prose prayers in which individuals address God directly in time of need" (see Eileen Schuller, "Prayer(s)," in The *Oxford Companion to the Bible*, ed. Bruce M. Metzger and Michael D. Coogan [New York: Oxford University Press, 1993], p. 607). Furthermore, Judaism's liturgy depends on prayer. An important ingredient in that liturgy, the Kaddish is a doxology, an expression of praise that honors the greatness of God. Of ancient origins—versions were known in the sixth century B.C.E.—this prayer does not refer explicitly to death, but it does express a yearning for peace and for the coming of God's kingdom "speedily and soon." Those themes help to explain why the Kaddish became a prayer for Jewish mourners, who recite it after the death of loved ones.

   Prayer played a vital part in the life of Jesus. With regularity the Gospels indicate that he took time to pray. According to one New Testament source (I Thessalonians. 5:17), Christians should "pray without ceasing." It is unlikely that anyone meets that standard, but Christian tradition and identity would scarcely be imaginable apart from prayer. No prayer resonates more deeply for Christians than the Lord's Prayer, which tradition holds that Jesus taught to his disciples. The New Testament—specifically Matthew 6:9–13 and Luke 11:1–4—is its source. In the version that most Christians know by heart, the Lord's Prayer asks God to "deliver us from evil." Recent translations refer to rescue from "the evil one," but in either case this prayer contains the hope and confidence that God can and will prevent evil from being ultimately overwhelming.
13. William James, *The Varieties of Religious Experience* (1902; reprint, Garden City, NY: Doubleday Image Books, 1978), p. 448.
14. See Thomas Hobbes, *Leviathan* (1651; reprint, Indianapolis, IN: Bobbs-Merrill, 1958), p. 107, and G. W. F. Hegel, *Introduction to The Philosophy of History*, trans. Leo Rauch (Indianapolis, IN: Hackett Publishing Company, 1988), p. 24. Hegel's *Philosophy of History* was originally published, posthumously, in 1840.
15. Hegel, *Introduction to The Philosophy of History*, p. 57.
16. Wiesel, *Night*, p. 64.
17. Ibid., p. 64.
18. The Holocaust forces one to be critical, to make qualifications, where generalizations are concerned. Charlotte Delbo, for example, was not at the Rosh Hashanah observance at Monowitz in 1944, but that non-Jewish woman experienced Auschwitz long enough to know that "one can turn a human being into a skeleton gurgling with diarrhea, without time or energy to think. ... People did not dream in Auschwitz, they were in a state of delirium. ... What did we speak of? Material, usable things. We had to omit anything that might awaken pain or regret. We never spoke of love." See Delbo's *Auschwitz and After*, trans. Rosette Lamont (New Haven, CT: Yale University Press, 1995), p. 168.
19. Ibid., p. 111.

20. For Wiesel's recollections on the latter point, see Elie Wiesel, *And the Sea Is Never Full: Memoirs 1969–*, trans. Marion Wiesel (New York: Alfred A. Knopf, 1999), p. 345. In his 1983 interview with Giuseppe Grieco, Levi discusses meeting Wiesel, "after forty years of separation," during the summer of that year. See "God and I," in Primo Levi, *The Voice of Memory: Interviews 1961–1987*, ed. Marco Belpoliti and Robert Gordon, trans. Robert Gordon (New York: The New Press, 2001), pp. 273–5.
21. Biographies of Levi include Carole Angier, *The Double Bond: Primo Levi, a Biography* (New York: Farrar, Straus and Giroux, 2002), Myriam Anissimov, *Primo Levi: Tragedy of an Optimist*, trans. Steve Cox (Woodstock, NY: Overlook Press, 1998), and Ian Thompson, *Primo Levi: A Life* (New York: Henry Holt and Company, 2003). For helpful commentary on Levi's thought, see Massimo Giuliani, *A Centaur in Auschwitz: Reflections on Primo Levi's Thinking* (Lanham, MD: Lexington Books, 2003).
22. Primo Levi, *Survival in Auschwitz: The Nazi Assault on Humanity*, trans. Stuart Woolf (1959; reprint, New York: Simon & Schuster, 1996), p. 17. My account of Levi and his reaction to Kuhn's prayer draws on "Raul Hilberg's 'Minutiae': Their Impact on Philosophical and Religious Inquiries after Auschwitz," my essay in *Perspectives on the Holocaust: Essays in Honor of Raul Hilberg*, ed. James S. Pacy and Alan P. Wertheimer (Boulder, CO: Westview Press, 1995), pp. 167–81.
23. Levi, *Survival in Auschwitz*, p. 127.
24. Ibid., p. 128.
25. Ibid., p. 129.
26. Ibid., p. 128.
27. Ibid., p. 125. Levi became aware that his life might have been spared during the October selection because "I was a chemist and because I was part of the factory workforce by then. In the factory section, there was a list with the names and numbers of some employees, mine included." Levi could never know for sure whether the presence of his name on that list might have granted him a reprieve. See "The Duty of Memory," Levi's 1983 interview with Anna Bravo and Federico Cereja, in *The Voice of Memory*, p. 242.
28. Levi, *Survival in Auschwitz*, p. 128.
29. Ibid., pp. 129–30. Interestingly, Levi does not indicate the language Kuhn used in his prayer or how he knew what Kuhn was saying, but clearly Kuhn's prayer left a deep impression on Levi. In the interview entitled "God and I" (pp. 275–6), Levi revealed his views about prayer in greater detail. They fit with his understanding of the gray zone and, in particular, with his responses to Kuhn's prayer. During what he calls "the great selection of 1944," which probably included the episodes surrounding Kuhn's prayer, Levi says that he had a "moment of religious temptation" when "I tried to commend myself to God, and I recall, with shame, having said to myself: 'No, you can't do this, you don't have the right. First, because you don't believe in God; secondly, because asking for favors, without having a special case, is the act of a *Mafioso.*' The moral of the story: I gave up the doubtful comfort of prayer, and I left it to chance, and whoever else it might be, to decide my fate." In Auschwitz, Levi stated, "I had seen suffering and dying all around me thousands of men more worthy than me, even innocent babies, and conversely, I had seen deplorable, most certainly malicious men survive. Thus salvation

and death did not depend on God but on chance." Even if in some sense God does exist, which Levi admitted was a possibility, he thought that God "is indifferent to the matters of mankind. In short, he isn't someone to pray to," and it would be wrong, Levi added, "to invent a God to talk to."

30. See Ferdinando Camon, *Conversations with Primo Levi*, trans. John Shepley (Marlboro, VT: Marlboro Press, 1989), pp. 67–8.

31. Elie Wiesel, *All Rivers Run to the Sea: Memoirs*, trans. Marion Wiesel (New York: Alfred A. Knopf, 1995), pp. 84–5.

32. See *The C. L. R. James Reader*, ed. Anna Grimshaw (Oxford: Blackwell Publishers, 1992), pp. 143 and 151. James's allusion to Hegel was brought to my attention by Paul Buhle, "The New Scholarship of Comics," *The Chronicle of Higher Education*, May 16, 2003, p. B7. To the best of my knowledge, James does not document the Hegel text he has in mind, but a likely source is *The Logic of Hegel*, 2nd edn., trans. William Wallace from Hegel's *Encyclopedia of the Philosophical Sciences* (Oxford: Oxford University Press, 1959), p. 375. In Wallace's translation, Hegel refers to "the old man who utters the same creed as the child, but for whom it is pregnant with the significance of a lifetime."

10   The Holocaust, Genocide, and the "Logic" of Racism

1. My use of the term *"logic"* requires some explanation. In this chapter, I use it primarily to signify a conceptual web or configuration, not a series of deductions from principles or a set of inferences from empirical data. The "logic" of racism—and the "logic" of genocide too—may include elements of both kinds, but as used here *"logic"* connotes a pattern of thinking and planning, a mapping of relationships among ideas and policies that associate congenially with each other. There are entailments and implications in these patterns and relationships. One idea, one policy, does lead to another, but the relationships are more organic and dialectical than linear and one-directional. My use of scare quotes around the term *"logic"* is not intended to minimize the power or authority that these patterns of thought can have. They both can be immense. But I use the scare quotes to make clear that the "logic" of racism and genocide is less than fully rational, disguised as rational though it may be.

With regard to my claim that the term *race* has done far more harm than good, I find significant support in the instructive series of articles on race that appeared in *Daedalus* 134, 1 (Winter 2005): 5–116. Especially pertinent are the contributions by Kenneth Prewitt, Jennifer L. Hochschild, George M. Fredrickson, and the philosopher Ian Hacking. Harmful though the very concept of race has been, one cannot—as this chapter shows—be rid of it altogether, because the idea has to be invoked to deconstruct and subvert it and to resist the harm it has done. Hacking's essay "Why Race Still Matters" (pp. 102–16) is especially important. Noting recent research that seems to link certain diseases and some medical treatments with racially identifiable populations, Hacking warns that such statistical correlations, helpful though they may prove to be, are neither equivalent to nor sufficient for claims that "races are real kinds, denoting essentially different kinds of people." Nevertheless, he adds, the recent scientific and medical findings may provide opportunities in which "racists will try to exploit the racial difference" (p. 109).

Thus, race still matters because the concept must continue to be very carefully watched and examined as inquiry proceeds. What follows in this chapter draws on contributions I have made in my edited volume *Genocide and Human Rights: A Philosophical Guide* (New York: Palgrave Macmillan, 2005).

2. Danilo Kiš, *Garden, Ashes*, trans. William J. Hannaker (Chicago, IL: Dalkey Archive Press, 2003), pp. 34, 37, 39. The discussion of *Garden, Ashes* draws on my contributions to David Patterson and John K. Roth, eds., *Fire in the Ashes: God, Evil, and the Holocaust* (Seattle: University of Washington Press, 2005).

3. Kiš, *Garden, Ashes*, p. 169.

4. The United Nations Convention on the Prevention and Punishment of the Crime of Genocide is reprinted in Carol Rittner, John K. Roth, and James M. Smith, eds., *Will Genocide Ever End?* (St. Paul, MN: Paragon House, 2002), pp. 209–11.

5. Major excerpts from Himmler's speech are reprinted in Paul Mendes-Flohr and Yehuda Reinharz, eds., *The Jew in the Modern World: A Documentary History*, 2nd ed. (New York: Oxford University Press, 1995). See especially, p. 685.

6. Linda Melvern, "Identifying Genocide," in Rittner, Roth, and Smith, eds., *Will Genocide Ever End?*, p. 101.

7. For the quotations that follow, see Kiš, *Garden, Ashes*, pp. 168–70.

11 Will Genocide Ever End?

1. R. G. Collingwood, *An Autobiography* (Oxford: Oxford University Press, 1939), p. 79. The opening paragraphs of this chapter draw on my book *Holocaust Politics* (Louisville, KY: Westminster John Knox Press, 2001), pp. 27–32. This chapter is also adapted from contributions I have made to my edited volume *Genocide and Human Rights: A Philosophical Guide* (New York: Palgrave Macmillan, 2005).

2. Emil Fackenheim, "The Holocaust and Philosophy," *The Journal of Philosophy* 82 (October 1985): 505.

3. In addition to Fackenheim and Lang, a representative list of philosophers whose work has been centrally concerned with the Holocaust would include the following: Theodor W. Adorno, Giorgio Agamben, Jean Améry, Robert Antelme, Hannah Arendt, Alain Badiou, Richard Bernstein, Maurice Blanchot, Martin Buber, Albert Camus, Jacques Derrida, Jonathan Glover, Norman Geras, Leonard Grob, Roger Gottlieb, Philip Hallie, Karl Jaspers, Hans Jonas, Steven Katz, Sarah Kofman, Emmanuel Levinas, Jean-François Lyotard, Avishai Margalit, André Mineau, Susan Neiman, Gillian Rose, Alan Rosenbaum, James Watson, and Edith Wyschogrod. Depending on how broadly the term *philosopher* is understood, the list above could be augmented by very important thinkers such as Charlotte Delbo, Primo Levi, Richard Rubenstein, and Elie Wiesel.

4. Raphael Lemkin, *Axis Rule in Occupied Europe: Laws of Occupation, Analysis of Government, Proposals for Redress* (Washington, DC: Carnegie Endowment for International Peace, 1944), p. 79.

5. Omer Bartov, "Extreme Violence and the Scholarly Community," *International Social Science Journal* 54 (December 2002): 509.

6. For more on this topic, see Richard L. Rubenstein and John K. Roth, *Approaches to Auschwitz: The Holocaust and Its Legacy*, rev. edn. (Louisville, KY: Westminster John Knox Press, 2003).

7. Several of the following paragraphs are adapted from my contributions to Dinah L. Shelton, ed., *The Encyclopedia of Genocide and Crimes against Humanity* (Detroit, MI: Macmillan Reference, 2004).

8. See, for example, Richard J. Bernstein, *Radical Evil: A Philosophical Interrogation* (Cambridge: Polity Press, 2002) and Susan Neiman, *Evil in Modern Thought: An Alternative History of Philosophy* (Princeton, NJ: Princeton University Press, 2002).

9. Bartov, "Extreme Violence and the Scholarly Community," p. 511.

10. As Nicholas D. Kristof pointed out, the UN figure is only an estimate of death "from non-violent causes." The total mortality has been difficult to ascertain, partly because of a lack of cooperation from the Sudanese government. Kristof noted that "independent estimates exceed 220,000—and the number is rising by about 10,000 per month." See Kristof's article, "The Secret Genocide Archive," *New York Times*, February 23, 2005. Kristof ended his editorial in a telling way: "During past genocides against Armenians, Jews and Cambodians, it was possible to claim that we didn't fully know what was going on. This time, President Bush, Congress and the European Parliament have already declared genocide to be under way. And we have photos. This time, we have no excuse."

11. See Warren Hoge, "International War-Crimes Prosecutor Gets List of 51 Sudan Suspects," *New York Times*, April 6, 2005.

12. It came as no surprise that the Sudanese government responded to the Congressional action by issuing a press release on July 23, 2004. Contending that the US Congress had "trivialized the horrific concept of 'genocide,' " the statement claimed further that "the Government of Sudan is cooperating fully with all efforts to bring aid and relief to all of Darfur's displaced people." The press release is available through the Internet at: http://www. sudanembassy.org/asp/print.asp?ID=291. Neither of the Sudanese assertions noted above can withstand scrutiny. Both are false.

13. See the transcript of the candidates' first debate in the 2004 presidential campaign, which took place in Coral Cables, Florida, on September 30, 2004, *New York Times*, October 1, 2004.

14. Some members of the US Congress have done much better. One thinks of Ed Royce (R-CA), who chairs the House of Representatives Subcommittee on Africa. Both he and his committee have spoken forcefully about the genocide in Darfur. See also the important editorial, "Stop the Genocide," coauthored by US Senators Jon S. Corzine (D-NJ) and Sam Brownback (R-KS), *Washington Post*, January 11, 2005, p. A15. Corzine and Brownback wrote the Senate resolution that identified the Darfur atrocities as genocide.

15. See "Annan Warns Chaos Looms in Violent Darfur," *New York Times*, December 6, 2004.

16. See Colum Lynch, "UN Panel Finds No Genocide in Darfur but Urges Tribunals," *Washington Post*, February 1, 2005, p. A1. It should be added that the UN study found that the Sudanese government and the Janjaweed had committed human rights abuses and war crimes that warranted prosecution in the International Criminal Court, which might also determine that those

acts took place "with genocidal intent." On April 5, 2005, UN Secretary General Kofi Annan handed the International Criminal Court a confidential list of 51 persons, including Sudanese government officials, who are key suspects in the mass killing and devastation that have taken place in Darfur. That step opens the door for Darfur-related war crimes trials in The Hague.

17. The report on Sudan is available through the Internet at: http://www.state.gov/g/drl/rls/hrrpt/2004/41628.htm.

18. The following paragraphs are adapted from my contributions to David Patterson and John K. Roth, eds., *After-Words: Post-Holocaust Struggles with Forgiveness, Reconciliation, Justice* (Seattle: University of Washington Press, 2004) and Carol Rittner, John K. Roth, and James M. Smith, eds., *Will Genocide Ever End?* (St. Paul, MN: Paragon House, 2002).

19. Elie Wiesel, *One Generation After*, trans. Lily Edelman and the author (New York: Avon Books, 1972), pp. 72–3.

20. Reprinted by permission of Hank Knight.

21. See Michael Bazyler, "Using Civil Litigation to Achieve Some Justice," in Rittner, Roth, and Smith, eds., *Will Genocide Ever End?*, p. 156.

22. Stanton and Dallaire made these comments at the Aegis Trust–British Foreign and Commonwealth Office (BFCO) Genocide Prevention Conference, an international inquiry that took place at the Beth Shalom Holocaust Centre in England on January 22–25, 2002. This conference included participants from government, the military, non-governmental organizations, and universities, as well as genocide survivors. See also Roméo Dallaire, *Shake Hands with the Devil: The Failure of Humanity in Rwanda*, with Brent Beardsley (Toronto: Random House Canada, 2003).

23. Pervanic was one of the genocide survivors who participated in the Aegis–BFCO Genocide Prevention Conference on January 22–25, 2002.

12 The Holocaust and the Common Good

1. Adrienne Rich, *An Atlas of the Difficult World: Poems 1988–1991* (New York: W. W. Norton, 1991), p. 6. The epigraph for this chapter is found on p. 6 as well. Portions of this chapter are adapted from my *Holocaust Politics* (Louisville, KY: Westminster John Knox Press, 2001).

2. Rich, *An Atlas of the Difficult World*, p. 11.

3. Ibid.

4. Ibid., p. 45.

5. Ibid., p. 36.

6. Ibid., p. 52.

7. William Styron, *Sophie's Choice* (New York: Random House, 1979), p. 25.

8. Ibid., p. 217.

9. Ibid., p. 493.

10. For elaboration on these points, see two books by David S. Wyman, *Paper Walls: American and the Refugee Crisis, 1938–1941* (Amherst: University of Massachusetts Press, 1968) and *The Abandonment of the Jews: America and the Holocaust, 1941–1945* (New York: Pantheon Books, 1984).Two other reliable resources on this topic are Michael Berenbaum, *The World Must Know: The History of the Holocaust as Told in the United States Holocaust Memorial Museum* (Boston, MA: Little, Brown and Company, 1993), and Deborah E. Lipstadt,

Beyond Belief: The American Press and the Coming of the Holocaust (New York: The Free Press, 1986).

11. Wyman, *The Abandonment of the Jews*, p. 12.
12. Ibid., p. 15.
13. Allan A. Ryan, Jr., *Quiet Neighbors: Prosecuting Nazi War Criminals in America* (San Diego: Harcourt Brace Jovanovich, 1984), p. 344.
14. See Ralph Ellison's introduction to the thirtieth anniversary edition of his *Invisible Man* (New York: Vintage Books, 1982), p. xv.
15. Ibid., p. x.
16. Langston Hughes, "Let America Be America Again," in *American Ground: Vistas, Visions, and Revisions*, ed. Robert H. Fossum and John K. Roth (New York: Paragon House Publishers, 1988), p. 350.
17. Styron, *Sophie's Choice*, p. 483.
18. Ibid., pp. 513, 515.
19. My account of Le Chambon relies on two works by Philip Hallie: *Lest Innocent Blood Be Shed: The Story of Le Chambon and How Goodness Happened There* (New York: HarperPerennial, 1994) and *In the Eye of the Hurricane: Tales of Good and Evil, Help and Harm* (Middletown, CT: Wesleyan University Press, 1997).
20. Albert Camus, *The Plague*, trans. Gilbert Stuart (New York: Vintage Books, 1991), p. 308.
21. For more detail about the themes mentioned in this paragraph and below, see Hallie, *In the Eye of the Hurricane*, pp. 56–83 and his contribution, "Cruelty: The Empirical Evil," in Paul Woodruff and Harry A. Wilmer, eds., *Facing Evil: Confronting the Dreadful Power behind Genocide, Terrorism, and Cruelty* (LaSalle, IL: Open Court, 2001).
22. Hallie, "Cruelty," p. 120.
23. Hallie, *In the Eye of the Hurricane*, p. 54.
24. Hallie, "Cruelty," p. 120.
25. Ibid., pp. 128–9.

Epilogue: Standing Here

1. William Stafford, "Meditation," in *The Darkness Around Us Is Deep: Selected Poems of William Stafford*, ed. Robert Bly (New York: HarperCollins, 1993), p. 123.
2. William Stafford, "Being a Person," in *Even in Quiet Places: Poems by William Stafford* (Lewiston, ID.: Confluence Press, 1996), p. 89. This poem is one in a small collection called *The Methow River Poems*.

Select Bibliography

As indicated by this book's endnotes, many sources have informed my work. Listed below are books, primarily recent ones, that have decisively influenced my thinking in *Ethics During and After the Holocaust*.

Adorno, Theodor W. *Can One Live after Auschwitz?: A Philosophical Reader*. Edited by Rolf Tiedemann. Stanford, CA: Stanford University Press, 2003.

Améry, Jean. *At the Mind's Limits: Contemplations by a Survivor on Auschwitz and Its Realities*. Translated by Sidney Rosenfeld and Stella P. Rosenfeld. New York: Schocken Books, 1986.

Barnett, Victoria. *Bystanders: Conscience and Complicity during the Holocaust*. Westport, CT: Praeger, 2000.

Bartov, Omer. *Mirrors of Destruction: War, Genocide, and Modern Identity*. New York: Oxford University Press, 2000.

———. *Murder in Our Midst: The Holocaust, Industrial Killing, and Representation*. New York: Oxford University Press, 1996.

Bauer, Yehuda. *Rethinking the Holocaust*. New Haven, CT: Yale University Press, 2001.

Browning, Christopher R. *Nazi Policy, Jewish Workers, German Killers*. Cambridge: Cambridge University Press, 2000.

———. *Ordinary Men: Reserve Police Battalion 101 and the Final Solution in Poland*. New York: HarperCollins, 1992.

Browning, Christopher R., with contributions by Jürgen Matthäus. *The Origins of the Final Solution: The Evolution of Nazi Jewish Policy, September 1939–March 1942*. Lincoln: University of Nebraska Press, 2004.

Camus, Albert. *The Plague*. Translated by Gilbert Stuart. New York: Vintage Books, 1991.

Delbo, Charlotte. *Auschwitz and After*. Translated by Rosette C. Lamont. New Haven, CT: Yale University Press, 1995.

Eizenstat, Stuart E. *Imperfect Justice: Looted Assets, Slave Labor, and the Unfinished Business of World War II*. New York: Public Affairs, 2003.

Garrard, Eve and Geoffrey Scarre, eds. *Moral Philosophy and the Holocaust*. Burlington, VT: Ashgate Publishing Company, 2003.

Geras, Norman. *The Contract of Mutual Indifference: Political Philosophy after the Holocaust*. London: Verso, 1999.

Glass, James M. *Jewish Resistance during the Holocaust: Moral Uses of Violence and Will*. New York: Palgrave Macmillan, 2004.

Glover, Jonathan. *Humanity: A Moral History of the Twentieth Century*. New Haven, CT: Yale University Press, 2000.

Goldhagen, Daniel Jonah. *A Moral Reckoning: The Role of the Catholic Church in the Holocaust and Its Unfulfilled Duty of Repair*. New York: Alfred A. Knopf, 2002.

Haas, Peter J. *Morality after Auschwitz: The Radical Challenge of the Nazi Ethic*. Philadelphia, PA: Fortress Press, 1988.

Hallie, Philip. *In the Eye of the Hurricane: Tales of Good and Evil, Help and Harm*. Middletown, CT: Wesleyan University Press, 1997.

Hallie, Philip. *Lest Innocent Blood Be Shed: The Story of the Village of Le Chambon and How Goodness Happened There*. New York: Harper Perennial, 1994.

Hayes, Peter. *From Cooperation to Complicity: Degussa in the Third Reich*. Cambridge: Cambridge University Press, 2004.

Haynes, Stephen. *Reluctant Witnesses: Jews and the Christian Imagination*. Louisville, KY: Westminster John Knox Press, 1995.

Hilberg, Raul. *The Destruction of the European Jews*. Third edition. New Haven, CT: Yale University Press, 2003.

———. *Perpetrators Victims Bystanders: The Jewish Catastrophe 19.33–1945*. New York: HarperCollins, 1992.

———. *The Politics of Memory: The Journey of a Holocaust Historian*. Chicago, IL: Ivan R. Dee, 1996.

———. *Sources of Holocaust Research: An Analysis*. Chicago, IL: Ivan R. Dee, 2001.

Kiš, Danilo. *Garden, Ashes*. Translated by William J. Hannaher. Chicago, IL: Dalkey Archive Press, 2003.

Kluger, Ruth. *Still Alive: A Holocaust Girlhood Remembered*. New York: The Feminist Press, 2001.

Kofman, Sarah. *Rue Ordener, Rue Labat*. Translated by Ann Smock. Lincoln: University of Nebraska Press, 1996.

———. *Smothered Words*. Translated by Madeleine Dobie. Evanston, IL: Northwestern University Press, 1998.

Koonz, Claudia. *The Nazi Conscience*. Cambridge, MA: Harvard University Press, 2003.

Kuntz, Dieter, ed. *Deadly Medicine: Creating the Master Race*. Washington, DC: United States Holocaust Memorial Museum, 2004.

Lang, Berel. *Post-Holocaust: Interpretation, Misinterpretation, and the Claims of History*. Bloomington, IN: Indiana University Press, 2005.

Lemkin, Raphael. *Axis Rule in Occupied Europe: Laws of Occupation, Analysis of Government, Proposals for Redress*. Washington, DC: Carnegie Endowment for International Peace, 1944.

Levi, Neil and Michael Rothberg, eds. *The Holocaust: Theoretical Readings*. New Brunswick, NJ: Rutgers University Press, 2003.

Levi, Primo. *The Drowned and the Saved*. Translated by Raymond Rosenthal. New York: Summit Books, 1988.

———. *Survival in Auschwitz*. Translated by Stuart Wolff. New York: Collier Books, 1976.

———. *The Voice of Memory: Interviews 1961–1987*. Edited by Marco Belpoliti and Robert Gordon and translated by Robert Gordon. New York: The New Press, 2001.

Levinas, Emmanuel. *Entre Nous: On Thinking-of-the-Other*. Translated by Michael B. Smith and Barbara Harshav. New York: Columbia University Press, 1998.

———. *Ethics and Infinity: Conversations with Philippe Nemo*. Translated by Richard A. Cohen. Pittsburgh, PA: Duquesne University Press, 1985.

———. *Totality and Infinity: An Essay on Exteriority*. Translated by Alphonso Lingis. Pittsburgh: Duquesne University Press, 1969.

Perechodnik, Calel. *Am I a Murderer? Testament of a Jewish Ghetto Policeman*. Edited and translated by Frank Fox. Boulder, CO: Westview Press, 1996.

Petropoulos, Jonathan and John K. Roth, eds. *Gray Zones: Ambiguity and Compromise in the Holocaust and Its Aftermath*. New York: Berghahn Books, 2005.

Power, Samantha. *"A Problem from Hell": America and the Age of Genocide.* New York: Basic Books, 2002.

Rubenstein, Richard L. *The Cunning of History: Mass Death and the American Future.* New York: Harper & Row, 1975.

Stafford, William. *Even in Quiet Places.* Lewiston, ID: Confluence Press, 1996.

Totten, Samuel, William S. Parsons, and Israel Charny, eds. *A Century of Genocide: Critical Essays and Eyewitness Accounts.* Second edition. New York: Routledge, 2004.

Wiesel, Elie. *Night.* Translated by Stella Rodway. New York: Bantam Books, 1982.

Woodruff, Paul and Harry A. Wilmer, eds. *Facing Evil: Confronting the Dreadful Power behind Genocide, Terrorism, and Cruelty.* La Salle, IL: Open Court, 2001.

Index